MENTAL CAPACITY ACT
MANUAL

AUSTRALIA
Law Book Co.
Sydney

CANADA and USA
Carswell
Toronto

HONG KONG
Sweet & Maxwell Asia

NEW ZEALAND
Brookers
Wellington

SINGAPORE and MALAYSIA
Sweet & Maxwell Asia
Singapore and Kuala Lumpur

MENTAL CAPACITY ACT MANUAL

by

Richard M. Jones M.A. (Kent and Brunel),
Solicitor, C.Q.S.W.

President, Institute of Mental Health Act Practitioners
Consultant, Morgan Cole, Solicitors

THOMSON

SWEET & MAXWELL

344.044 JON PG

Published in 2005 by
Sweet & Maxwell Ltd of
100 Avenue Road, Swiss Cottage,
Londong NW3 3PF
www.sweetandmaxwell.co.uk
Typeset and printed in Great Britain by Hobbs, Totton, Hampshire

No natural forests were destroyed to
make this product: only farmed
timber was used and re-planted.

ISBN 0 421 918 209

**A catalogue record for this book is
available from the British Library.**

PREFACE

The Mental Capacity Act 2005 is a measure which is likely to touch the lives of everyone because, at some point, all adults will probably be affected by a lack of capacity to make decisions relating to their everyday lives, either personally, or through contact with people who are unable to make decisions for themselves. As the Government has noted, a

"wide range of conditions can result in incapacity to take decisions. In some cases, the capacity to take decisions is never attained (for example in the case of some people with a learning disability). In other cases, capacity is attained but is subsequently lost. This may occur for a number of reasons, including medical disorders or traumatic injury. The loss of capacity may be temporary for example during a toxic confusional state, which might result from an illness, or use of drugs. In some cases, capacity may fluctuate during periods when they are well, but may lose it during periods of illness. Finally, the loss of capacity may be permanent, as for example in some cases of dementia or the persistent vegetative state" (*Who Decides? Making Decisions on Behalf of Mentally Incapacitated Adults*, Cm. 3803, para.2.1).

The following factors can be said to have driven the process that cumulated in the passing of the Act: the legal context, demographic tends and improvements in healthcare, the community care policy, and the protection of human rights.

The legal context

As is pointed out in the "Introduction and General Note" to the Act, the legal context that confronted the Law Commission when it commenced its investigation into the adequacy of legal procedures for decision-making on behalf of mentally incapacitated adults was most unsatisfactory. It was described as "one of incoherence, inconsistency and historical accident" (Law Comm. No.231, para.2.45). The High Court had attempted to respond to this situation by using the doctrine of necessity and the declaratory jurisdiction to determine the legality of action proposed to be taken in respect of a mentally incapacitated person, but this approach, which is aimed at responding to individual problems, was ill-suited to developing a coherent legal framework It was clear that the law did not offer sufficient protection either for the mentally incapacitated, or for those who look after them.

Demographic trends and improvements in healthcare

The number of elderly people is rising steadily in the population. The mental faculties of the elderly often decline with age and the number of persons suffering from dementia, which leads to a progressive loss of mental capacity, is increasing markedly. More than 700,000 people in the United Kingdom are estimated to suffer from dementia and this is projected to rise to around 840,00 by 2010 (The

Alzheimer's Society (January 2004)). Recommendation 1035 (1986) of the Parliamentary Assembly of the Council of Europe on ageing of populations in Europe noted that during the period from 1990 to 2020:

"increases of 20% and more are expected in the 45–60 age group and of 15–20% in the 65 and over and there will be a disproportionate growth in the number of very old people, aged 80 and over, which would be one-third of the size of this group".

In the United Kingdom context, the House of Lords Select Committee on Economic Affairs estimated that the proportion of the population aged 65 or over as a percentage of those aged 16–64 would be 24.4% in 2000, 32.8% in 2025, and 39.2% in 2050 (Session 2002–03, 4th Report, *Aspects of the Economics of an Ageing Population*, Vol.1, p.10).

Medical advances, in particular the development of antibiotics, have saved the lives of many people who would in earlier times have died from disease or trauma. Some of those who survive will do so with impaired mental capacity or even, exceptionally, lapse into a persistent vegetative state. In the case of Tony Bland, a young man who as a result of being crushed at the Hillsborough disaster was in a persistent vegetative state, Lord Browne-Wilkinson expressed his concern about the "scale of the problem that is presented by modern technological developments" and said that it seemed to him "imperative that the moral, social and legal issues raised by this case should be considered by Parliament" (*Airedale NHS Trust v Bland* [1993] 1 All E.R. 821 at 878, 879, HL). Also, as the Law Commission noted, the

"achievements of medical science have also created difficult dilemmas about the appropriate measure of medical care which should be given at the end of life, particularly where unconscious or incapacitated people have, in advance, indicated an unwillingness to be kept alive once their health has deteriorated" (Law Comm. No.231, para.2.38).

A further concern in the medical context was the recognition that certain procedures involving the mentally incapacitated were almost certainly unlawful. The most prevalent example was the practice of carrying out research on a person who was mentally incapable of consenting to participating in it, and where that person would receive no benefit from the results of the research.

The community care policy

The community care policy comprises two distinct threads. The first relates to the policy of discharging mentally disordered people from large, isolated long-stay hospitals into community based provision. This has lead to significant changes to the ways in which such people are cared for. The second thread concerns the manner in which social care needs of the population should be assessed and provided for. The White Paper *Caring for People: Community Care in the Next Decade and Beyond* (1989) Cm. 849, states at para.1.1:

"Community care means providing the services and support which people who are affected by problems of ageing, mental illness, mental handicap or physical or sensory disability need to be able to live as independently as possible in their own homes, or in 'homely' settings in the community. The Government is firmly committed to a policy of community care which enables such people to achieve their full potential."

One of the consequences of this approach, which has been delivered through the legislative framework of the National Health Service and Community Care Act 1990, has been the emphasis on avoiding institutional care for elderly and disabled people unless their particular needs positively require such an outcome.

The combination of these two policy initiatives has lead to a decrease in reliance on institutional care for the mentally disabled. Institutional care tends to encourage a paternalistic approach to meeting patient/resident needs, while community based care increases the opportunities for mentally disabled individuals to make many of the decisions that occur in everyday life either by themselves or with support. Some of the decisions that may be required to be taken will raise the question of whether the person concerned possesses the required level of mental capacity to make the decision in question. If the answer is in the negative, disputes, in particular about the most appropriate living situation for the person, can sometimes arise between relatives, or between relatives and a public authority.

The protection of human rights

The Act is indicative of a growing shift in attitude toward those who, for whatever reason, lack the mental capacity to make key decisions for themselves. In particular, there has been a growing international recognition of the unacceptability of discrimination against the mentally disabled. In 1971, the United Nations proclaimed the Declaration of the Rights of Mentally Retarded Persons. Its seven paragraphs read:

"1. The mentally retarded person has, to the maximum degree of flexibility, the same rights as other human beings.

2. The mentally retarded person has a right to proper medical care and physical therapy and to such education, training, rehabilitation and guidance as will enable him to develop his ability and maximum potential.

3. The mentally retarded person has a right to economic security and to a decent standard of living. He has a right to perform productive work or to engage in any other meaningful occupation to the fullest possible extent of his capabilities.

4. Whenever possible, the mentally retarded persons should live with his own family or with foster parents and participate in different forms of community life. The family with which he lives should receive assistance.

5. The mentally retarded person has a right to a qualified guardian when this is required to protect his personal well-being and interests.

6. The mentally retarded person has a right to protection from exploitation, abuse and degrading treatment. If prosecuted for any offence, he shall have a right to due process of law with full recognition being given to his degree of mental responsibility.

7. Whenever mentally retarded persons are unable, because of the severity of their handicap, to exercise all their rights in a meaningful way or it should become necessary to restrict or deny some or all of these rights, the procedure used for that restriction or denial of rights must contain proper legal safeguards against every form of abuse. This procedure must be based on an evaluation of the social capability of the mentally retarded person by qualified experts and must be subject to periodic review and to the right of appeal to higher authorities."

Although a Declaration of the United Nations is not legally binding, the Declaration on the Rights of Mentally Retarded Persons was supported by the UK Government when it was adopted by the General Assembly. The Declaration can therefore be categorised as identifying non-binding "soft law" principles which provide guidance to the UK Government when it legislates in this field. Despite is dated terminology, the Declaration represents an important milestone in that it established some important rights, in particular the person with a learning disability has "the same rights as other human beings" which cannot be restricted without due process that "must contain proper legal safeguards against every form of abuse". The Law Commission paid "careful regard" to aspects of the Declaration when it made its final report (Law Comm. No.231, para.2.27). The philosophy that lies behind the Declaration is one of minimum intervention in the lives of the learning disabled, consistent with providing proper care and protection and maximum help to enable them to realise their full potential and make best use of their abilities. Many countries have enacted legislation embodying its principles: see *Report on Incapable Adults,* Scottish Law Commission, Cm. 2962, para.1.5.

Subsequent to the 1971 Declaration, the General Assembly proclaimed the Declaration on the Rights of Disabled Persons in 1975, and adopted twenty-five "Principles for the protection of persons with mental illness and the improvement of mental health care" (Resolution 46/119 of December 17, 1991). Principle 23.1 requires States to "implement [the] Principles through appropriate legislative, judicial, administrative, educational and other measures, which they shall review periodically." In the European context, Recommendation No.(99)4 of the Committee of Ministers on Principles Concerning the Legal Protection of Incapable Adults, and the Convention on Human Rights and Biomedicine, together with its Additional Protocol, are reproduced as Annexes A to C.

The only international instrument against which UK law can be judicially tested is the European Convention on Human Rights. Although the Convention is not part of substantive domestic law, the Human Rights Act 1998 makes Convention rights enforceable in domestic courts. The Joint Committee on Human Rights said that the provisions of the Draft Mental Incapacity Bill:

"engage a wide range of [Convention] rights, including the right to respect for family life, the right to property, and the right to be free of degrading treatment. In our view, however, the safeguards built into the Draft Bill are sufficient to ensure that there is no significant risk of the implementation of the Draft Bill leading to an incompatibility with any of them" (Session 2002–03, 15th Report, *Scrutiny of Bills and Draft Bills: Further Progress Report* (HL 149/ HC 1005), para.4.7).

Further reports of the Joint Committee were more questioning of whether particular provisions of the Bill risked violating either Arts 2, 3, 5, or 8 of the Convention. Generally speaking, the Committee was satisfied with the responses that it received from the Government either in terms of amendments to the Bill, or from assurances the it received regarding the contents of the Code of Practice (Session 2004–05, 4th Report (HL 26/HC 224), Ch.4).

Another aspect of the rights based approach to the provision of services has been an increasing demand for the mentally incapacitated to enjoy the benefits of a lay advocate. In particular, it is considered that the support of an advocate would be beneficial in respect of an incapacitated person who did not enjoy the benefits of an involvement with caring relatives.

Running in tandem with the development of a rights agenda for the mentally incapacitated has been a gradual abandonment of the paternalistic approach to medical provision for the mentally capacitated, and a growing recognition of the principle of patient autonomy. The House of Lords Select Committee on Medical Ethics (1993–94) commented that the principle of patient autonomy "has become important in relation to medical treatment as the relationship between doctor and patient has changed to one of partnership" (HL 21–1, para.40). One manifestation of this trend has been the recognition at common law of the right of a capacitated patient to make a "living will". At the European level, the importance of patients being empowered to make informed choices in healthcare is reflected in the European Charter of Patients' Rights which proposes fourteen rights that all patients in Europe should be granted. The Charter, which was developed by the Italian patients' rights organisation Cittadinazattiva—Active Citizens Network, was launched in Rome in 2002.

Ten years elapsed between the publication of the Law Commission's Mental Incapacity Bill on February 28, 1995 and the Mental Capacity Act receiving its Royal Assent on April 7, 2005. This delay can be partly explained by the sensitivity of successive Governments to concerns that had been expressed by a number of bodies about the prospect of the provisions on advance decisions enabling euthanasia to be introduced "by the backdoor". This concern, which was a recurring issue throughout the parliamentary debates on the Bill, led to the enactment of s.62. The fact that the legislation had been the subject of detailed scrutiny over a number of years did not prevent the Bill being amended frequently during its passage through Parliament. Although the amendments improved the Bill, they did not ameliorate the following concerns:

- The fact that the Act provides for advance decisions to be made orally will inevitably result in many purported oral advance decisions being invalid because they will not be applicable to the treatment in question for one or more of the reasons set out in s.25(4).

- There is much to be said in favour of the opinion of House of Lord's Select Committee on Medical Ethics that advance decisions should be advisory only. A number of witnesses to the Joint Committee pointed out that healthy patients tend not to make the same choices as sick ones.

- Although the potential for the donee of a lasting power of attorney to act in a manner which is contrary to the best interests of the donor was recognised by the Government, the Act does not provide sufficient safeguards to protect the donor from such acts.

Apart from these concerns, there can be no doubt that the Mental Capacity Act represents a major advance in that it provides a comprehensive statutory framework for assisting those lacking capacity to make decisions for themselves wherever possible and for proper decisions to be made by others when that is not possible. However, the framework could prove to be an empty vessel if it is not "accompanied by changes in attitude which recognise the rights of those lacking capacity and the need to instil respect and good practice in dealing with them" (Joint Committee, para.30).

Richard Jones
Penarth
June, 2005
email: richard.jones2@morgan-cole.com

CONTENTS

TABLE OF CASES

MENTAL CAPACITY ACT 2005

(2005 c.9)

CONTENTS

Part 2 — THE COURT OF PROTECTION AND THE PUBLIC GUARDIAN

An Act to make new provision relating to persons who lack capacity; to establish a superior court of record called the Court of Protection in place of the office of the Supreme Court called by that name; to make provision in connection with the Convention on the International Protection of Adults signed at the Hague on 13th January 2000; and for connected purposes.   [7th April 2005]

PROGRESS OF THE BILL
    Hansard, HL Vol.667, col.1333 (1R).
    Hansard, HC Vol.422, col 928 (1R); Vol.425 col.22 (2R), (Prog), (MR), (Carry-over Motion); Vol.428, cols 101 (1R), 1531 (Prog), (RS); Vol.432, cols 1362 (Prog), (Lords' Amendments), 1641 (Royal Assent); Vol.668 cols 11 and 42 (2R); Vol.669 cols 102, 191, 734 (Comm), 1101 (MfA); Vol. 670, cols 845 (MfA), 1275, 1441 and 1483 (Rep.); Vol.671, cols 412 (3R), 950 (Royal Assent).

INTRODUCTION AND GENERAL NOTE

    The Law Commission's Fourth Programme of Law Reform (1989, Law Com. No. 185) proposed an investigation into the adequacy of legal and other procedures for decision-making on behalf of mentally incapacitated adults. There followed an extensive consultation exercise in the course of which the Commission published the following consultation papers.

● Mentally Incapacitated Adults and Decision-Making: An Overview (CP No.119)
● Mentally Incapacitated Adults and Decision-making: A New Jurisdiction (CP No.128)
● Mentally Incapacitated Adults and Decision-Making: Medical Treatment and Research (CP No.129)
● Mentally Incapacitated and Other Vulnerable Adults: Public law Protection (CP No.130)

The current state of the law was described by the Commission in para.1.1 of its Final Report "Mental Incapacity" (Law Com. No.231) which was published in March 1995:

"It is widely recognised that, in this area, the law as it now stands is unsympathetic and full of glaring gaps. It does not rest on clear or modern foundations of principle. It has also failed to keep up with developments in our understanding of the rights and needs of those with mental disability."

The Report sought to provide:

"A new set of coherent answers to a single question. The question, put simply, is 'who decides?' Although it may be asked in a variety of situations and for a variety of reasons, it arises whenever a person lacks the mental capacity to make a legally effective decision for himself or herself. There are various supplementary questions which must then be put. 'On what basis?' and 'with what formalities?' are examples of these. The types of decision which may be called for can be divided into three broad categories: 'personal welfare' decisions, 'health care' decisions and 'financial' decisions" (para.2.1).

A draft "Mental Incapacity Bill" was appended to the Report. This was intended to "provide a unified and comprehensive scheme within which people can make decisions for themselves" (para.3.1).

Lord Mackay, the Lord Chancellor, announced in January 1996 that the "Government has decided not to legislate on the basis of the Law Commission's proposals in their current form and has also concluded that it would be inappropriate to make any proposals to Parliament in the absence of full public consultation" (Lord Chancellor's Department, Press Notice, January 16, 1996).

The incoming Labour Government issued a consultation paper *"Who Decides? Making Decisions on Behalf of Mentally Incapacitated Adults"*, Cm.3803 (1997) which was based on the Commission's proposals. It also took into account the report of the House of Lords Select Committee on Medical Ethics (HL Paper 21-1) which had considered the issue of advance statements about healthcare. The consultative paper sought views on a possible framework for providing protection for mentally incapacitated adults and those who look after them, and for providing an organised framework of law to manage the welfare and affairs of mentally incapacitated adults. The consultation resulted in over 4,000 responses being received. The Government's response to the consultation was published in October 1999 as *"Making Decisions: The Government's proposals for making decisions on behalf of mentally incapacitated adults"*, Cm.4465 (1999). The proposals were largely based on the Law Commission's recommendations. The Lord Chancellor, Lord Irvine, announced in November 1999 that the Government had decided to bring forward legislation "to empower mentally incapacitated adults, so far as can safely be allowed, to make provision for the care they want before they lose capacity, and to ensure that when decisions come to be made about their care and welfare, they contain adequate safeguards and protection, they are made consistently and in line with each individual's particular best interests" (speech to the Law Society's Conference on Mental Incapacity, November 10, 1999).

Judicial support for legislation was expressed in a number of cases. In *F (Adult: Court's Jurisdiction), Re* [2000] 2 F.L.R. 512, CA, Butler-Sloss P. said at 524:

"The assumption of jurisdiction by the High Court on a case-by-case basis does not, however, detract from the obvious need expressed by the Law Commission and by the Government for a well-structured and clearly defined framework of protection of protection of vulnerable, mentally incapacitated adults, particularly since the whole essence of declarations under the inherent jurisdiction is to meet a recognised individual problem and not to provide general guidance for mentally incapacitated adults. Until Parliament puts in place that defined framework, the High Court will still be required to help out where there is no other practicable alternative."

A "Draft Mental Incapacity Bill" (Cm.5859-1) was presented to Parliament in June 2003. In July 2003 the House of Commons and House of Lords appointed a Joint Committee to scrutinise the Draft Bill. The Joint Committee's Report, which contained 99 recommendations and was mainly supportive of the principles underlying the draft Bill, was published in two volumes in November 2003 (HL Paper 189-1, 2; HC 1083-1, 2). The Government's response to the report was published in February 2004 (Cm.6121). The great majority of the Joint Committee's recommendations were accepted by the Government.

Several witness to the Joint Committee suggested that the title "Mental Incapacity Bill" was inappropriate and had negative consequences and preferred "Mental Capacity Bill" which they saw as a more accurate description of the Bill as well as more positive and reassuring. The Joint Committee considered that the Bill "should avoid the pejorative implications of incapacity and instil confidence in those it is intended to serve" and recommended "that consideration should be given to changing the Bills title to 'Mental Capacity Bill'" (paras 362-364). The Government accepted this recommendation.

The objectives of the legislation were explained by the Secretary of State for Constitutional Affairs and Lord Chancellor, Lord Falconer, when he moved the second reading of the Bill:

"The Bill seeks to do six main things. First, it allows adults to take as many decisions as they can for themselves and, in any event, to put them at the centre of the decision-making process about themselves.

Secondly, when adults fear that they may not be able to take decisions about their medical treatment in the future, it allows them, if they wish, and subject to effective safeguards, to make decisions in advance of incapacity about whether treatment should be carried out or continued.

Thirdly, where adults cannot make decisions and have not made any decision in advance about their own personal welfare or other property or affairs, the Bill ensures that the decisions which are made for them are made in their best interests.

Fourthly, where an adult lacks capacity to make a decision for himself about serious medical treatment, accommodation in a hospital or care home, or other residential accommodation, and they have no friends or family to be consulted, the Bill will require the relevant NHS body or local authority to appoint an independent [mental capacity advocate] to support the person in these most difficult decisions.

Fifthly, the Bill will provide protection against subsequent legal liability for those carers who have honestly and reasonably sought to act in the best interests of the person for whom they have cared.

Finally, the Bill will provide clarity and safeguards around the carrying out of research in relation to people who lack capacity" (*Hansard*, HL Vol.668, col.12).

The view of the Joint Committee on Human Rights is that the legislation "should be broadly welcomed from a human rights perspective, because it enhances the ability of people who lack capacity to make their own decisions where they can and makes it more likely that sound decisions will be made on their behalf where they cannot make those decisions for themselves" (Fourth Report, HL 26/HC 224, para.4.5).

Research into the operation of the Adults with Incapacity (Scotland) Act 2000 (asp 4) found that lack of publicity about the Act and how it might benefit adults and carers was perceived as one of the main barriers to access (*The Adults with Incapacity (Scotland) Act 2000: Learning from Experience* (2004), Scottish Executive).

Territorial Extent

This Act only extends to England and Wales. Two exceptions are set out in s.68(5).

Territorial Application: Wales

The National Assembly for Wales may make regulations under ss.30 and 34 and issue guidance under s.32(3). It may also make regulations under ss.35, 36, 37 and 41. Section 68(2) provides that ss.30-41 will come into force by order made by National Assembly. Section 43(1) provides that the National Assembly must be consulted by the Lord Chancellor before a code of practice is prepared or revised.

Matters not covered by this Act

The most significant omission from the Act relates to the recommendations that the Law Commission made in Pt IX of its Final Report for the protection of vulnerable people at risk. In particular, the Commission recommended that, where local authorities have reason to believe that a vulnerable person in their area is suffering or is likely to suffer significant harm or serious exploitation, they should be under a statutory duty to investigate and to provide or arrange community care services or to take other action to protect that person (Law Comm. No.231, para.9.16).

Appointees

If an incapacitated person has little capital and receives income only from state benefits, the necessary financial arrangements can be made under reg.33 of the Social Security (Claims and Payment) Regulations 1987 (SI 1987/1968) which provides that the Secretary of State may appoint someone aged 18 or over (the "appointee") to act on behalf of the claimant. The appointee has no power to deal with the claimant's capital but can:

a   exercise any rights and duties that the claimant has under the social security legislation;
b   receive any benefits payable to the claimant; and
c   deal with the money received on the claimant's behalf in the interests of the claimant or his or her dependants.

Concern has been expressed about the nature of the enquiries conducted before appointments are made, and about the absence of regular supervision or monitoring of the performance of appointees: see R. Lavery and L. Lundy "The Social Security Apointee System" (1994) Journal of Social Welfare and Family Law, 313-327.

The Government resisted amendments to the Bill which would have brought the appointee system under the jurisdiction of the Court of Protection. However Baroness Andrews, speaking during the committee stage in the House of Lords, said:

"The Bill has enabled us to take stock of the arrangements for appointees and to improve them in the light of the Bill's principles. Officials and Ministers from the Department for Constitutional Affairs and Department for Work and Pensions have been discussing how they can use the Bill to improve the appointeeship system ...

During the process a DWP official - a benefits official - will visit the person lacking capacity and the prospective appointee. The official needs to be sure that the person does in fact lack the capacity to look after their own benefits, and that the appointee will act in their best interests. That process will be enhanced by the Bill and the code of practice. For example, it will be useful for the officials carrying out those visits to have the benefit of the extra advice on assessing capacity. DWP and DCA officials will work together to ensure that DWP guidance reflects the principles of the Bill and places best interests at its heart.

In addition DWP acknowledges that the question of monitoring needs to be addressed, and it will look at options for introducing a monitoring system. With half a million appointees, that is not going to be easy; but it is clearly important, and there will be visits, paper reviews, targeted monitoring - all those sorts of things can be looked at in the light of the Bill. DWP will act quickly to revoke appointments where allegations of mismanagement are made (*Hansard*, HL Vol.668, col.1463).

COMMENCEMENT

The Mental Capacity Act 2005 received Royal Assent on April 7, 2005.

ABBREVIATIONS

"ANH":	artificial nutrition and hydration
"Draft Code of Practice":	the first draft Code of Practice on the Mental Capacity Bill published by the Department for Constitutional Affairs in September 2004
"EPA":	Enduring Powers of Attorney
"Explanatory Notes":	Explanatory notes on the Mental Capacity Bill prepared by the Department for Constitutional Affairs and the Department of Health
"IMCA":	independent mental capacity advocate
"Joint Committee":	House of Lords, House of Commons, Joint Committee on the Draft Mental Incapacity Bill, Session 2002-3
"LPA":	lasting power of attorney
"Oral and written evidence":	House of Lords, House of Commons, Joint Committee on the Draft Mental Incapacity Bill, Session 2002-3, Volume II: Oral and written evidence, HL Paper 189-II, HC 1083-II
"the Bill":	the Mental Capacity Bill
"the court":	the Court of Protection
"the 1983 Act":	the Mental Health Act 1983 (c.20)
"the 1985 Act":	Enduring Powers of Attorney Act 1985 (c.29)

Throughout the Act, the capital letter "P" is used to refer to a person who lacks capacity or is believed to lack capacity, and the capital letter "D" is used to refer to a person exercising powers in relation to P

PART 1

PART 1   PERSONS WHO LACK CAPACITY

The principles

1.   The principles

(1) The following principles apply for the purposes of this Act.

(2) A person must be assumed to have capacity unless it is established that he lacks capacity.

(3) A person is not to be treated as unable to make a decision unless all practicable steps to help him to do so have been taken without success.

(4) A person is not to be treated as unable to make a decision merely because he makes an unwise decision.

(5) An act done, or decision made, under this Act for or on behalf of a person who lacks capacity must be done, or made, in his best interests.

(6) Before the act is done, or the decision is made, regard must be had to whether the purpose for which it is needed can be as effectively achieved in a way that is less restrictive of the person's rights and freedom of action.

GENERAL NOTE

The Joint Committee recommended that a statement of principles should appear on the face of the Act. The Committee believed "that such a statement inserted as an initial point of reference could give valuable guidance to the courts, as well as helping non-lawyers to weigh up difficult decisions. Evidence given to us indicates that this be welcome to a wide range of those who have to deal with the problems of substitute decision-making in practice. We also believe that such a statement would be valuable in helping to frame the Codes of Practice based upon the [Act]" (para.43).

The status of this section is that decisions and actions carried out under the Act should be tested against the principles which act as benchmarks for decision makers. Although there is no duty placed on persons or bodies to apply the principles, a failure to do so could be cited in legal proceedings as evidence of unlawful conduct.

The principles reflect the position that obtained at common law.

Subsection (2)

This establishes the fundamental principle that persons over the age of 16 (s.2(5)) are assumed to be mentally capable of making their own decisions. This assumption of personal autonomy can only be over-ridden if the person concerned is assessed as lacking the mental capacity to make a particular decision for him or herself at the relevant time. The formula to be used when making the assessment is set out in s.3. In legal proceedings, the burden of proof will fall on the person who asserts that capacity is lacking.

Subsection (3)

This provision is expanded upon in s.3(2).

The Explanatory Notes suggest that "all practicable steps" could include "making sure the person is in an environment in which he is comfortable or involving an expert in helping him his views" (para.20). The Joint Committee said that such steps "might include using specific communication strategies, providing information in [a] more accessible form, or treating an underlying mental disorder to enable a person to regain capacity" (para.70). Providing information over time may allow a person to assimilate information more completely, thereby maximising their actual understanding. Resource constraints are clearly relevant to the practicability of the assistance that might be required.

During the second reading debate in the House of Lords, Lord Brennan cited a dramatic example of the impact that appropriate help can have on the ability of a disabled person to communicate:

"[A] client whom I represented had for 12 years, while being able to walk and grunt but not talk, been treated as a zombie, because his family did not believe that he was capable of any cognitive function. After obtaining a judgment on liability and getting an interim payment, at the second meeting with a speech therapist who knew about communication my client was able to converse with her. When challenged by me in conference, he readily spelt the word 'encyclopaedia'. Yet his family - his carers - were convinced for 12 years that his life was pretty well worthless" (HL Vol.668, col.84).

Although all practicable steps must be taken to help a person make a decision, those assisting the person must beware of subjecting the person to undue influence. In the context of consent to medical treatment, Lord Donaldson M.R. said in *T (Adult: Refusal of Treatment), Re* [1992] 4 All E.R. 649, 662 that while it is acceptable for the patient to receive advice or for the patient to have been subject to the strong persuasion of others in reaching a decision, such persuasion must not "overbear the independence of the patient's decision". His Lordship identified the real question in each case as being: "does the patient really mean what he says or is he merely saying it for a quiet life, to satisfy someone else or because the advice and persuasion to which he has been subjected is such that he can no longer think and decide for himself? In other words, is it a decision expressed in form only, not in reality?" His Lordship identified two aspects of the effect of outside influence that could be of "crucial importance": the strength of will of the patient and the relationship of the "persuader" to the patient. With regard to the former, a patient who is "very tired, in pain or depressed will be much less able to resist having his will overborne than one who is rested, free from pain and cheerful". With regard to the relationship between the persuader and the patient, his Lordship spoke of the potential strength of the parental and marital relationship, especially with regard to arguments based on religious belief. Other outside influences that could vitiate a person's consent include fraud, misrepresentation and duress.

Research into the decision-making capabilities of persons with learning disabilities has shown that the presentation of information in a user-friendly manner makes it possible to move some people from being assessed as incapable to being assessed as capable (M.J.Gunn, J.G.Wong, I.C.H.Clare and A.J. Holland, "Decision-making capacity", Medical Law Review (1999), 7(3), 269-306). Confirmation that capacity is not static, even among patients who have engaged in self-harm, is contained in a study which found that the number of patients judged to have capacity increased significantly following the presentation of an information sheet about the specific treatment being proposed, together with a verbal explanation (R. Jacob, I.C.H .Clare, A.J. Holland, P.C. Watson, C. Maimaris and M .J. Gunn "Self-Harm, Capacity, and Refusal of Treatment: Implications for Emergency Medical Practice", Emergency Medical Journal (in press)).

Guidance on creating the right environment for assessing capacity is given in *Assessment of Mental Capacity: Guidance for Doctors and Lawyers*, BMA / Law Society (2004), para.2.3.

Subsection (4)

This provision underpins the right to personal autonomy by preserving the right of a person to make an irrational, unusual or eccentric decision which, viewed objectively, is not in that person's best interests without the person being treated as being mentally incapable by virtue of that decision alone. It does not prevent a capacity assessment being undertaken in respect of a person who makes an unwise decision, a series of unwise decisions, a decision that puts that person at risk, or who makes a decision which does not reflect that person's values, beliefs or approach to risk-taking. The making of such decisions might suggest that the person is susceptible to undue influence, or it could be an indication of inadequate understanding or a lack of information being provided to the person about the decision in question.

That the nature of the decision taken might be indicative of a lack of capacity on the part of the decision maker was emphasised by Kennedy L.J. in *Masterman-Lister v Brutton & Co* [2002] EWCA Civ 1889; [2003] 3 All E.R. 162, where his Lordship said at para.54 that although the role of the court was the investigation of capacity not outcomes, outcomes "can often cast a flood of light on capacity"

In the context of consent to medical treatment, Lord Donaldson MR said:

"Prima facie every adult has the right and capacity to decide whether or not he will accept medical treatment, even if a refusal may risk permanent injury to his health or even lead to premature death. Furthermore, it matters not whether the reasons for the refusal were rational or irrational, unknown or even non-existent. This is so notwithstanding the very strong public interest in preserving the life and health of all citizens" *(T (Adult: Refusal of Treatment), Re* [1992] 4 All E.R.649, CA, at 664).

Butler-Sloss P, in confirming that a mentally competent person is entitled to refuse treatment even if she does not give good reasons for doing so, said that "there is a point at which refusal and irrationality, as others might see it, tips the usually competent person over into a situation where the person, for however long or short a period, is actually unable to see through the consequences of the act, because that capacity to see through those consequences is inhibited by the panic situation in which the patient finds [her]self ." *(Bolton Hospitals NHS Trust v O* [2003] 1 F.L.R. 824, para.15).

The approach taken in this provision is consistent with the finding of the European Court of Human Rights in *Winterwerp v Netherlands* (1979-80) 2 E.H.R.R. 387, para.37, that Art.5 of the European Convention on Human Rights does not permit the detention of a person "simply because his views or behaviour deviate from the norms prevailing in a particular society."

Subsection (5)

The best interest principle, which must guide all actions done for or decisions made on behalf a person who lacks capacity, is expanded upon in s.4.

A clinician who follows a valid and applicable advance decision (see ss.24-26) is not acting "for or on behalf of a person who lacks capacity", he or she is acting on the instructions of a capacitated individual. It follows that the best interests principle does not apply to such decisions and healthcare professionals must comply with a valid and applicable advance decision, even though they do not consider that it would be in the patient's best interests to do so.

Subsection (6)

Someone making a decision or acting on behalf of a mentally incapacitated person must consider whether it is possible to decide or act in a way that would interfere less with the person's rights and freedom of action, or whether there is a need to act at all. Put another way, the intervention should be proportional to the particular circumstances of the case. As only "regard" must be had to this principle, an option which is not the least restrictive option can still be in the person's best interests.

The Parliamentary Under-Secretary of State for Constitutional Affairs gave the following example of an approach that would satisfy this principle: "A care assistant might be worried about residents with dementia wandering into the kitchen of the establishment unsupervised in case they come into contact with cleaning fluids. However, to steer them away from the kitchen would be unnecessary if staff ensured that all dangerous liquids were locked in a cupboard. That would not interfere with the freedom of action of the person suffering from dementia" (St.Comm.A, col.25).

Preliminary

2. People who lack capacity

(1) For the purposes of this Act, a person lacks capacity in relation to a matter if at the material time he is unable to make a decision for himself in relation to the matter because of an impairment of, or a disturbance in the functioning of, the mind or brain.

(2) It does not matter whether the impairment or disturbance is permanent or temporary.

(3) A lack of capacity cannot be established merely by reference to—

(a) a person's age or appearance, or

(b) a condition of his, or an aspect of his behaviour, which might lead others to make unjustified assumptions about his capacity.

(4) In proceedings under this Act or any other enactment, any question whether a person lacks capacity within the meaning of this Act must be decided on the balance of probabilities.

(5) No power which a person ("D") may exercise under this Act—

(a) in relation to a person who lacks capacity, or

(b) where D reasonably thinks that a person lacks capacity,

is exercisable in relation to a person under 16.

(6) Subsection (5) is subject to section 18(3).

DEFINITIONS
    "enactment": s.64(1)

GENERAL NOTE
    This section sets out the Act's definition of a person who lacks capacity, bearing in mind the assumption is that a person has capacity (s.1(2)). The definition applies for "the purposes of this Act" only. Schedule 6 makes consequential amendments to statutes to ensure that the definition contained in this Act is used in relation to other relevant proceedings. Common law definitions of capacity, such as the capacity to make a will (*Banks v Goodfellow* (1869-70) L.R. 5 Q.B. 549) and to marry (*Park, In the Estate of* [1954] P. 89), are not affected.
    If a person satisfies the "diagnostic test" set out in this section, that person's capacity to make the particular decision in question is assessed using the formula set out in s.3. If the person fails to satisfy the diagnostic test, there can be no finding of incapacity for the purposes of this Act.
    The Law Commission proposed a "diagnostic threshold" to ensure that the test of capacity "is stringent enough not to catch large numbers of people who make unusual or unwise decisions" The Commission was also concerned that there "may also be a small number of cases where a finding of incapacity could lead to action which could amount to 'detention' as defined in the European Convention on Human Rights" (Law Com. No.231, para.3.8).

Subsection (1)
    Impairment of, or a disturbance in the functioning of, the brain or mind. A wide range of conditions can result in incapacity to make decisions. In some cases, the capacity to take decisions is never attained (for example a person born with a severe leaning disability). In other cases, capacity is attained but is subsequently lost, either on a temporary or permanent basis. The Explanatory Notes state that the diagnostic test contained in this provision could "cover a range of problems, such as psychiatric illness, learning disability, dementia, brain damage or even a toxic confusional state, as long as it has the necessary effect on the functioning of the mind or brain, causing the person to be unable to make the decision" (para.22). It will "clearly also apply to patients with grave physical illnesses, which, by reason of vital organ failure and consequent biochemical disturbances, will cause either confusion or impairment of consciousness" (Dr Fiona Randall, Oral and written evidence, Ev 301). It could also cover people who are suffering from the effects of pain, shock or exhaustion.

Subsection (2)
    The temporary nature of P's incapacity matters for the purposes of decision making because a decision should be delayed if the person's mental capacity might return and the delay would be consistent with the person's best interests (see s.4(3)). Temporary loss of capacity could be caused by the effect of excessive alcohol consumption, the misuse of drugs, the nature of a person's mental disorder, the effect of prescribed medication or an emotional crisis. Also see the note on s.24(1).

Subsection (3)
    This provision, which was added at report stage in the House of Lords, is aimed at preventing unjustified assumptions being made about a person's mental capacity. It "gives further emphasis to the Bill's principle that everyone should be assumed to have capacity until it is shown that they do not. For example, it is not acceptable to say, on the assumption that someone has a learning disability, that he cannot or will not want to make decisions about where to live", *per* Baroness Andrews (*Hansard*, HL Vol.670, col.1319). Also see the notes to s.4(1).

Subsection (4)
    "The balance of probability standard means that a court is satisfied an event occurred if the court considers that, on the evidence, the occurrence of the event was more likely than not", *per* Lord Nicholls in *H (Minors) (Sexual Abuse: Standard of Proof), Re* [1996] A.C. 563 at 586.

Subsections (5) and (6)
    Although the powers under this Act only generally arise where the person lacking capacity is 16 or over, powers in relation to property might be exercised in relation to a younger person who has disabilities

which will cause the incapacity to last into adulthood (see s.18(3)). Any overlap with the jurisdiction under the Children Act 1989 (c.41) can be dealt with by order made under s.21.

3. Inability to make decisions

(1) For the purposes of section 2, a person is unable to make a decision for himself if he is unable—

(a) to understand the information relevant to the decision,

(b) to retain that information,

(c) to use or weigh that information as part of the process of making the decision, or

(d) to communicate his decision (whether by talking, using sign language or any other means).

(2) A person is not to be regarded as unable to understand the information relevant to a decision if he is able to understand an explanation of it given to him in a way that is appropriate to his circumstances (using simple language, visual aids or any other means).

(3) The fact that a person is able to retain the information relevant to a decision for a short period only does not prevent him from being regarded as able to make the decision.

(4) The information relevant to a decision includes information about the reasonably foreseeable consequences of—

(a) deciding one way or another, or

(b) failing to make the decision.

DEFINITIONS
"emergency worker": s.2(3)

GENERAL NOTE
This section sets out the test for determining whether a person is "unable to make a [particular] decision" and therefore lacks capacity for the purposes of this Act (see s.2). The approach taken is a "functional" approach to capacity as the definition relates to the ability of the person to make a particular decision at a particular moment in time, not on the person's ability to make decisions generally. The functional approach can be contrasted with the "outcome" approach which uses the consequence of the decision-making process as the criterion for determining capacity, and the "status" approach under which a person's capacity is determined by his or her membership of a specific population, such as those who have a specific psychiatric diagnosis. With regard to the status approach T.Grisso and P.Appelbaum have pointed out that a "patient may be psychotic, seriously depressed, or in a moderately advanced stage of dementia, yet still found competent to make some or all decisions" (*Assessing Competence to Consent to Treatment* (1998), p.18). The rejection of the outcome approach was emphasised in *Masterman-Lister v Jewell* [2002] EWHC 417 (QB); [2002] W.T.L.R. 563, at para.19 where Wright J said that "in principle, legal capacity depends on understanding rather than wisdom; the quality of the decision is irrelevant as long as the person understands what he is deciding". This approach is reflected in s.1(4). The appropriateness of adopting the functional approach has been confirmed by research that has shown that people with mild intellectual disabilities may have the capacity to make some financial decisions but not others (W.M.I. Suto , I.C.H. Clare, A.J. Holland and P.C. Watson "Capacity to make financial decisions among people with mild intellectual disabilities", Journal of Intellectual Disability Research (2005) 49, 199-209).

The functional approach, which allows individuals to have the maximum decision-making powers possible, reflects the position that has obtained under common law. In *Masterman-Lister v Brutton & Co* [2002] EWCA Civ 1889; [2003] 3 All E.R. 163, Chadwick L.J. said at paras 57-58:

"English law requires that a person must have the necessary mental capacity if he is to do a legally effective act or to make a legally effective decision for himself The authorities are unanimous in support of two broad propositions. First, that the mental capacity required by the law is capacity in relation to the transaction which is to be effected. Second, that what is required is the capacity to understand the nature of that transaction when it is explained."

This functional approach allows for a temporary loss of capacity, for example, unconsciousness following a road traffic accident, and for persons to lack capacity in relation to one matter but not in relation to another (perhaps more complex) matter. A fresh capacity assessment would need to be made in respect of every decision that the person might be required to make. A striking example of a situation where a person was found to be capable of making a decision in relation to one matter, but not in relation to another is the deceased who on the same day was found by Karminski J. to have had capacity to marry (*Park, In the Estate of* [1954] P. 89), and by Pearce J and a jury not to have had capacity to make a will (*Park, Culross v Park* (1950) Times, December 2, 1950) (cited by Munby J. in *Sheffield City Council v E* [2004] EWHC 2808 (Fam) at para.25).

If there is any doubt as to whether a parson lacks capacity, this should be decided on a balance of probabilities (s.2(4)). A person who wishes to challenge a finding of capacity can, if the matter cannot be resolved by discussion, mediation or the provision of a second opinion, make an application to the Court of Protection for a declaration (s.15(1)(a)).

The person who is required to assess an individual's capacity will be the person who is contemplating making a decision on behalf of the person who is to be assessed. The assessment of a person's capacity to make most day-to-day decisions will be made by the appropriate carer and will not require the involvement of a professional. Where consent to medical treatment is required, the doctor proposing the treatment is responsible for the capacity assessment. If a professional, such as a psychiatrist or a psychologist, is brought in to assist the potential decision-maker with an assessment of the person's capacity to make a complex or serious decision, the ultimate decision about capacity is that of the potential decision-maker and not the professional whose role is that of an advisor. The Draft Code of Practice at para.3.37 suggests that any of the following factors "might indicate the need for professional involvement:

- The gravity of the decision and its consequences.
- Where the person concerned disputes a finding of incapacity.
- Where there is disagreement between family members, carers and/or professionals as to the person's capacity.
- Where the person concerned is expressing different views to different people, perhaps through trying to please each or tell them what s/he thinks they want to hear.
- Where the person's capacity to make a particular decision may be subject to challenge, either at the time the decision is made or in the future - for example a person's testamentary capacity may be challenged after his or her death by someone seeking to contest the will.
- Where there may be legal consequences of a finding of capacity - for example in a settlement of damages following a claim for personal injury.
- The person concerned is repeatedly making decisions that put him/her at risk or resulted in preventable suffering or damage."

It is a striking fact that during the Parliamentary debates on the Bill no-one questioned the ability of professionals, let alone laypeople, to assess mental capacity. The available evidence suggests that professional competence in this area is poor (see the studies cited below). In the context of medical practice, T.Grisso and P.Appelbaum suggest that doctors approach the issue of capacity assessments intuitively:

"Whether they recognise it or not, most clinicians assess their patients' decision-making abilities as part of every encounter. Ordinarily, this occurs unconsciously, as clinicians take notice of patients' dress, demeanour, communicative skills, intelligence, ability to attend to a conversation, apparent understanding, and ability to reach a decision. Since we all assume, appropriately, that people with whom we deal are competent to make decisions about their own lives - indeed the law makes a similar assumption - only when are unconscious monitoring detects something unexpected do we attend to it directly" (above, p.61)

The authors suggest that the following factors alert clinicians to the need for a capacity assessment: abrupt changes in patients' mental states, patients' refusal of recommended treatment, patients' consent to specially invasive or risky treatment, and the presence of one or more risk factors to impaired decision making, such as diagnosis or age (above, pp.62-76) For a person to be assessed as being mentally incapable or making a decision he or she must: (1) be suffering from an impairment of, or disturbance in the functioning of, the mind or brain (s.2(1)); and (2) fail to satisfy any one of the requirements set out in paras (a)-(d) of subs.(1). Paragraphs (a),(b) and (c), which will cover the vast majority of cases, are taken from the decision of the Court of Appeal in *MB (Medical Treatment), Re* [1997] 2 F.L.R. 426 at 437, where Butler-Sloss L.J. identified the test of capacity in medical cases in the following terms:

"A person lacks capacity if some impairment or disturbance of mental functioning renders the person unable to make a decision whether to consent to or refuse treatment. That inability to make a decision will occur when:

a   the patient is unable to comprehend and retain the information which is material to the decision, especially as to the likely consequences of having or not having the treatment in question;
b   the patient is unable to use the information and weigh it in the balance as part of the process of arriving at the decision."

The finding of Lord Donaldson in *T (Adult: Refusal of Treatment), Re* [1992] 4 All E.R. 649 at 661 that the required capacity is the capacity which is commensurate with the gravity of the decision which the person is purporting to should be followed under this Act. Thus the more serious the decision, the greater the level of capacity required. To be valid, a consent must be truly that of the mentally capable person, given freely and uncontaminated by the undue influence of others. The nature of undue influence is considered in the note on s.1(3). Paragraph 3.1 of the *Reference Guide to Consent for Examination or Treatment* (Department of Health, 2001) considers the validity of consent given in a prison or psychiatric hospital environment:

"When patients are seen and treated in environments where involuntary detention may be an issue, such as prisons and mental hospitals, there is a potential for treatment offers to be perceived coercively, whether or not this is the case. Coercion invalidates consent and care must be taken to ensure that the patient makes a decision freely. Coercion should be distinguished from providing the patient with appropriate reassurance concerning their treatment, or pointing out the potential benefits of treatment for the patient's health. However, threats such as the withdrawal of any privileges or loss of remission of sentence for refusing consent, or using such measures to induce consent are not acceptable."

In *B (Consent to Treatment: Capacity), Re* [2002] EWHC 429 (Fam); [2002] 1 F.L.R. 1090, at para.100, Butler-Sloss P stressed the importance of distinguishing between capacity and best interests in the context of consent to medical treatment:

"If there are difficulties in deciding whether the patient has sufficient mental capacity, particularly if the refusal may have grave consequences for the patient, it is most important that those considering the issue should not confuse the question of mental capacity with the nature of the decision made by the patient, however grave the consequences. The view of the patient may reflect a difference in values rather than an absence of competence and the assessment of capacity should be approached with this firmly in mind. The doctors must not allow their emotional reaction to or strong disagreement with the decision of the patient to cloud their judgment in answering the primary question whether the patient has the mental capacity to make the decision."

A person's ambivalence about whether to receive medical treatment is only relevant to the issue of capacity "if, and only if, the ambivalence genuinely strikes at the root of the mental capacity of the patient", *per* Butler-Sloss P. in *B (Consent to Treatment: Capacity), Re* above, at para.35. In this case the President said at para.94: "Unless the gravity of the illness has affected the patient's capacity, a seriously disabled patient has the same rights as the fit person to respect for personal autonomy".

If there is concern or doubt about the mental capacity of a person to consent to medical treatment, that doubt should be resolved as soon as possible, by doctors within the hospital or NHS trust or by other normal medical procedures. In the meantime, while the question of capacity is being resolved, the person must be cared for in accordance with the judgment of the doctors as to the person's best interests. In the rare case where disagreement still exists about competence, it is of the utmost importance that the person is fully informed of the steps being taken, such as enlisting independent outside expertise, and made part of the process. Those in charge must not allow a situation of deadlock or drift to occur. If all appropriate steps to seek independent assistance from medical experts outside the hospital have failed, the hospital should not hesitate to make an application to the Court of Protection or seek the advice of the Official Solicitor (*NHS Trust v T (Adult Patient: Refusal of Medical Treatment)* [2004] EWHC 1279 (Fam), para.42).

A judge is not required to accept the evidence of psychiatrists as to a person's mental capacity (*W (Adult: Refusal of Medical Treatment), Re* [2002] EWHC Fam 901). In *Masterman-Lister v Jewell*, above, Wright J. said at para.16:

"Although the opinions of skilled and experienced medical practitioners are a very important element in the evidence to be considered by the court, that element has to be considered in conjunction with any other evidence that there may be about the manner in which the subject of the enquiry actually has conducted his everyday life and affairs."

Although the test set out in this section is easily understandable and, perhaps, gives the impression that the assessment of a person's mental capacity is a relatively straightforward task, the reality is that the assessment can sometimes be extremely difficult. Baroness Finlay of Llandaff gave evidence to the Joint Committee on this point:

"If I can give you two specific and very common instances, one where patients have been anxious, which is understandable because they are facing dying, and where the benzodiazepine group of drugs such as Midazolam are used to remove the churning drive of anxiety without sedating the patients so they can still function but they are relived in part of this desperate feeling of anxiety, butterflies and churning inside. With some of these patients you can have a conversation and they appear to understand everything that is said and have recall. The following day they have no recall whatsoever of that conversation. It may have been a few hours later in some patients. Another situation which arises is where patients' calcium goes up and that occurs in about ten per cent of all cancer patients. They become confused. That is a gradual onset and the outset is difficult to diagnose. They may appear to be arguing rationally but when their calcium level has been brought down and is treated they then are behaving differently and they have no recall of that previous conversation or the direction that they were trying to give in expressing what they wanted. Also they may completely change their mind which is a terribly important situation for a clinician. The difficulty is in judging whether they have capacity or not because at any one point in time the conversation appears to be logical and consequential There are lots of other situations which arise, particularly with patients on steroids where the steroids may have created a very mild steroid psychosis which can be difficult to diagnose and just presents as emotional immobility. Again, their thinking and perception is distorted" (Oral and Written Evidence, Ev 126).

This Act requires judgments to be made about a person's mental capacity by people without a clinical background who have had no training or experience in making such assessments. There must be a very considerable doubt as to their ability to do this. Similar doubts can be expressed about the competence of some medical practitioners to undertake this task. In its evidence to the Joint Committee, the Alzeheimer's Society emphasised the need for a skilled capacity assessment. One of its members wrote of her experiences:

"As a former nurse, my mother was extremely good at covering up her problems and was extremely plausible. Her doctor reacted with shocked amazement at our suggestion that my mother had dementia. - 'There's nothing wrong with your mother. I saw her only the other day and had a conversation with her. She's fine.' This was at a time when my mother was putting the electric kettle on the gas ring, entertaining phantom meetings of teachers in her front room, turning up at the hairdressers at 2a.m. and living on a diet of biscuits having forgotten how to cook" (Oral and Written Evidence, Ev 384).

Research into the application of the functional approach to capacity has been undertaken: see M.J.Gunn, J.G.Wong, I.C.H.Clare and A.J.Holland, "Decision-making capacity", Medical Law Review (1999) 7(3), 269-306. The authors concluded that the approach "can work, albeit the interface between legal definition and clinical practice is not a simple one to bridge" (at 306). Suto and her colleagues found that the quality of capacity assessment made by medical practitioners under Part VII of the 1983 Act, including those undertaken by psychiatrists, was poor and that most assessors relied on the status approach. The authors found little evidence of the use of the functional approach (W.M.I. Suto, I.C.H. Clare and A.J. Holland, "Substitute financial decision-making in England and Wales: a study of the Court of Protection" (2002) Journal of Social Welfare and Family Law (2002) 24(1), 37-54). There is also evidence that psychiatrists can be inconsistent in their approach to the assessment of patients' capacity to consent to treatment (A.Shah and S.Mukherjee, "Ascertaining Capacity to Consent: A survey of approaches used by psychiatrists", Medicine, Science and the Law; (2003) 43, 231-235). A study of the recognition of the mental incapacity of acutely ill medical hospital in-patients by clinical staff found that only a quarter of patients identified by the investigators as not having mental capacity were identified by the clinicians (V. Raymont, W. Bingley, A Buchanan, S. David, P. Hayward, S. Wessely, and M. Hotopf, "Prevalence of mental incapacity in medical inpatients and associated risk factors: cross sectional study" Lancet (2004); 364: 1421-27).

Subsection (1) para. (a)

The nature of understanding is considered by T.Grisso and P.Appelbaum, above, at p.38:

"As basic as the concept of understanding may seem, the psychological process related to it are not easily defined. A person's accurate assimilation of information involves a complex series of events. First the information must be received as presented, a process that is influenced not only by sensory integrity, but also by perceptual functions such as attention and selective awareness. Whatever is received then undergoes cognitive processing and is encoded in a manner consistent with the person's existing fund of information and concepts, which in turn influences how, and how will, the message is recorded and stored in the memory."

The authors point out that many medical conditions, as well as chronic mental disorders and disabilities, can "have a substantial negative influence on these functions" (p.39).

The information provided must include the information specified in subs.(4). As the information must be "relevant to the decision", the person should not be burdened with peripheral information. The information, which should be devoid of technical jargon, should be given in an appropriate manner in the person's first language (subs.(2)). All practicable steps should be taken to assist the person to understand the information (s.1(3)), with account being taken of any cultural or religious factors relating to the person which might inhibit communication.

In the context of consent to medical treatment, an explanation in "broad terms" of the nature of the procedure which is intended and its likely effects would be sufficient for the person's consent to be "real" (*Chatterton v Gerson* [1981] 1 Q.B. 432 at 442). In *R v Mental Health Act Commission Ex p. X* (1998) 9 B.M.L.R. 77 at 87, DC, Stuart-Smith L.J. said that he could not "accept that a patient must understand the precise physiological process involved before he can be said to be capable of understanding the nature and likely effects of the treatment or can consent to it". The finding in *Chatterton v Gerson* was followed by the House of Lords in *Sidaway v Board of Governors of the Bethlem Royal Hospital* [1985] 1 All E.R. 643, where it was held that the decision on what risks should be disclosed to a patient was primarily a matter of clinical judgment and in making that judgment a doctor was required to act in accordance with a practice accepted at the time as proper by a responsible body of medical opinion. It would not matter that there may be another body of responsible medical opinion which takes a different view. However, Lords Keith and Bridge, speaking with the majority, considered that the court might in certain circumstances come to the conclusion that disclosure of a particular risk was so obviously necessary to an informed choice on the part of the patient that no reasonably prudent doctor would fail to make it. This approach was confirmed by the House of Lords in *Bolitho (Deceased) v City and Hackney HA* [1997] 4 All E.R. 771, where it was held that in a rare case, if it could be demonstrated that the medical opinion was not capable of withstanding logical analysis, the judge would be entitled to hold that the body of opinion was not reasonable or responsible. *Sidaway* and *Bolitho* were considered by the Court of Appeal in *Pearce v United Bristol Healthcare NHS Trust* (1999) 48 B.M.L.R. 118, where Lord Woolf held at para.23 that:

"[I]f there is a significant risk which would affect the judgment of a reasonable patient then in the normal course it is the responsibility of a doctor to inform the patient of that significant risk, if the information is needed so that the patient can determine for him or herself as to what course that he or she should adopt."

Whether a risk is "significant" cannot be determined simply in terms of percentages. The doctor will have to:

" take into account all the relevant considerations, which include the ability of the patient to comprehend what he has to say to him or her and the state of the patient at the particular time, both from the physical point of view and the emotional point of view" (para.24).

If a patient asks about a risk, it is the doctor's legal duty to give an honest answer (per Lord Woolf at para.5).

In *R (A Minor) (Wardship: Medical Treatment), Re* [1991] 4 All E.R. 177, a case concerning the capacity of a child to consent to treatment, Lord Donaldson MR said at 187:

"[W]hat is involved is not merely an ability to understand the nature of the proposed treatment - in this case compulsory medication - but a full understanding and appreciation of the consequences both of the treatment in terms of intended and possible side effects and, equally important, the anticipated consequences of a failure to treat".

The treating doctor should therefore provide the patient with information about what would happen to the patient if the treatment is provided, the likely consequences to the patient if the treatment is not provided, and the risks and side effects of the treatment. In the studies examined by Diana Rose and her colleagues, approximately half of those who receive electroconvulsive therapy feel that they are given insufficient information about the procedure ("Information, consent and perceived coercion: patient's perspectives on electroconvulsive therapy", Br. J. Psychiatry (2005), 186, 54-59).

The General Medical Council's guidelines "Seeking Patients' Consent: The Ethical Considerations" state at para.10:

"You should not withhold information necessary for decision making unless you judge that disclosure of some relevant information would cause the patient serious harm."

A similar approach to the existence of a "therapeutic privilege" that allows for certain information to be withheld from patients is taken by the Code of Practice on the Mental Health Act at para.15.16. Given that the notion of professional paternalism has been effectively buried by the recommendations made by Learning from Bristol: the report of the public inquiry into children's heart surgery at the Bristol Royal Infirmary 1984-1995 (Cm.5207), it is suggested that Andrew Hockton is correct when he states that doctors invoke therapeutic privilege "at their peril" (*The Law of Consent to Medical Treatment*, 2002, para.1-002).

Subsection (1) para.(b)

Retain. See subs.(3).

Subsection (1) para.(c)

Understanding the information is not sufficient: the person must also be able to use the information as part of the process of arriving at a decision. In using the information, the person can be assisted by relevant professional advice (*Masterman-Lister v Brutton & Co* [2003] 3 All E.R. 162, CA), and by support from the person's care network. The Draft Code at para.3.12 offers the following examples of persons who able to understand, but not "use or weigh" the information:

"For example, a person suffering from anorexia may be able to understand rationally the consequences of not eating, but lack the capacity to weigh them against the desire not to eat and will decide not to eat regardless of whether he or she feels hungry, the time of day etc. Certain types of pathology seen after catastrophic brain damage, such as a massive stoke, can cause people, who are able to understand and absorb information, to take decisions or to act impulsively, regardless of the information available or their understanding of it."

In order to "use or weigh" information, the person must believe the information. In *B v Croydon HA* (1994) 22 B.M.L.R. 13, Thorpe J. said at 20 that in the context of consent to medical treatment there is a difference between outright disbelief (due to mental disorder) which meant being "impervious to reason, divorced from reality, or incapable of adjustment after reflection", and "the tendency which most people have when undergoing medical treatment to self assess and then puzzle over the divergence between medical and self assessment".

In *Re MB*, above, the court said that if a compulsive disorder or phobia from which the patient suffers dominates her thinking, the decision may not be a true one. In this case the patient's phobia to needles induced such panic in her that "at that moment the needle or mask dominated her thinking and made her quite unable to consider anything else" (at 431). Similar considerations apply if the patient's thinking is dominated by fear or pain.

Subsection (1) para.(d)

The rationale for this provision is explained in the Explanatory Memorandum at para.27:

"This is intended to be a residual category and will only affect a small group of persons, in particular some of those with the very rare condition of 'locked-in syndrome'. It seems likely that people suffering from this condition can in fact still understand, retain and use information and so would not be regarded as lacking capacity under subs.(1)(a)-(c). Some people who suffer from this condition can communicate by blinking an eye, but it seems that others cannot communicate at all. [This provision] treats those who are completely unable to communicate their decisions as unable to make a decision. Any residual ability to communicate (such as blinking an eye to indicate 'yes' or 'no' in answer to a question) would exclude a person from this category."

Although the blinking of an eye or the squeezing of a hand can be used to communicate a decision without undue difficulty, it would be less easy to use such methods to identify whether the person has understood and applied the information provided. In *AK (Adult Patient) (Medical Treatment: Consent), Re* [2001] 1 F.L.R. 129, a patient who could only communicate by blinking one eyelid was held to be mentally capable.

Subsection (2)

This provision, which expands upon the principle set out in s.1(3), was added at the third reading of the Bill so that there "is no longer any doubt: no one should be labelled incapable merely because insufficient efforts have been made to help him understand and communicate", *per* the Parliamentary Under-Secretary of State (*Hansard*, HC Vol.428, col.1632.

An explanation. The explanation must be sufficiently specific to enable the person to use or weigh the information as required by subs.(1)(c).

Subsection (3)
Short period. The person must be able to retain the information until the decision is made.

4. Best interests

(1) In determining for the purposes of this Act what is in a person's best interests, the person making the determination must not make it merely on the basis of—

  (a) the person's age or appearance, or

  (b) a condition of his, or an aspect of his behaviour, which might lead others to make unjustified assumptions about what might be in his best interests.

(2) The person making the determination must consider all the relevant circumstances and, in particular, take the following steps.

(3) He must consider—

  (a) whether it is likely that the person will at some time have capacity in relation to the matter in question, and

  (b) if it appears likely that he will, when that is likely to be.

(4) He must, so far as reasonably practicable, permit and encourage the person to participate, or to improve his ability to participate, as fully as possible in any act done for him and any decision affecting him.

(5) Where the determination relates to life-sustaining treatment he must not, in considering whether the treatment is in the best interests of the person concerned, be motivated by a desire to bring about his death.

(6) He must consider, so far as is reasonably ascertainable—

  (a) the person's past and present wishes and feelings (and, in particular, any relevant written statement made by him when he had capacity),

  (b) the beliefs and values that would be likely to influence his decision if he had capacity, and

  (c) the other factors that he would be likely to consider if he were able to do so.

(7) He must take into account, if it is practicable and appropriate to consult them, the views of—

  (a) anyone named by the person as someone to be consulted on the matter in question or on matters of that kind,

  (b) anyone engaged in caring for the person or interested in his welfare,

  (c) any donee of a lasting power of attorney granted by the person, and

  (d) any deputy appointed for the person by the court,

as to what would be in the person's best interests and, in particular, as to the matters mentioned in subsection (6).

(8) The duties imposed by subsections (1) to (7) also apply in relation to the exercise of any powers which—

  (a) are exercisable under a lasting power of attorney, or

  (b) are exercisable by a person under this Act where he reasonably believes that another person lacks capacity.

(9) In the case of an act done, or a decision made, by a person other than the court, there is sufficient compliance with this section if (having complied

with the requirements of subsections (1) to (7)) he reasonably believes that what he does or decides is in the best interests of the person concerned.

(10) "Life-sustaining treatment" means treatment which in the view of a person providing health care for the person concerned is necessary to sustain life.

(11) "Relevant circumstances" are those—

(a) of which the person making the determination is aware, and

(b) which it would be reasonable to regard as relevant.

DEFINITIONS

"treatment": s.64(1)

"lasting power of attorney": s.64(1)

"deputy": s.64(1)

"the court": s.64(1)

GENERAL NOTE

Section 1(5) establishes the principle that "an act done, or decision made, under this Act for or on be-half of a person who lacks capacity must be done, or made, in his best interests". This section sets out a checklist of factors which must be considered before the decision is made, or the act is carried out. In ef-fect, the checklist establishes the course of action that should be followed in order to reach a determina-tion whether a decison is in the person's best interests, a term which is not defined in this Act. It deals with the process of acquiring evidence, rather than specifying the criteria of best interests. A considerable latitude is therefore granted by thr deciosn-maker when reaching a reasonable belief as to where P's best interests lie. In its report on *Mental Incapacity*, the Law Commission acknowledged that "no statutory guidance could offer an exhastive account of what is in the persons best interests, the intention being that the individual person and his or her individual circumstances should always determine the result" (Law Com. No. 231, para.3.26). As well as being in the person's best interests, the decision must also satisfy the least restrictive option principle set out in s.1(6).

Any person or body that intervenes on behalf of P must believe that their act or decision is in that per-son's best interests and that belief will have to be reasonable (subs.(9)). The test of best interests is therefore an objective one. It is the best interests of P that is at issue, not the best interests of another. The test applies to all decisions made or actions taken under this Act, ranging from a decision of the Court of Protection to a minor decision made by an informal carer.

Only one course of action can be in the best interests of P. The practical effect of subs.(6) is to attempt to ascertain what P's subjective preference would have been had he or she been mentally capable. How-ever the effect of this is not to require the decision maker to make a form of substituted judgment on be-half of P as the matters itemised in subs.(6) must merely be considered by the decision-maker who may come to a decision which P would not have wanted. For example, "if someone had a lifelong aversion to needles, a decision could still be taken to give them the necessary injection when they were unconscious after a car crash", *per* the Parliamentary Under-Secretary of State, St.Comm. A, col.73. The concept of substituted judgment has been developed by the American courts and rejected by the English courts; see, for example the observations of Lord Goff and Lord Mustill in Airedale *NHS Trust v Bland* [1993] 1 All E.R.821 at 872-3, and 891-2 respectively.

The provisions of subss.(3)-(7) do not provide an exhaustive list of factors that need to be taken into account as the decision maker must consider "all the relevant circumstances" (subs.(2)). The assessment of a P's best interests is clearly going to be influenced by either the personal or professional relationship that the assessor has with P.

If a person wishes to challenge a determination made by the decision-maker as to what is in the best interests of P, an application can the made to the Court of Protection if all attempts to resolve the conflict through discussion and/or mediation fail.

Best interests and medical treatment

In the context of medical treatment, a patient's best interests are not limited to best medical interests (Re M.B. (Medical Treatment) [1997] 2 F.L.R. 426, CA); they encompass "medical, emotional and all other welfare issues" (per Butler-Sloss P. in *A (Mental Patient: Sterilisation), Re* [2000] 1 F.L.R. 549 at 555). In *Y (Mental Patient: Bone Marrow Donation), Re* [1996] 2 F.L.R. 787, Connell J. held that it was in the best interests of an incompetent patient to donate bone marrow to her gravely ill sister. Having heard evidence that the death of the sister would have a particularly adverse effect upon the mother, with whom the patient enjoyed a very close relationship, and, in particular, would significantly handicap her ability to visit the patient, his Lordship held that the procedure would be to the patients "emotional, psychological and social benefit".

The sanctity of life is a fundamental principle and there is a very strong presumption in favour of a course of action which will prolong life (*B (A Minor) (Wardship: Medical Treatment), Re* [1981] 1 W.L.R. 1421). Lord Goff said in *Airedale NHS Trust v Bland* [1993] 1 All E.R. 821 at 865 and 866:

"...the fundamental principle is the principle of the sanctity of human life - a principle long recognised not only in our own society but also in most, if not all, civilised societies throughout the modern world, as is indeed evidenced by its recognition both in Art.2 of the European Convention on Human Rights and in Art. 6 of the International Covenant on Civil and Political Rights

But this principle, fundamental though it is, is not absolute We are concerned with circumstances in which it may be lawful to withhold from a patient medical treatment or care by means of which his life may be prolonged. But here too there is no absolute rule that the patient's life must be prolonged by such treatment or care, if available, regardless of the circumstances."

This approach is illustrated by the case of *D (Medical Treatment: Mentally Disabled Patient), Re* [1998] 2 F.L.R. 22 where Sir Stephen Brown P. granted a declaration that "notwithstanding the [patient's] inability to consent to or refuse medical treatment, it is lawful as being in the best interests of the patient that the [NHS Trust] do not impose haemodialysis upon him in circumstances in which, in the opinion of the medical practitioners responsible for such treatment, it is not reasonable practicable so to do". This was a case where it had proved to be impossible to treat a gravely ill, physically protesting, incompetent patient. The doctors had sought a declaration to protect themselves from any liability arising from a failure to carry out the treatment.

In *W Healthcare NHS Trust v H* [2004] EWCA Civ 1324, reference was made to the following passage from para.1.2 of the BMA's "Withholding and Withdrawing Life Prolonging Medical Treatment: Guidance for decision making" (2000):

"Where, however, the disability is so profound that individuals have no or minimal levels of awareness of their own existence and no hope of recovering awareness the question arises as to whether continuing to provide treatment aimed at prolonging that life would provide a benefit to them."

The Court of Appeal has held that the touchstone of best interests in this context would be whether the continuation of life would be intolerable for the patient. Brooke L.J. said at para.30:

"English law, as it stands at present, places a very heavy burden on those who are advocating a course which would lead inevitably to the cessation of a human life."

In making this finding, the court followed the approach taken by Munby J. in *R. (on the application of Burke) v General Medical Council* [2004] EWHC 1879 (Admin) at para.116:

"If the patient is incompetent, the test is best interests. There is a very strong presumption in favour of taking steps which will prolong life, and save in exceptional circumstances, or where the patient is dying, the best interests of the patient will normally require such steps to be taken. In case of doubt that doubt falls to be resolved in favour of the preservation of life. But the obligation is not absolute. Important as the sanctity of life is, it may have to take second place to human dignity. In the context of life-prolonging treatment the touchstone of best interests is intolerability. So if the life-prolonging treatment is providing some benefit it should be provided unless the patient's life, if thus prolonged, would from the patient's point of view be intolerable"

The Lord Chancellor said at the second reading of the Bill in the House of Lords that "in some cases it will be in the best interests of the person to withhold treatment or to give palliative care that might incidentally shorten life" (*Hansard*, HL Vol.668, col.15). In support of this approach, he quoted from the Roman Catholic Archbishop of Cardiff who said:

"it is not the church's position that life must be sustained at all costs. On the contrary, one can quite reasonably, and consistently with one's responsibilities for oneself and others, decide to refuse treatment - even life sustaining treatment - which one judges burdensome or futile, knowing that forgoing the treatment will shorten one's life."

When considering the best interests of a patient concerning a possible kidney transplantation, it is the duty of the court "to assess the advantages and disadvantages of the various treatments and management options, the viability of each such option and the likely effect each would have on the patient's best interests and, I would add, his enjoyment of life"; *per* Butler-Sloss P. in *A Hospital NHS Trust v S* [2003] EWHC 365 (Fam) at para.47.

In *Re A*, above, Thorpe L.J. said at 560:

"[T]he first instance judge with the responsibility to make an evaluation of the best interests of a claimant lacking capacity should draw up a balance sheet. The first entry should be of any factor or factors of actual benefit Then on the other sheet the judge should write any counterbalancing dis-benefits to the applicant Then the judge should enter on each sheet the potential gains and losses in each instance making some estimate of the extent of the possibility that the gain or loss might accrue. At the end of that exercise the judge should be better placed to strike a balance between the sum of the certain and possible gains against the sum of the certain and possible losses. Obviously, only if the account is in relatively significant credit will the judge conclude that the applicant is likely to advance the best interests of the claimant".

In *Re A*, the question whether third party interests, such as the interests of potential sexual partners of the patient, should ever be considered in a case concerned with the best interests of a patient was left open. During the Bill's passage through Parliament, the BMA sought assurances that it would be possible to conduct a diagnostic test on an incapacitated person primarily for the benefit of a family member in the case of genetic diseases, or to a nurse or doctor if a needlestick accident had occurred during the person's treatment. The Minister of State responded to these concerns as follows:

"[T]he Bill will allow for acts whose primary purpose is to benefit a third party, provided that those acts are in P's best interests. I reassure the House that the interpretation of best interests could be broader than P's medical best interests. I can confirm that the Bill will not prevent a genetic test for a familial cancer, for example, that might not be essential to P's medical care but would provide considerable benefit to some other family member. Similarly, HIV testing would be lawful if there were a needlestick injury to a nurse involved in P's care and if a timely diagnosis of HIV status would be in P's best interests, so that treatment could be started. There is the ability for a medical professional in those circumstances - if they reasonably think that a person might have HIV/AIDS or hepatitis C and they might have been affected by it - to request a test so that treatment of P could start" (*Hansard*, HC Vol.428, col.1601).

Although it is likely that a court would confirm the lawfulness of the assurances given by the Minister, the best interests principle would not be satisfied in a situation where the procedure in question resulted in no tangible or intangible benefit to P. It could be argued in a situation where the primary purpose of the intervention is to benefit a third party that an intangible benefit would be the desire of P, had he or she been capable, to be seen to be "a normal decent person, acting in accordance with contemporary standards of morality" (*C (Spinster and Mental Patient), Re* [1991] 3 All E.R. 866, *per* Hoffmann J. at 870).

Where there is no alternative treatment available for a mentally incapacitated patient and the disease is progressive and fatal, it is reasonable to consider experimental treatment with unknown benefits and risks, but without significant risks of increased suffering to the patient, in cases where there is some chance of benefit to the patient (*Simms v Simms* [2002] EWHC Fam 2734; [2003] 1 All E.R. 669) Butler-Sloss P. said at para.57: "A patient who is not able to consent to pioneering treatment ought not to be deprived of the chance in circumstances where he would be likely to consent if he had been competent". Her Ladyship stressed at para.64 that in such cases the views of the family of the patient about the proposed treatment would carry great weight in the wider considerations of the best interests test.

Although, in the absence of an appropriate lasting power of attorney, the next of kin of a mentally incapable patient has no legal right either to consent or to refuse treatment on behalf of the patient, it is not necessarily undesirable for such consent to be sought if the interests of the patient will not be adversely affected by any consequential delay. This is because "contact with the next of kin may reveal that the patient has made an anticipatory choice which, if clearly established and applicable in the circumstances - two major 'ifs' - would bind the practitioner (*NHS Trust v T (Adult Patient: Refusal of Medical Treatment)*, above, *per* Lord Donaldson MR at 649).

The General Medical Council describes the best interests' principle in *Seeking patients' consent: the ethical considerations*, 1999, at para.25:

"In deciding what options may be reasonably considered as being in the best interests of a patient who lacks capacity to decide, [the treating doctor] should take into account:

- options for treatment or investigation which are clinically indicated;
- any evidence of the patient's previously expressed preferences, including an advance statement;
- your own and the health care team's knowledge of the patient's background, such as cultural, religious, or employment considerations;
- views about the patient's preferences given by a third party who may have other knowledge of the patient, for example the patient's partner, family, carer, or a person with parental responsibility;
- which option least restricts the patient's future choices, where more than one option (including non-treatment) seems reasonable in the patient's best interest".

In the absence of a valid and applicable advance decision, the supposed view of the patient, as identified by relatives, will be no more than a factor to be taken into account in determining where his or her best interests lie.

Subsection (1)

Although the Government resisted an amendment to insert an anti-discrimination principle in s.1 for technical reasons and because it "would be inconceivable that giving someone less favourable treatment because of his disability, sex, age, race or sexual orientation could ever be considered to be in his best interests" (*per* the Parliamentary Under-Secretary of State (*Hansard*, HL Vol.668, col.1194)), the question of including some form of anti-discrimination or equal consideration provision in the Bill was a recurrent theme in the Parliamentary debates. The Government's response to this concern was to amend this provision at report stage in the House of Lords to "make sure that no one began a best interests determination with unjustified assumptions or prejudices. [The provision now] makes it clear that decision-making must start from a blank slate. People cannot say, 'She is very old so it is not necessary to give her this treatment' or, 'He has very severe physical disabilities, so it is obviously not in his best interests to have an operation'. Instead there must be a full and objective best interests assessment in every situation", *per* Baroness Andrews (*Hansard*, HL Vol.670, col.1320).

A person's best interests. The best interests criterion does not apply to advance decisions: see the note on s.1(5).

Appearance. This covers "visible medical problems, disabilities, the colour of someone's skin, religious dress, and so on", *per* Baroness Andrews, above.

Condition. The condition could be temporary.

Subsection (2)

All the relevant circumstances. In the Bill as originally drafted, this phrase read "all the circumstances appearing to him to be relevant". The amendment, together with the addition of subs.(11), were made in order to emphasise the objective nature of the best interests test (*Hansard*, HC Vol.428, col.1631).

In particular. None of the considerations set out in the indicative "checklist" contained in subss.(3)-(7) take precedence over any other consideration. The Government's view is the "any prioritising of factors within the best interests checklist would have the effect of unnecessarily fettering the application of all factors in the checklist. We believe that the checklist as it is in the draft Bill is sufficiently flexible to allow the factors to be applied to any particular individual in their particular circumstances" (*The Government Response to the Scrutiny Committee's Report on the draft Mental Incapacity Bill*, (Cm.6121)).

Subsection (3)

If the person is likely to regain his or her capacity at some point in the future, the decision should be postponed until then if such a delay is consistent with the person's best interests. Paragraph 4.16 of the Draft Code of Practice identifies the following factors "which may indicate that a person may regain capacity :

- The cause of the incapacity can be treated, either by medication or some other form of treatment or therapy.
- The incapacity may decrease in time (for example where caused by the effects of medication or alcohol, or following a sudden shock).
- People may learn new skills or be subject to new experiences which increase their capacity to make certain decisions, for example, a young adult with learning disabilities who leaves his parental home to live in supported accommodation and gains new skills as a result.
- The person may have a condition which causes capacity to fluctuate (such as some forms of mental illness) so it may be possible to arrange for the decision to be made during a lucid interval.
- A person previously unable to communicate may learn a new form of communication."

Subsection (4)

This provision complements the principle contained in s.1(3). The decision-maker might wish to seek the help of others when complying with this obligation to involve the person to the fullest practicable extent in both the decision-making process and the consequences of the decision.

Reasonably practicable. This is an objective requirement. "[T]here will always be cases where, for urgent or non-emergency reasons, it would be inappropriate and not in a person's best interests to delay acting, which is why the words 'reasonably practicable' are in clause 4(4). It is also unrealistic to expect all people affected by the Bill to be able to participate in decisions. The Bill applies to people in a coma, as well as to those who are seriously distressed or who need urgent care. While in some cases it would be possible to wait until the person is capable of making the decision themselves, in other cases it clearly would not", *per* the Parliamentary Under-Secretary of State, St. Comm. A, col.92.

Improve his ability to participate. Using communication support where this is appropriate.

Subsection (5)

This provision was inserted at the Committee stage in the House of Lords in an attempt to respond to the concern of those who considered that decisions concerning life-sustaining treatment could lead to euthanasia by omission. Its purpose is to "make it absolutely clear that no person, whether doctor, attorney, deputy or court, can, when making a best interests determination, have the motive of causing death, regardless of what would be in his best interests" (Joint Committee on Human Rights, Fourth Report, Session 204-2005, Appendix 4, para.41). The Joint Committee expressed its concern that proving the motive of a person making a best interests determination will in practice "be extremely difficult" (para.4.42). This concern was shared by some members of the House of Lords who drew a distinction between intent, which can be objectively identified by examining the act, and motive, which is a state of mind which cannot be objectively verified: see, for example, Lord St John of Fawsley (*Hansard*, HL Vol.668, cols 1167-1170.

The Parliamentary Under-Secretary of State said that this provision "does not change the law as it stands at the moment. But it does put it beyond doubt. All that matters is that the decision maker considers the range of treatment options available and the patient's objective best interests in respect of those treatments. [Subsection (5)] cannot be interpreted to mean that doctors are under an obligation to provide, or to continue to provide, life-sustaining treatment where that treatment is not in the best interests of the patients. That is the case even when the patient's death is foreseen" (H.C. Vol.670, cols.1293-1294).

If there is any ambiguity in either an advance decision or a lasting power of attorney about a purported refusal of life-sustaining treatment, the treatment should be provided.: see s.11(8) and *HE v A Hospital NHS Trust* [2003] EWHC 1017 (Fam); [2003] 2 F.L.R. 408, noted under s.24. Also see *W Healthcare NHS Trust v H* [2004] EWCA Civ 1324, above.

Life-sustaining treatment. Is defined in subs.(10).

Subsection (6)

The factors set out in this provision cannot determine the decision: they must be considered by the decision-maker and weighed against other factors. In the absence of a written record, it may be difficult to establish whether the decision-maker has taken these factors into account when reaching the decision.

Paragraph (a)

"Wishes and feelings" about a particular issue can be expressed orally, in writing, or through behaviour. The past or present wishes and feelings of the person would normally carry substantial weight in the determination of that person's best interests. Although the person may lack mental capacity, he or she may be able to indicate present wishes and feelings or preferences through expressions of pleasure or distress. These indications, which might be accessed through the use of psychological techniques, should be given serious consideration by the decision maker. As the incapacity might have the effect of altering the person's perception about what he or she might find acceptable, where past wishes and feelings conflict with present wishes and feelings, greater weight should be given to the latter.

The person's wishes and feelings must be considered by the decision-maker who could be faced with the task of balancing a person's wishes and feelings against a contrary course of action which is objectively believed to be in that person's best interests. For example, the person could have been subject to significant psychological strain when the wishes and feelings were expressed. The Draft Code of Practice states at para.4.21: "[I]t is important to recognise that the person's wishes and feelings will not automatically control the outcome. The 'best interests' principle is a fundamental principle, requiring what is best for the person." There will clearly be occasions when, having undertaken the consultations set out in subs.(7), it would be difficult for the decision-maker to establish whether the person's past expression of wishes and feelings as reported by others represent that person's actual wishes and feelings expressed at that time. This situation is likely to occur when the reporter has a vested interest in the decision. It is also important for the decision-maker to be alert to the possibility of the person's expression of his or her past or present wishes and feelings having been subject to the undue influence of another (see the note on s.l(3)).

The context within which the wishes and feelings were expressed should be carefully examined, *e.g.* a person might have expressed a desire not to live at a time when he or she was clinically depressed or was ignorant about the true prognosis of an illness or of the treatment that could be offered. The person might also have been misinformed about a crucial component of an issue that was being considered. It is also the case that a person's wishes and feelings can undergo dramatic shifts due to a change of personal perspective. One disabled witness to the Joint Committee wrote that she had had a settled wish that she wanted to die "that lasted about ten years, and during the first five of those years I made serious suicide attempts several times. I was saved only because my friends refused to accept my view that my life had no value, and made sure I received emergency treatment in hospital, which was given against my will. Then I was extremely angry with them; now I am eternally grateful What has changed is not my medical condition, but my outlook on life. If advance decisions had been legally binding then, I have no doubt that I would have written one" (Alison Davis, Oral and written evidence, Ev 359).

Relevant written statement. The purpose of the words in parenthesis "is to clarify that if someone with capacity has written down their wishes and feelings in respect of a matter, including positive preferences, those must be explicitly taken into account in a best-interests determination", *per* the Parliamentary Under-Secretary of State (*Hansard*, HC Vol.670, col.1442. In the context of medical treatment, where someone has sought to make a written advance decision that does not qualify under ss.24 and 25, but there is a reasonable belief that the written statement is an expression of the person's wishes, it must be taken into account. The more specific and well thought-out the statement, the more likely it will be persuasive in determining best interests. Also see the note on "advance statements" in the General Note to s.24.

Paragraph (b)

Beliefs and values may be evidenced by factors such as the person's cultural background, religious and/or political affiliation, memberships of societies, subscriptions to charitable causes and known past behaviour and expressions of conviction.

Paragraph (c)

Other factors. Such as emotional bonds, family obligations or concern for others. If there are no such factors, the assumption should be that the person would be "a normal decent person, acting in accordance with contemporary standards of morality" (*C (Spinster and Mental Patient), Re* [1991] 3 All E.R. 866 at 870).

Subsection (7)

If there is no-one apart from a paid carer in the categories set out in this provision with whom it would be appropriate to consult about P's best interests, an independent mental capacity advocate must be consulted in the situations set out in ss.37-39. The decision-maker must bear in mind P's right to confidentiality when undertaking the consultation(s).

The decision-maker must *consider* consulting the persons listed. Such persons may be able to assist with providing information relevant to the issues set out in subs.(6). The consultations might also disclose to existence of an advance decision made by P. Whether it is "practicable and appropriate" to undertake the consultation will depend upon a number of factors including the urgency of the decision (no consultation may be possible in an emergency) and the nature of the decision (consultation would not be required for trivial decisions such as whether to watch television). The views of the consultees about the person's best interests may differ from the person's own views as identified under subs.(6)(a).

A decision-maker must be able to justify a decision that it was not "practicable and appropriate" to consult someone identified in this provision. The meaning of "practicable" was considered by Sir Hugh Griffiths in *Owen v Crown House Engineering* [1973] 3 All E.R.618, NIRC at 622:

"It is important not to equate 'practicable' with 'possible'. When considering whether a course of action is possible, it is not permissible to consider the results of that course of action; if it can be done, it must be done. But when considering whether a course of action is practicable it may be permissible to look at the end result. Like so many other words of the English language, 'practicable' will take considerable colour from the context in which it is used."

The weight to be given to the views expressed by the consultees will depend on a number of factors including the extent of their knowledge of P, the amount of contact that they have with P, and their relationship with P. It should be noted that studies have shown that relatives' perception of the patient's likely views often differ substantially from the patient's own wishes; see, for example, A.B. Seckler *et al*, "Substituted judgment: how accurate are proxy predictions?" Ann Intern Med 1991; 115(9):743-5.

Paragraph (b)

Carers UK in its evidence to the Joint Committee expressed concern that this provision gives "equal decision-making weight to both professionals and to carers" (Oral and written evidence, Ev 338). There have been occasions when the sustained opposition of family carers to the firmly held views of professionals about the care needs of an incapacitated person has been proved to have been correct; see, for example, the "Report on an Investigation into Complaint No.02/C/17068 against Bolton Metropolitan Borough Council" (November 2004).

Interested in his welfare. The decision-maker should consider the nature of the interest and its motivation before consulting persons in this category. The Parliamentary Under-Secretary of State for Constitutional Affairs said that an advocate could fall into this category (St. Comm. A, col.100).

Subsection (8)

This applies the duties contained in this section to the following situations: (1) any decision made by a donee acting under a lasting power of attorney; and (2) where the person concerned does not in fact lack capacity but where the decision-maker reasonably believes the person lacks capacity.

Subsection (9)

If the decision-maker, having satisfied the requirements of subss.(1)-(7) reasonably believes that what has been done or decided is in the best interests of the P, he or she will have complied with this section. Reasonable belief is an objective test and the decision-maker will therefore need to identify objective reasons to support the contention that he or she believed that the decision was in the P's best interests.

Subsection (10)

This provision was subject to a Government amendment to delete the word "his" before "life" because "in the case of a pregnant woman we want to ensure that the life of the baby, not only the life of the mother, must be considered", *per* the Parliamentary Under-Secretary of State (*Hansard*, HL Vol.668, col.1184).

5. Acts in connection with care or treatment

(1) If a person ("D") does an act in connection with the care or treatment of another person ("P"), the act is one to which this section applies if—
    (a) before doing the act, D takes reasonable steps to establish whether P lacks capacity in relation to the matter in question, and
    (b) when doing the act, D reasonably believes—
        (i) that P lacks capacity in relation to the matter, and
        (ii) that it will be in P's best interests for the act to be done.
(2) D does not incur any liability in relation to the act that he would not have incurred if P—
    (a) had had capacity to consent in relation to the matter, and
    (b) had consented to D's doing the act.
(3) Nothing in this section excludes a person's civil liability for loss or damage, or his criminal liability, resulting from his negligence in doing the act.
(4) Nothing in this section affects the operation of sections 24 to 26 (advance decisions to refuse treatment).

GENERAL NOTE

The aim of this section is to clarify aspects of the common law principle of necessity which enable decisions to be taken for people who lack capacity. It does not create any new powers of intervention or duties to act, but offers protection against civil and criminal liability for certain acts done in connection with the care or treatment of P and which would normally require that persons consent, *e.g.* helping P to dress, wash or to eat, entering P's house, and providing P with medical treatment. Such acts, which could be performed by a range of professional and lay people, are not limited to "day to day" or emergency situations, as they could include, for example, performing a serious planned operation on P. Without the protection of this section, such acts could amount to civil wrongs, such as trespass, or crimes, such as assault. Liability for negligent acts is unaffected (subs.(3)). Subject to the limitations set out in s.6, this section enables steps to be taken on behalf of P by family members, carers, and health and care professionals without the need for any formal authority or involvement of the Court of Protection as long as the steps are in the P's best interests.

There is no requirement for decisions taken to be documented or for any person or body to be informed of the decisions taken. The protection will apply in any setting where P is being cared for or where services are being provided to him or her, *e.g.* at P's home, a care home, a day centre or a hospital. As one person does not have power to act to the exclusion of others, it is likely that a number of persons will be acting under the powers contained in this section during the course of a day. It is unrealistic to expect lay carers, who are unlikely to have received any training on this Act, to undertake a capacity assessment and a best interests determination in respect of every decision that needs to be taken in respect of P.

The established common law position that no-one has the power to make decisions on behalf of a mentally incapacitated person is unchanged (*F v West Berkshire HA* [1989] 2 All E.R. 545, HL) as this section does not confer power on anyone to make substitute decisions on behalf of the person or to give substitute consent. As a large number of people are unlikely to have made provision for their incapacity through creating lasting powers of attorney, the "operational reality of [this section] is likely to be crucial" (Joint Committee, para.l03).

A decision made by either a donee under a lasting power of attorney or a deputy appointed by the court will take priority over any action that might be taken under this section (s.6(6)).

The point at which it would be unwise to rely on the protection provided by this section, and when an application should be made to the Court of Protection for an order or to have a deputy appointed is unclear. Applications should be made to the court in cases where it is proposed either to withhold or withdraw artificial nutrition and hydration from patients in a permanent vegetative state or to perform a non-therapeutic sterilisation on a mentally incapacitated patient, as both of these procedures clearly raise serious issues relating to the person's best interests. Prior to this Act, the courts required these proposals to be brought before the High Court to enable a declaration to be sought as to the lawfulness of the treatments. The Draft Code of Practice states that other cases likely to be referred to the court include "those involving ethical dilemmas in untested areas, or where there are otherwise irresolvable conflicts between professionals, or between professionals and family members" (para.5.24).

This provision does not provide any procedural safeguards aimed at preventing the inappropriate use of "section 5 acts". If there is concern about the manner in which P is being cared for, consideration could be given to invoking the multi-agency adult protection procedure. In extreme cases, the offence of ill-treatment or wilful neglect might be committed (see s.44).

Subsection (1)

Paragraph (a) emphasises the Act's "ethos of empowerment and personal autonomy, and the key obligation of all carers to support and maximise the decision-making capacity of the person who lacks capacity", *per* the Parliamentary Under-Secretary of State for Constitutional Affairs, St. Comm. A, col.107.

The draft Code of Practice at para.5.5 offers the following non-exhaustive list of "examples of acts in connection with care or treatment:

(a) Acts in connection with personal care -

i   acts of physical assistance such as washing, dressing, attending to personal hygiene, feeding, physically putting someone in a car (*e.g.* in order to take them to see their doctor)
ii other assistance, such as doing the shopping, buying essential goods, arranging services required for the person's care.
iii clearing someone's house when they have moved into residential care, washing someone's clothes, taking their car to the garage to be repaired.

(b) Acts in connection with health care and treatment:

i   diagnostic examinations and tests
ii Medical and dental treatment

iii   other healthcare procedures (such as the taking of a blood or other bodily samples, chiropody, phy-
siotherapy)
iv   nursing care."

A person. Including a person who instructs another to act. This section does not specify who has the
authority to take a particular decision or to undertake a particular act.

Does an act. Acting on a reasonable belief that P lacks capacity, and having concluded that there are
reasonable grounds for believing that the decision or act is in P's best interests. The steps taken to establish
the reasonableness of the belief and the reasonableness of the grounds will reflect the status of the decision-maker and the significance of the decision being taken: a healthcare professional would be expected
to adopt a more rigorous approach than a lay carer, and a routine care intervention would require less
investigation than a serious medical decision. It will also be the case that the urgency of the action required, for example, the provision of emergency medical treatment, will dictate the extent of the steps that
can be taken.

Care. This term is not defined. Payment for something that is arranged for P's care or treatment is provided for by s.8.

Treatment. Includes a diagnostic or other procedure (s.64(1)).

Reasonably believes. Formal assessments of capacity will rarely be required with most day to day decisions, but D must be able to identify objective reasons to explain why he or she believes P lacks capacity.
The starting point is a presumption of capacity (s.1(2)). The other relevant principles set out in s.1 should
also be applied.

Lacks capacity. In relation to the particular decision that needs to be made. Many of those who will
be making a judgment about P's capacity, using the test set out in s.3, will be lay people.

Best interests. The checklist contained in s.4 must be followed, and the least restrictive principle contained in s.1(6) should be applied. The amount of time devoted to ascertaining the best interests of P will,
in non-urgent cases, depend upon the seriousness of the decision under consideration.

Subsection (3)

Consent is not a defence to a claim in the tort of negligence and there are some criminal offences, such
as manslaughter, which depend on a finding of negligence as defined in civil law. This provision therefore
makes it clear that liability for negligence is unaffected by this section.

Subsection (4)

A valid and applicable advance decision relating to the person's healthcare is unaffected by this section
which gives no protection from liability if the decision is not followed.

6.   Section 5 acts: limitations

(1) If D does an act that is intended to restrain P, it is not an act to which
section 5 applies unless two further conditions are satisfied.
(2) The first condition is that D reasonably believes that it is necessary to do
the act in order to prevent harm to P.
(3) The second is that the act is a proportionate response to—
(a) the likelihood of P's suffering harm, and
(b) the seriousness of that harm.
(4) For the purposes of this section D restrains P if he—
(a) uses, or threatens to use, force to secure the doing of an act which P
resists, or
(b) restricts P's liberty of movement, whether or not P resists.
(5) But D does more than merely restrain P if he deprives P of his liberty
within the meaning of Article 5(1) of the Human Rights Convention
(whether or not D is a public authority).
(6) Section 5 does not authorise a person to do an act which conflicts with a
decision made, within the scope of his authority and in accordance with this
Part, by—

(a) a donee of a lasting power of attorney granted by P, or
(b) a deputy appointed for P by the court.
(7) But nothing in subsection (6) stops a person—
    (a) providing life-sustaining treatment, or
    (b) doing any act which he reasonably believes to be necessary to prevent a
       serious deterioration in P's condition,
while a decision as respects any relevant issue is sought from the court.

DEFINITIONS
  "the Human Rights Convention": s.64(1)
  "public authority": s.64(1)
  "lasting power of attorney": s.64(1)
  "deputy": s.64(1)
  "the court": s.64(1)
  "life-sustaining treatment": s.64(1)

GENERAL NOTE
  This section sets two important limitations to the protection from liability given to "section 5 acts".
  The first (subss.(1) to (5)) relates to restraint, which is defined in subs.(4). Restraint can only be used when: (1) the person using it reasonably believes that it is necessary to prevent harm to P and; (2) its use is proportionate both to the likelihood and seriousness of the harm. The restraint must also be in P's best interests (s.1(5)). Restraint that does not meet these conditions is unlawful. The practical result of this is that only the minimum amount of restraint for the shortest duration should be used to prevent the harm occurring. This reflects the "least restrictive option" principle in s.1(6).
  It would be lawful to use a reasonable amount of force under the authority of this section to ensure, for example, that P attended at a hospital for necessary treatment even if P was not compliant to being taken to the hospital. Prior to this Act, a non-compliant incapacitated person would be the subject of an application under the Mental Health Act 1983 if the person required hospitalisation for treatment for a mental disorder, and the common law doctrine of necessity would have been invoked if that person required hospitalisation for a physical disorder. Both situations now come within the scope of this section, although the 1983 Act would need to be invoked in repect of a patient who required treatment for mental disorders if the degree of force used constituted a deprivation of the patient's liberty.
  This section, together with s.5, provides authority for treating P's mental disorder in a hospital setting as an informal patient, even if P's liberty was restricted (subs.(4)(b)), as long as P is not being deprived of his or her liberty in that hospital. The use of restraint which results in P being deprived of his or her liberty would constitute a violation of P's rights under Art. 5 of the European Convention of Human Rights: see subs.(5) and *HL v United Kingdom* (2005) 40 E.H.R.R. 32, ECHR. This issue is discussed in the notes to s.28.
  If the steps taken to control the activities P in a care home, amount to a deprivation of his or her liberty, the patient's rights under Art.5 will have been violated: see *HL v United Kingdom*, above. Although a guardianship application made under s.7 of the 1983 Act does not provide authority for depriving P of his or her liberty, it is suggested that such an application should be made as this would:

  i   provide a degree of protection for P through the formal reviewing of his or her situation on the renewal of the guardianship;
  ii   provide explicit authority for P to be returned to the designated place of residence under the guardianship if he or she went absent from that place without authority; and
  iii be evidence of the good faith of those who are responsible for P's care.

  In cases where there is a significant conflict between the local authority that is responsible for P's placement in a care home and the patient's carers as to where P should reside, or where a significant use of restraint is required in order to prevent P from leaving the care home, an application should by made to the Court of Protection for a declaration as to the lawfulness of the action taken in respect of P.
  Although this provision does not provide for the restraint of P in order to prevent harm to others, such action is authorised under common law powers to prevent a breach of the peace. Restraining P from causing harm to others could be justified under this provision if it was considered that P's actions would provoke a reaction that would cause harm to P. If there is concern about the manner in which a donee of a

lasting power of attorney or a court appointed deputy is restraining P, a complaint may be made to the Public Guardian (s.58(1)(h)).

The second limitation (subss.(6) and (7)) is that a valid decision by a donee or a deputy takes priority over any action which might be taken under s.5. There is an important proviso to this limitation. If there is a dispute as to whether a decision of a donee or deputy either prevents life-sustaining treatment being given to P or might cause a serious deterioration of Ps condition, action can be taken to sustain life or prevent serious deterioration while the dispute is referred to the Court of Protection.

Subsection (1)

Restrain. Acts of restraint could include steadying P's shaking arm to enable an injection to be given safely, holding P down whilst administering a sedative, using reasonable force to take P to hospital to receive necessary treatment, using barriers to prevent P from falling out of bed, preventing P from running into the road, putting a car seatbelt on P, telling P that he will be restrained if he persists in a particular activity, securing the external doors of a care home to prevent P from leaving, assisting P to undress, and preventing P from harming himself.

The Government did not adopt the recommendation of the Joint Committee on Human Rights that the use or threat of force or other restrictions of liberty of movement be expressly confined to emergency situations for the following reason:

"Sometimes it is not always in a person's best interests for matters to be left until it is an urgent situation. For example, restraint may be necessary in order to undertake a diagnostic procedure. If such a procedure is left until there is an urgent need or an emergency, then the resulting harm to the person may be worse. If a person needs treatment for a bad tooth, it will generally be in that person's best interests to be restrained, and to have the tooth treated, rather than to wait until it is so bad as to count as an emergency requiring intervention" (Letter from the Parliamentary-Under Secretary of State to the Chair of the Committee, December 16, 2004, Annex, para.4).

Subsection (2)

Harm. This term, which is not defined, is not confined to physical harm. It could include preventing P from causing financial harm to him or her self by, for example, restraining P from ripping up bank notes. It could also include the prevention of psychological harm by, for example, restraining P from acting in a manner which could result in him or her suffering verbal abuse from members of the public.

Subsection (3)

Proportionate response. In terms of both the degree and duration of the restraint. It follows that (a) the minimum amount of restraint should be used in order to prevent harm occurring, and (b) the level of restraint used should diminish as the risk of harm diminishes. The draft Code of Practice provides the following example at para.5.32:

"[A] carer may need to keep hold of the arm of a person with learning disabilities while crossing a road, but it would not be a proportionate response to stop the person going outdoors at all. It may be appropriate to have a secure lock on a door leading to a road, but it would not be a proportionate response to lock someone in a bedroom all the time because they have a tendency to wander out onto the busy main road."

The extent of force or compulsion that may become necessary in ensuring that medical treatment can be provided to a mentally incapacitated patient can only be judged in each individual case and by health professionals. It may become for them a balance between continuing treatment that is forcibly opposed and deciding not to continue with it (*MB (Medical Treatment), Re* [1997] 2 F.L.R. 426, CA, at 439). In *R. (on the application of Wilkinson) v Broadmoor Hospital* [2001] EWCA Civ 1545; [2002] 1 W.L.R. 419, Hale L.J. said at para.64 that where a mentally incapacitated patient is "actively opposed to a course of action, the benefits which it holds for him will have to be carefully weighed against the disadvantages of going against his wishes, especially if force is required to do this".

The Department of Health and Department of Education and Skills has issued "Guidance on restrictive physical interventions for people with learning disabilities and autistic spectrum disorder, in health, education or social care settings" (July 2002). This guidance was issued under s.7 of the Local Authority Social Services Act 1970 (c.42).

Subsection (4)

This definition includes verbal restraint, such as threatening P with the use of force, and locking P in a room even if P does not indicate any objection to the confinement.

Restricts P's liberty. But not deprive P of his or her liberty. Restrictions on P's liberty are not confined to emergency situations: P could be subjected to restrictions of his or her liberty for an indefinite period without such restrictions constituting a deprivation of his or her liberty.

Subsection (5)

This provision was added to the Bill at the report stage in the House of Lords because the Fourth Report of the Joint Committee on Human Rights at para.4.9 wanted the Bill to confirm expressly that actions amounting to the deprivation of liberty do not fall within the definition of "restraint".

This Act cannot be used to subject P to a deprivation of liberty, as neither s.5 nor s.6 satisfy the requirements of Art.5 of the European Convention on Human Rights. The distinction between a deprivation of liberty and a mere restriction of liberty is not always easy to determine: see the General Note to s.28.

Subsection (6)

If a carer or doctor wishes to challenge a decision made by a donee or deputy on the ground that the decision of the donee or deputy is not in P's best interests, an application could be made to the Court of Protection. In the absence of such action, the decision of the donee or deputy must be respected as a failure to do so would be unlawful.

Does an act. It is submitted that this phrase includes an instruction to another to do an act.

Subsection (7)

This provision does not apply where a complaint has been made to the Public Guardian under s.58(1)(h) about the decision of the donee or deputy.

Life-sustaining treatment. Is defined in s.4(10).

7.   Payment for necessary goods and services

(1) If necessary goods or services are supplied to a person who lacks capacity to contract for the supply, he must pay a reasonable price for them.

(2) "Necessary" means suitable to a person's condition in life and to his actual requirements at the time when the goods or services are supplied.

GENERAL NOTE

In general, a contract entered into by a person who lacks capacity (P) is voidable and can be set aside if the other person knew or must be taken to have known of the lack of capacity. Under s.3(2) of the Sale of Goods Act 1979 (c.54), this rule does not apply if "necessaries" are supplied and P must pay a "reasonable price" for the goods. There is also a matching common law rule about "necessary" services. This section combines these rules to set out a single statutory rule to cover "necessary" goods and services. Subsection (2) repeats the established legal definition of what is "necessary". Thus, for example, a cleaner who carries on cleaning the house of P, who has a progressive dementia, can expect to be paid. As P lacks the capacity both to order or to pay for necessaries, ss.5 and 8 allows for a carer to do both.

At the committee stage in the House of Lords, the Government resisted an amendment to extend the existing powers to set aside a contract made by a person who lacks capacity to a situation where: (1) the other party was not aware of the incapacity; and (2) the contract can be set aside without loss to the other party, or where the person lacking capacity has been persuaded to enter into a plainly disadvantageous contract. However, the Government committed itself at report stage "to carrying out scoping research work to assess whether there is a problem arising from the current law and, if so, the extent of that problem. This will take into account people who lack capacity and the broader group of vulnerable consumers more generally. The Department of Constitutional Affairs will also commit to working with the Department of Trade and Industry as part of the implementation strategy of the Bill to ensure that policy on consumer strategy, credit and indebtedness is sensitive to the needs of consumers who lack capacity", *per* the Parliamentary Under-Secretary of State (*Hansard*, HL Vol.670, cols 1471-1472).

Subsections (2)

Condition in life. This means the living circumstances of P, in particular the standard of life that P enjoys. The draft Code of Practice states at para.5.36 that "while food, drink and clothing are necessary for everyone, the actual requirements for the type of food or the style or amount of clothing will vary according to their individual circumstances or 'condition in life'".

8. Expenditure

(1) If an act to which section 5 applies involves expenditure, it is lawful for D—
    (a) to pledge P's credit for the purpose of the expenditure, and
    (b) to apply money in P's possession for meeting the expenditure.
(2) If the expenditure is borne for P by D, it is lawful for D—
    (a) to reimburse himself out of money in P's possession, or
    (b) to be otherwise indemnified by P.
(3) Subsections (1) and (2) do not affect any power under which (apart from those subsections) a person—
    (a) has lawful control of P's money or other property, and
    (b) has power to spend money for P's benefit.

DEFINITIONS
    "property": s.64(1)

GENERAL NOTE
    If D, acting under s.5, arranges something for P's care or treatment that costs money then D can either promise that P will pay (*i.e.* D may pledge the credit of P), use money which P has in his possession, pay himself back from P's money in his possession or consider him or herself owed by P. Nothing in this section allows D to gain access to P's funds where they are held by a third party such as a bank or building society. Such funds cannot be accessed until formal steps are taken, such as registering a relevant power of attorney, or making an application to the Court of Protection for a deputy to be appointed or for a single order to be made. This section does not authorise D to sell any of P's property or to gain access to any of P's assets other than cash that is in P's possession.
    D cannot make a decision that conflicts with a decision made by either a donee of a lasting power of attorney ("LPA") or a deputy (s.6(6)).
    D could be appointed under reg.33 of the Social Security (Claims and Payments) Regulations 1987 (SI 1987/ 1968) to be the "appointee" to act on behalf of P. Appointeeship is considered in the Introduction and General Note to this Act.
    Concerns were expressed to the Joint Committee that the wide scope of this provision allows for the financial abuse of P. Although there is no requirement placed on D to keep records of the financial transactions undertaken on behalf of P, it would clearly be sensible for D to do so.

Subsection (3)
    This recognises that people may have control over P's money or property by other routes, for example by virtue of being appointed as P's appointee. A donee or a deputy appointed by the court could also have lawful control over P's money.

Lasting powers of attorney

9. Lasting powers of attorney

(1) A lasting power of attorney is a power of attorney under which the donor ("P") confers on the donee (or donees) authority to make decisions about all or any of the following—
    (a) P's personal welfare or specified matters concerning P's personal welfare, and

(b) P's property and affairs or specified matters concerning P's property and affairs,

and which includes authority to make such decisions in circumstances where P no longer has capacity.

(2) A lasting power of attorney is not created unless—
    (a) section 10 is complied with,
    (b) an instrument conferring authority of the kind mentioned in subsection (1) is made and registered in accordance with Schedule 1, and
    (c) at the time when P executes the instrument, P has reached 18 and has capacity to execute it.

(3) An instrument which—
    (a) purports to create a lasting power of attorney, but
    (b) does not comply with this section, section 10 or Schedule 1,

confers no authority.

(4) The authority conferred by a lasting power of attorney is subject to—
    (a) the provisions of this Act and, in particular, sections 1 (the principles) and 4 (best interests), and
    (b) any conditions or restrictions specified in the instrument.

DEFINITIONS
  "property": s.64(1)

GENERAL NOTE

A power of attorney is a legal document under which one person (the donor) empowers another person (the attorney or donee) or persons to act in his or her stead, either generally or for specific purposes. An act done by a donee can be treated as an act done by the donor, so as to affect the donor's relations with third parties. Prior to the Enduring Powers of Attorney Act 1985 (c.29), a power of attorney would be automatically revoked if the donor lost mental capacity. That Act introduced Enduring Powers of Attorney which enabled donors to continue to act on behalf of the donor's property and affairs after the donor ceased to have capacity if certain formalities were satisfied. This section, together with ss.10-14, creates a new form of power of attorney, a "lasting power of attorney". These replace the EPA and the 1985 Act is repealed by Sch.7. A key distinction between an EPA and a LPA is that the former were confined to the donor's property and affairs, while the latter can also extend to personal welfare matters, which can include health care decisions (s.11(7)(c)). The legal effect of existing EPAs is preserved and integrated into the scheme of this Act by s.66(3) and Sch.4. A person with mental capacity who has made an EPA before this Act comes into force can either destroy it and then make a LPA, or can do nothing. An EPA cannot be made after this Act has come into force (s.66(3)). The power to make an ordinary power of attorney under the Powers of Attorney Act 1971 (c.27) is unaffected by this Act.

A LPA can only be executed by a mentally capable adult (subs.(2)(c)), and it will only be valid if it complies with s.10, and the instrument conferring the authority is made in the prescribed form and registered with the Public Guardian in accordance with Sch.1 (subss.(2)(a)(b),(3)). The Public Guardian is required to establish and maintain a register of LPAs (s.58(1)(a)), and will receive reports from donees (s.56(1)(f)). The Public Guardian can investigate a complaint about the way in which a donee is exercising his or her powers (s.58(1)(h)). This function can be discharged in co-operation with other persons who are involved in the care of treatment of P (s.58(2)).

The Court of Protection would only become involved if the registration of the LPA is disputed. By making an LPA, the donor (P), confers on the donee or donees authority to make decisions about P's personal welfare and/or property and affairs or specified matters concerning those areas. The authority to make decisions includes, where appropriate, the authority to act on decisions made (s.64(2)). The LPA must include authority for the donee/s to make decisions when P no longer has capacity to make those decisions (subs.(1)). The donee/s must act in P's best interests (s.1(5)) and comply with any conditions or restrictions that P has put in the LPA (subs.(4)). It is submitted that the donee acts as the statutory agent of P; see further the General Note to ss.10 and 19.

If P wishes, a LPA relating to P's property and affairs can operate as an "ordinary" power of attorney while P has mental capacity as long as it will continue to have effect after P loses capacity. Section

11(7)(a) prevents a personal welfare LPA having similar effect: it can only be used once the donor has lost capacity.

Separate LPAs can be created for welfare and financial matters. In her evidence to the Joint Committee, the Health Minister acknowledged the need, in some cases, to appoint different donees in relation to different types of decision:

"From the health care side it may be that people might want different attorneys for different decisions. Somebody that you trust with your finances may not be the same as somebody that you wanted to make decisions about your health and welfare" (Q754).

The Joint Committee expressed its concern about evidence that it has received "indicating that financial abuse occurs in approximately 10-15% of cases involving EPAs. Further evidence estimated that that abuse was as high as 20%" (para.138). These figures relate to unethical conduct. It is estimated that 2%-3% of cases involve criminal conduct (Oral and written evidence, Ev 188). This Act attempts to reduce the risk of financial abuse by requiring an LPA to be executed and registered before it can be used (see subs.(2)), thereby reducing the difficulties associated with the monitoring of EPAs. A report prepared for the Public Guardianship Office, "The role of the Public Guardianship Office in safeguarding vulnerable adults against financial abuse" (undated) by Hilary Brown et al, suggests that further action will be required to tackle the financial abuse of incapacitated persons who are subject to LPAs. There are also potential conflicts of interest between P and the donee in relation to welfare matters. For example, a decision by the donee to authorise the placement of P in a care home might have the effect of diminishing the potential inheritance of the donee. The powers of the Court of Protection in relation to LPAs are set out in ss.22 and 23. They include the power to revoke a LPA if the donee is not acting in P's best interests (s.22(3)(4)).The Public Guardian can receive reports from donees (s.58(1)(f)).

Baroness Andrews outlined the manner in which the Act can be utilised to prevent financial abuse by donees:

"[D]onors of financial LPAs will be advised that they can, if they so choose, stipulate in their financial LPA that they wish the [donee] to provide annual accounts to the Public Guardian or to any other third party for checking. That is a front-line defence. Therefore, the Public Guardian can check accounts not only if he is asked to do so but also if someone raises a concern. Concerns can be raised by different sorts of objectors at all stages. If an objector raises concerns about a prospective [donee] at the registration stage, the Court may add a requirement for the [donee] to lodge accounts if that would alleviate the concerns of the objector. That is a second line of defence.

Anyone can raise a concern with the Office of the Public Guardian if they fear that an attorney of a registered LPA is not acting properly. The Court will then be able to direct that the [donee] should lodge accounts. We believe that is robust. They could be 'on-off' accounts or annual accounts. They could be lodged with the Court, a solicitor, an accountant or, indeed, a third party.

In the broader context the Code of Practice makes it clear to financial [donees] that they should keep accounts. We intend to issue guidance to reinforce that message" (*Hansard*, HL Vol.669, cols 771-772).

The House of Lords Select Committee on Medical Ethics in its comments on proxy decision-making on healthcare matters, observed that, "whilst the idea of the patient appointed proxy is in many ways attractive, it is vulnerable to the same problems as advance directives, and indeed to a greater degree" (HL Paper 21-1, para.268). The Committee observed that personal relationships are not immutable, and that the choice of proxy might soon become out of date. The Committee also noted the practical difficulties of ascertaining what choice the patient would have made, that previous statements of preference form an unreliable basis for future decisions, and the difficulty in ensuring the objectivity of the proxy (even when acting in good faith).

Subsection (1)

All or any. An LPA can relate to personal welfare matters, to property and affairs, or to both. A donee will be provided with protection by ss.5 and 6 for acts done outside the scope of the LPA.

Personal welfare. The draft Code of Practice at para.6.7 states that the "types of decisions that welfare donees could be authorised to take, and the powers the LPA would confer on them, might include any or all of the following:

● Decisions on where the donor should live.
● Giving or refusing consent to medical examination and/or treatment.
● Arranging for the donor to access medical, dental or optical treatment.
● Applying for and having access to confidential documents and personal information relating to the donor held by any organisation, such as medical records or personal files held by social services autho-

rities."

A welfare LPA which gives general powers to the donee would include all of the above powers. A welfare LPA which is not drafted in general terms can either specify the powers that the donee is granted, or can specify the types of decisions that the donee is not empowered to make.

Property and affairs. Means "business matters, legal transactions and other dealing of a similar kind" (*F v West Berkshire HA* [1989] 2 All E.R. 545, HL, *per* Lord Brandon at 554). The draft Code of Practice at para.6.13 states that the "types of decisions or actions financial donees could be authorised to take, and the powers an LPA would confer on them, might include any or all of the following:

- Buying or selling property (land, buildings or other assets).
- Opening, closing or operating any bank, building society or other account containing the donor's funds.
- Giving access to financial information to others concerning the donor.
- Claiming, receiving and using on the donor's behalf all benefits, pensions, allowances, rebates etc to which the donor may be entitled (unless someone else had already been appointed to do this and everyone wanted that arrangement to continue).
- Receiving any income, inheritance or other entitlement of the donor.
- Dealing with the donor's tax affairs.
- Paying the donors mortgage, rent and / or household expenses.
- Making appropriate arrangements to insure, maintain and repair the donor's property.
- Investing the donor's savings in interest bearing accounts, bonds, stocks and shares or any other form of investment.
- Making gifts on the donor's behalf [but see s.12].
- Pay for private medical care and / or residential care or nursing home fees.
- Using the donor's income or capital to purchase a vehicle or any aids, adaptations or equipment required by the donor where these are not provided free of charge.
- Borrowing money on behalf of the donor and repaying interest and capital on any loan taken out by the donor or donee on his / her behalf.
- Making provision for any person for whom the donor might be expected to provide if he did not lack capacity, such as a spouse and dependant children."

A financial LPA may grant the donee general powers, in which case the donee will be authorised to undertake any of the acts set out above. As an alternative, the donor might wish to grant the donee specific powers, or could specify the types of decisions the donee is not empowered to make.

Subsection (2) (c)

Reached 18. This ensures that there is no overlap with the Children Act 1989 or the wardship jurisdiction of the High Court.

Subsection (2) (c)

Any conditions or restrictions. Even if the condition or restriction, viewed objectively, does not serve the best interests of P.

10. Appointment of donees

(1) A donee of a lasting power of attorney must be—
   (a) an individual who has reached 18, or
   (b) if the power relates only to P's property and affairs, either such an individual or a trust corporation.

(2) An individual who is bankrupt may not be appointed as donee of a lasting power of attorney in relation to P's property and affairs.

(3) Subsections (4) to (7) apply in relation to an instrument under which two or more persons are to act as donees of a lasting power of attorney.

(4) The instrument may appoint them to act—
   (a) jointly,
   (b) jointly and severally, or
   (c) jointly in respect of some matters and jointly and severally in respect of others.

(5) To the extent to which it does not specify whether they are to act jointly or jointly and severally, the instrument is to be assumed to appoint them to act jointly.

(6) If they are to act jointly, a failure, as respects one of them, to comply with the requirements of subsection (1) or (2) or Part 1 or 2 of Schedule 1 prevents a lasting power of attorney from being created.

(7) If they are to act jointly and severally, a failure, as respects one of them, to comply with the requirements of subsection (1) or (2) or Part 1 or 2 of Schedule 1—

  (a) prevents the appointment taking effect in his case, but

  (b) does not prevent a lasting power of attorney from being created in the case of the other or others.

(8) An instrument used to create a lasting power of attorney—

  (a) cannot give the donee (or, if more than one, any of them) power to appoint a substitute or successor, but

  (b) may itself appoint a person to replace the donee (or, if more than one, any of them) on the occurrence of an event mentioned in section 13(6)(a) to (d) which has the effect of terminating the donee's appointment.

DEFINITIONS

"lasting power of attorney": s.64(1)
"property": s.64(1)
"trust corporation": s.64(1)
"bankrupt": s.64(3)

GENERAL NOTE

This section sets out requirements relating to the appointment of donees and how they should act. An individual donee must be an adult and, if the LPA relates to property and affairs, not be a bankrupt (subss.(1)(a),(2)). A trust corporation, as well as an individual, can be appointed as donee to a LPA that relates only to property and affairs (subs.(1)(b)). If an individual is appointed, it is important for the donor to be confident that the chosen donee would be likely to act in his or her best interests when performing functions under this Act. The Act does not place an obligation on a donee to accept appointment.

A donee acts as the agent of the donor. Under the law of agency, an act of an agent done within the scope of his authority binds his principal, in this case P. As an agent the donee is bound by a number of common law duties toward P, including the duty to act with due care and skill, to act in good faith, not to delegate his or her functions to another, to keep the donor's affairs confidential apart from where the disclosure of information is allowed by the LPA or is otherwise required, to keep accounts of monies received and paid on P's behalf, and not to permit his or her own interests to conflict with the duties owed to P. The donee also has a duty to act within the scope of the LPA (s.9(4)(b)), and to comply with any directions that the Court of Protection might make. For a comprehensive account of the law of agency, see Francis M.B. Reynolds and William Bowstead, *Bowstead and Reynolds on Agency*, (18th ed., Sweet & Maxwell, London, 2005).

In this Act references to making decisions, in relation to a donee, include, where appropriate, acting on decisions made (s.64(2)).

Any concerns about the way in which the donee in undertaking his or her functions, including a concern that the donee might lack mental capacity, should be reported to the Public Guardian or, if criminal behaviour is suspected, the police. The Public Guardian may decide to direct a Court of Protection Visitor to visit P and/or the donee (s.58(1)(d)). Also see the note on adult protection procedures in s.42.

The draft Code of Practice at para.6.32 suggests the following as "signs that are sufficient to raise concerns that a donee may be exploiting the donor or failing to act in the donor's best interests:

● The denial of relatives or friends of access to the donor - either active denial by the donee or where the donor suddenly refuses visits or telephone calls from family members or longstanding friends for no apparent reason.
● Sudden unexplained changes in living arrangements, such as where someone moves in to care for an elderly person with whom they have had little previous contact.

- The denial of access to a medical practitioner or care worker to see the donor.
- Unpaid bills, such as arrears of residential care or nursing home fees.
- The opening of credit card accounts for the donor by the donee.
- Expenditure that is not obviously related to the donor's needs.
- Unusual or extravagant expenditure by the donee.
- The transfer of assets to another country."

A number of witnesses to the Joint Committee expressed their concern about the situation that could arise when a donee who is a close relative of P appears not to be acting in the best interests of the P because of a conflict of interest. This difficulty was said to be "not common but neither is it rare" (Oral and written evidence, Ev 472). An example of how such a conflict can arise has been given by Baroness Finlay:

"A lady aged 59 was very ill. Her family appeared to be very concerned about her pain and constantly asked for her diamorphine to be increased. However, we remained unconvinced that her pain was really that severe. In fact, the patient declined increasing doses of diamorphine. Her 60th birthday arrived and was passed with minimal celebration, after which the family visited very little. She became depressed and spoke to one of the night nurses, explaining that the problem was that on her 60th birthday, her fixed-term life insurance policy expired. The family would not now inherit what they thought they would if she had died, and if her drugs had been duly increased" (*Hansard*, HL Vol.642, col.766).

Donees who are close relatives might not accurately reflect P's wishes as studies have shown that relatives' perception of the patient's likely views often differ substantially from the patient's own wishes; see, for example, A.B. Seckler et al, "Substituted judgment: how accurate are proxy predictions?" Ann Intern Med 1991; 115(9): 743-5.

In its "*Response to the Scrutiny Committee's Report on the draft Mental Incapacity Bill*" (Cm.6121), the Government recognised "that there may be potential for conflict of interest in an LPA" and agreed "that donors should be given information about this and more generally about the seriousness of making an LPA".

Subsection (1)

Trust corporation. Is defined in the Trustee Act 1925 (c.19), s.68(1) as "the Public Trustee or a corporation either appointed by the court in any particular case to be a trustee, or entitled by rules made under s.4(3) of the Public Trustee Act 1906 (c.55), to act as custodian trustee."

Subsection (2)

The Parliamentary Under-Secretary of State announced that the Government had "decided that the Office of the Public Guardian will check to see if prospective financial attorneys are bankrupt when an LPA is registered" (*Hansard*, HL Vol.668, col.1417). If the donee is bankrupt, then the LPA will be invalid.

Subsection (4)

This provides that where two or more people are appointed as donees, they may be appointed either to act jointly (so that they must all join together in any decision), or to act jointly and severally (which means that they can act independently or all together) or to act jointly in respect of some matters and jointly and severally in respect of others. The donor therefore "has all possible options when wanting to appoint more than one donee", *per* the Parliamentary Under-Secretary of State (*Hansard*, HL Vol.670, col.1473. If the donor does not specify, it will be assumed that the donees were appointed jointly (subs.(5)).

Subsection (6)

For joint attorneys, any breach by one of them of the requirements concerning how LPAs are made will prevent a LPA from being created.

Subsection (7)

Where donees are appointed jointly and severally, a breach by one of them of the requirements concerning how LPAs are made will only prevent the appointment taking affect in his or her case; a valid LPA is created in respect of the other donee(s).

This enables a donor to provide in the LPA for the replacement of the donee(s) on the occurrence of an event mentioned in s.13(6)(a)-(d) which would normally terminate a donee's powers. One of these events is the death of the donee. It would therefore be possible for a donor to appoint his spouse as donee, but nominate his child as a replacement donee. Under para.(a), a donee cannot be given power by the LPA to choose a successor.

11. Lasting powers of attorney: restrictions

(1) A lasting power of attorney does not authorise the donee (or, if more than one, any of them) to do an act that is intended to restrain P, unless three conditions are satisfied.

(2) The first condition is that P lacks, or the donee reasonably believes that P lacks, capacity in relation to the matter in question.

(3) The second is that the donee reasonably believes that it is necessary to do the act in order to prevent harm to P.

(4) The third is that the act is a proportionate response to—
   (a) the likelihood of P's suffering harm, and
   (b) the seriousness of that harm.

(5) For the purposes of this section, the donee restrains P if he—
   (a) uses, or threatens to use, force to secure the doing of an act which P resists, or
   (b) restricts P's liberty of movement, whether or not P resists,
or if he authorises another person to do any of those things.

(6) But the donee does more than merely restrain P if he deprives P of his liberty within the meaning of Article 5(1) of the Human Rights Convention.

(7) Where a lasting power of attorney authorises the donee (or, if more than one, any of them) to make decisions about P's personal welfare, the authority—
   (a) does not extend to making such decisions in circumstances other than those where P lacks, or the donee reasonably believes that P lacks, capacity,
   (b) is subject to sections 24 to 26 (advance decisions to refuse treatment), and
   (c) extends to giving or refusing consent to the carrying out or continuation of a treatment by a person providing health care for P.

(8) But subsection (7)(c)—
   (a) does not authorise the giving or refusing of consent to the carrying out or continuation of life-sustaining treatment, unless the instrument contains express provision to that effect, and
   (b) is subject to any conditions or restrictions in the instrument.

DEFINITIONS
   "lasting power of attorney": s.64(1)
   "the Human Rights Convention": s.64(1)
   "treatment": s.64(1)
   "life-sustaining treatment": s.64(1)

GENERAL NOTE
   Subsections (1)-(6) place restrictions on the use of restraint by donees similar to those that apply to "section 5 acts" (see s.6) and deputies (see s.20). Reference should be made to the notes on s.6.
   Under subs.(7), a personal welfare LPA:

a   can only take effect after P loses capacity. Decision making will therefore fluctuate between the donor and donee in cases where the donor has fluctuating capacity. It is also the case that P could be capable of making some simple personal welfare decisions, but not other, more complex, decisions. This could give rise to considerable practical difficulties. A healthcare professional who is proposing to provide medical treatment for P must also assess P's capacity. Any dispute between donee and the professional about the assessment of P's capacity that remains unresolved should be referred to the Court of Protection for a declaration under s.15(1)(a);

b   is subject to any advance decision that P has made; and

c   can authorise the donee to give or refuse consent to the carrying out or continuation of health care for P. This power is subject to any conditions or restrictions in the LPA and to subs.(8) which prohibits the donee from refusing life-sustaining treatment for P unless the LPA expressly allows for this. A LPA does not provide the donee with a power to demand that a specific form of medical treatment be provided to P.

In order to make a healthcare decision on behalf of P, the donee will have had to have received the same information about the nature of the treatment being proposed and its consequences as P would have received had he or she had been mentally capable. The power to make a LPA which enables the donee to make healthcare decisions has been criticised on the ground that patients' views about the medical treatment that they would wish to receive are not fixed; they adapt to circumstances; see further the note on s.25(4)(c). An application to the Court of Protection should be made if the donee is asked to consent to a non-therapeutic treatment, such as an organ donation, if such treatment is not specified in the LPA.

The fact that the donee has the power to refuse medical treatment on behalf of P represents a significant change in the doctor patient relationship in that a non-medical donee can override the doctor's clinical judgment as to what treatment his or her patient should receive. If a doctor wishes to challenge a decision made by a donee not to consent to treatment for P, the doctor could consider making an application to the Court of Protection for on order overriding the donee's decision on the ground that the donee was not acting in P's best interests. But as the briefing note on the Mental Capacity Bill by the Catholic Bishops' Conference of England and Wales (July 2004, at para.24) notes, how many doctors "will have the time, energy and motivation to ask a court to override a [donee] whose determination of best interests appears to them to be defective or questionable?" If the decision of the donee to refuse treatment either stops the doctor from providing life-sustaining treatment or would be likely to lead to a serious deterioration in P's condition, the treatment can continue until the decision of the court is made (s.6(6),(7)).

It is submitted that a donee cannot refuse the provision of basic care for P, such as the provision of hydration and nutrition by non-artificial means and keeping P clean, because the cessation of such care would never be in P's best interests.

If an urgent healthcare decision needs to be taken in respect of P and there is no time to contact the donee, the healthcare professional should proceed to treat P in his or her best interests and then report to the donee.

Siubsection (6)
See the note to s.6(5).

Subsection (7)
Make decisions. See s.64(2).

Subsection (8)
The power of a donee to prevent life-sustaining treatment to be given to P, which is subject to the restriction contained in s.4(5), was the subject of considerable criticism during the Bill's passage through Parliament. For example, Earl Howe said:

"In very many cases - perhaps the majority - the doctor and the [donee] will be in agreement about what is in the patient's best interests, and no problem will therefore arise. The problems arise when doctor and [donee] are in disagreement.

Both of them are required under the Bill to work in the patient's best interests. But the interpretation of 'best interests' is open to difference. What the Bill is saying is that, in the worst case, [a donee] with no medical knowledge whatever can take it on himself to gainsay a doctor whose professional advice is that the patient whose life is at stake should receive certain treatment. It might be perfectly possible for the [donee] to maintain, with some justification, that his decision to refuse consent was taken in the best interests of P. But the doctor, who had close knowledge and experience of the treatment, might not think that a fair and reasonable view of best interests.

What happens then? The Bill allows the doctor to seek a ruling from the Court [of Protection] where there is such disagreement. But let us take the example of a doctor who has no previous knowledge of the patient and who is confronted by a [donee] with no medical expertise and articulates his views plausibly and forcefully. Are we going to imagine that every doctor in that position will have the strength of purpose and the degree of self-belief to refer the matter to the Court? I find that unlikely. Doctors are professional people, but they are also human. I very much fear that some will be browbeaten into agreeing to a course of action that runs contrary to their better judgment" (*Hansard*, HL Vol.670, col.1484).

This provision is compatible with Art.2 of the European Convention on Human Rights which provides for a "right to life" because the donee is chosen by a competent adult and can only act under this Act in the best interests of that person.

12. Scope of lasting powers of attorney: gifts

(1) Where a lasting power of attorney confers authority to make decisions about P's property and affairs, it does not authorise a donee (or, if more than one, any of them) to dispose of the donor's property by making gifts except to the extent permitted by subsection (2).

(2) The donee may make gifts—

    (a) on customary occasions to persons (including himself) who are related to or connected with the donor, or

    (b) to any charity to whom the donor made or might have been expected to make gifts,

if the value of each such gift is not unreasonable having regard to all the circumstances and, in particular, the size of the donor's estate.

(3) "Customary occasion" means—

    (a) the occasion or anniversary of a birth, a marriage or the formation of a civil partnership, or

    (b) any other occasion on which presents are customarily given within families or among friends or associates.

(4) Subsection (2) is subject to any conditions or restrictions in the instrument.

DEFINITIONS
  "lasting power of attorney": s.64(1)
  "property": s.64(1)

GENERAL NOTE
  This section limits the power of a donee of a financial LPA to dispose of P's property by making gifts. Only gifts coming within the categories set out in subs.(2) are allowed. The donee must also act in accordance with any conditions or restrictions on his or her power to make gifts which are specified in the LPA, and satisfy the best interests criterion (s.1(5)). The court has power to authorise gifts that are more substantial than those permitted by subs.(2) if satisfied that these would be in P's best interests (s.23(4)).

Subsection (2)
  Not unreasonable. This is for the donee to determine. The donee is not required to obtain consent from anyone before making the gift. The authorisation of the Court of Protection should be obtained if it is proposed to make a substantial gift in order to reduce P's tax liability.

Subsection (3)
  Any other occasion. Taking into account P's past and present wishes and feelings (s.4(6)(a)).

13. Revocation of lasting powers of attorney etc

(1) This section applies if—
(a) P has executed an instrument with a view to creating a lasting power of attorney, or
(b) a lasting power of attorney is registered as having been conferred by P,
and in this section references to revoking the power include revoking the instrument.

(2) P may, at any time when he has capacity to do so, revoke the power.

(3) P's bankruptcy revokes the power so far as it relates to P's property and affairs.

(4) But where P is bankrupt merely because an interim bankruptcy restrictions order has effect in respect of him, the power is suspended, so far as it relates to P's property and affairs, for so long as the order has effect.

(5) The occurrence in relation to a donee of an event mentioned in subsection (6)—
(a) terminates his appointment, and
(b) except in the cases given in subsection (7), revokes the power.

(6) The events are—
(a) the disclaimer of the appointment by the donee in accordance with such requirements as may be prescribed for the purposes of this section in regulations made by the Lord Chancellor,
(b) subject to subsections (8) and (9), the death or bankruptcy of the donee or, if the donee is a trust corporation, its winding-up or dissolution,
(c) subject to subsection (11), the dissolution or annulment of a marriage or civil partnership between the donor and the donee,
(d) the lack of capacity of the donee.

(7) The cases are—
(a) the donee is replaced under the terms of the instrument,
(b) he is one of two or more persons appointed to act as donees jointly and severally in respect of any matter and, after the event, there is at least one remaining donee.

(8) The bankruptcy of a donee does not terminate his appointment, or revoke the power, in so far as his authority relates to P's personal welfare.

(9) Where the donee is bankrupt merely because an interim bankruptcy restrictions order has effect in respect of him, his appointment and the power are suspended, so far as they relate to P's property and affairs, for so long as the order has effect.

(10) Where the donee is one of two or more appointed to act jointly and severally under the power in respect of any matter, the reference in subsection (9) to the suspension of the power is to its suspension in so far as it relates to that donee.

(11) The dissolution or annulment of a marriage or civil partnership does not terminate the appointment of a donee, or revoke the power, if the instrument provided that it was not to do so.

DEFINITIONS
"lasting power of attorney": s.64(1)
"property": s.64(1)
"bankrupt": s.64(3)
"trust corporation": s.64(1)

GENERAL NOTE

This section identifies the way in with an LPA can be revoked, whether before or after registration.

P can revoke an LPA at any time while he or she has capacity to do so (subs.(2)). P's bankruptcy will revoke a LPA that relates to P's property and affairs, but not a personal welfare LPA or that part of a LPA giving authority to make personal welfare decisions (subs.(3)). An interim bankruptcy restrictions order merely suspends a financial LPA (subs.(4)).

The events relating to the donee which are set out in subs.(6) terminate his or her appointment and also revoke the LPA, apart from when the terms of the LPA replace the donee or where the donee is acting jointly and severally with others and, after the event, there is at least one remaining donee (subs.(7)).

Subsection (2)

P might have the capacity to revoke the power by, for example, saying "I don't want X deciding things for me any more", but not have the capacity to make the decision in question. This power can be exercised during a period of temporary capacity.

Subsection (3)

Bankruptcy. See s.64(3) and (4).

Subsection (4)

Bankruptcy restrictions orders. These are provided for in Sch.4A of the Insolvency Act 1986 (c.45).

Subsection (6)

Bankruptcy of the donee. But see subss.(8)-(10).

Dissolution or annulment of a marriage, or civil partnership. But see subs.(11). A civil partnership is a registered relationship between two people of the same sex which ends only on death, dissolution or annulment, as provided for in the Civil Partnership Act 2004.

Lack of capacity of the donee. Although the matter is not free from doubt, it is submitted that a temporary incapacity of the donee would not revoke the LPA.

14. Protection of donee and others if no power created or power revoked

(1) Subsections (2) and (3) apply if—

   (a) an instrument has been registered under Schedule 1 as a lasting power of attorney, but

   (b) a lasting power of attorney was not created,

whether or not the registration has been cancelled at the time of the act or transaction in question.

(2) A donee who acts in purported exercise of the power does not incur any liability (to P or any other person) because of the non-existence of the power unless at the time of acting he—

   (a) knows that a lasting power of attorney was not created, or

   (b) is aware of circumstances which, if a lasting power of attorney had been created, would have terminated his authority to act as a donee.

(3) Any transaction between the donee and another person is, in favour of that person, as valid as if the power had been in existence, unless at the time of the transaction that person has knowledge of a matter referred to in subsection (2).

(4) If the interest of a purchaser depends on whether a transaction between the donee and the other person was valid by virtue of subsection (3), it is conclusively presumed in favour of the purchaser that the transaction was valid if—

   (a) the transaction was completed within 12 months of the date on which the instrument was registered, or

(b) the other person makes a statutory declaration, before or within 3 months after the completion of the purchase, that he had no reason at the time of the transaction to doubt that the donee had authority to dispose of the property which was the subject of the transaction.

(5) In its application to a lasting power of attorney which relates to matters in addition to P's property and affairs, section 5 of the Powers of Attorney Act 1971 (c. 27) (protection where power is revoked) has effect as if references to revocation included the cessation of the power in relation to P's property and affairs.

(6) Where two or more donees are appointed under a lasting power of attorney, this section applies as if references to the donee were to all or any of them.

DEFINITIONS
  "lasting power of attorney": s.64(1)
  "purchaser": s.64(1)
  "property": s.64(1)

GENERAL NOTE
  This section provides legal protection to donees and others who act on invalid LPAs.
  Subsection (1) outlines the situations to which subss.(2) and (3) apply. It gives protection to donees and others who rely on registered LPAs which later turn out to be invalid. The protection applies whether or not the registration has been cancelled. Broadly, both donees and third parties will be protected from legal liability if they were unaware that the LPA was invalid.
  Subsections (4) and (5) deal with property. If either para.(a) or (b) of sub.(4) is satisfied, a purchaser of property from a donee of an invalid LPA will be protected unless the purchaser was aware of the invalidity.

General powers of the court and appointment of deputies

15. Power to make declarations

(1) The court may make declarations as to—
  (a) whether a person has or lacks capacity to make a decision specified in the declaration;
  (b) whether a person has or lacks capacity to make decisions on such matters as are described in the declaration;
  (c) the lawfulness or otherwise of any act done, or yet to be done, in relation to that person.

(2) "Act" includes an omission and a course of conduct.

DEFINITIONS
  "the court": s.64(1)

GENERAL NOTE
  This section provides the Court of Protection with the power to make declarations about whether an individual has mental capacity, and whether an act or proposed act was or would be lawful. A declaration may be refused on the ground that no such declaration is needed. For example, in *H (Mental Patient: Diagnosis), Re* (1993) 1 F.L.R. 28, the judge held that a C.T. scan for a schizophrenic patient with a suspected brain tumour was not one of those cases where it was either necessary or desirable to grant a declaration. He did not wish to "send a signal" that this and similar procedures should be delayed pending a costly application to the court.
  The power to make declarations regarding a person's capacity is likely to be exercised where: (a) healthcare professionals cannot resolve a dispute about a person's capacity to make a serious decision regarding the provision of medical treatment; or (b) there is a dispute as to whether a person was mentally

capable when either an advance decision or a lasting power of attorney was made. Declarations regarding the lawfulness of an act are likely to be made most frequently in cases involving controversial or particularly serious decisions regarding the provision of medical treatment for the incapacitated person. Subsection (2) confirms that the court can be asked to make declarations on an omission to act (for example, the withholding or withdrawing of medical treatment), as well as on a course of conduct. As a superior court of record, the Court of Protection has the same powers as the High Court (see s.45(1)).

The Declaratory Jurisdiction of the High Court

As the Court of Protection's jurisdiction to make declarations is founded on the inherent jurisdiction of the High Court to make declarations, an account of the development of this jurisdiction in so far as it relates to personal welfare matters is given below.

The question of the lawfulness of treating patients who are incapable of giving consent because they are unconscious in circumstances where the operation or other treatment cannot safely be delayed until consciousness is recovered or because they are deemed to be mentally incapable of making a decision whether to receive treatment was considered in the House of Lords in *F v West Berkshire HA* [1989] 2 All E.R. 545. Their Lordships held that:

1   Under the common law doctrine of necessity a doctor can lawfully operate on, or give other treatment to, adult patients who are incapable, for one reason or another, of consenting to his doing so, provided that the operation or other treatment concerned is the best interests of such patients. The operation or other treatment will be in the best interests of patients if, but only if, it is carried out in order either to save their lives or ensure improvement or prevent deterioration in their physical or mental health. Lord Brandon said at 551: "in many cases it will not only be lawful for doctors, on the grounds of necessity, to operate on or give other medical treatment to adult patients disabled from giving their consent: it will be their common law duty to do so".
2   A doctor will be deemed to have acted in the best interests of a mentally incapable patient and will be immune from liability in trespass to the person if he establishes that he acted in accordance with a practice accepted at the time as proper by a responsible body of medical opinion skilled in the particular form of treatment in question (*Bolam v Friern Hospital Management Committee* [1957] 2 All E.R. 118 applied).
3   Special considerations apply in the case of an operation for the sterilisation of an adult woman who is physically perfectly healthy or of an operation on an organ transplant donor because such treatments cannot be considered to be either curative or prophylactic. No court now has jurisdiction either by statute or derived from the Crown as parens patriae to give or withhold consent to such operations in the case of a mentally incapable adult. However, the High Court does have jurisdiction to make a declaration that the proposed operation is lawful on the ground that in the circumstances it is in the best interests of the patient. Although a declaration is not necessary to establish the lawfulness of the operation, in practice the court's jurisdiction should be invoked prior to the operation taking place, since a declaration would establish by judicial process whether the proposed operation was in the best interests of the patient and therefore lawful.

The purpose of the declaratory jurisdiction was explained by Sir Thomas Bingham MR in *S (Hospital Patient: Court's Jurisdiction) (No.1), Re* [1996] Fam. 1 at 18:

"[I]n cases of controversy and cases involving momentous and irrevocable decisions, the courts have treated as justicable any genuine question as to what the best interests of a patient require or justify. In making these decisions the courts have recognised the desirability of informing those involved whether a proposed course of conduct will render them criminally or civilly liable; they have acknowledged their duty to act as a safeguard against malpractice, abuse and unjustified action; and they have recognised the desirability, in the last resort, of decisions being made by an impartial independent tribunal."

Subsequent to the decision in *F*, the courts have held that declarations in respect of mentally incapable patients should also be applied for in the following circumstances: where it is proposed to sterilise a male patient (*A (Mental Patient: Sterilisation), Re* [2000] 1 F.L.R. 549, CA), and where it is proposed to withdraw artificial feeding from a patient in a persistent vegetative state (*Airedale NHS Trust v Bland* [1993] 1 All E.R. 821, HL), where there is doubt about the mental capacity of the patient (*St George's Healthcare NHS Trust v S* [1998] 3 All E.R. 673), where it was anticipated that force might have to be used to administer an anaesthetic to a patient who required a CT scan (*Doncaster and Bassetlaw Hospitals NHS Trust v C* [2004] EWHC 1657 (Fam Div)), and where it is proposed to harvest bone marrow from the patient (*Y (Mental Patient: Bone Marrow Donation), Re* [1996] 2 F.L.R. 787). Declarations have been also been applied for in a number of cases where it was proposed to sterilise a mentally incompetent patient. The test for making an application for a declaration in such cases was established by Sir Stephen Brown P. in *GF (Medical Treatment), Re* [1992] 1 F.L.R. 293 when he said at 294:

"I take the view that no application for leave to carry out [a sterilisation] operation need be made in cases where two medical practitioners are satisfied that the operation is (1) necessary for therapeutic purposes, (2) in the best interests of the patient, and (3) there is no practicable, less intrusive means of treating the condition."

In *LC (Medical Treatment: Sterilisation), Re* [1997] 2 F.L.R. 258, Thorpe J held that leave to perform the sterilisation operation could not be justified upon the basis of some vague and unsubstantiated fear that the patient would be exposed to the risks of pregnancy from which she is presently protected. A similar approach was taken in *S (Medical Treatment: Adult Sterilisation, Re* [1998] 1 F.L.R. 994, where Johnson J. refused to grant a declaration on an application by the patient's mother in "the absence of any risk [of pregnancy] that can be called identifiable rather than speculative". A sterilisation can be in the best interests of the patient even if the risk of pregnancy is small (*W (An Adult: Mental Patient) (Sterilisation), Re* [1993] 1 F.L.R. 381).

In *An NHS Trust v D* [2003] EWHC 2793 (Fam Div), Coleridge J. considered the following question: when should an NHS Trust make an application to the High Court for a declaration that the proposed termination of the pregnancy of a mentally incapacitated patient is lawful? His Lordship held that where there is any doubt as to either the mental capacity of the patient or whether the termination would be in her best interests, an application to the court should be made. In particular, the following circumstances would ordinarily warrant the making of an application:

1   Where there is a dispute as to capacity, or where there is a realistic prospect that the patient will regain capacity, following a response to treatment, within the period of her pregnancy or shortly thereafter;
2   Where there is a lack of unanimity amongst the medical professionals as to the best interests of the patient;
3   Where the procedures under s.1 of the Abortion Act 1967 (c.87) have not been followed (*i.e.* where two medical practitioners have not provided a certificate);
4   Where the patient, members of her immediate family, or the foetus's father have opposed, or expressed views inconsistent with, a termination of the pregnancy; or
5   Where there are other exceptional circumstances (including where the termination may be the patient's last chance to bear a child).

If any case is considered to fall anywhere near the boundary line in relation to any of the above criteria, it should for the avoidance of doubt be referred to the court (*S (Adult Patient: Sterilisation: Patient's Best Interests), Re* [2001] Fam. 15, *per* Thorpe L.J. at 32).

It is essential for protocols to be put in place to deal with the possible termination of the pregnancy of patients in psychiatric hospitals. Such protocols should be designed to address the issue in good time and should ensure that the patient is referred at an early stage to independent legal advice whether from the Official Solicitor or from the solicitor who represented her at the Mental Health Review Tribunal (*SS (Medical Treatment: Late Termination), Re* [2002] 1 F.L.R. 445).

Declarations can be applied for in respect of treatment in the future (*NHS Trust v T (Adult Patient: Refusal of Medical Treatment)* [2004] EWHC 1279 (Fam Div); [2005] 1 All E.R. 387). In this case Charles J. confirmed that an interim declaration could be made pursuant to CPR Part 25.1(1)(b). His Lordship said at para.45 that when the court is faced with an emergency situation where treatment cannot be delayed because of an imminent high risk to life the court should make every effort to ensure that the person who it is proposed should be treated in reliance of any declaration has an opportunity to make representations (either directly or indirectly) to the court (and thus in cases of emergency out of hours to the Duty Judge). It would then be for the Judge to decide on capacity and then if appropriate on best interests by applying the normal civil standard on the best evidence then available. It is submitted that in extreme emergencies where there is no time to seek the assistance of the court, any doubt that may exist about the patient's capacity must be resolved in favour of society's interest in upholding the concept that all human life is sacred and that it should be preserved if at all possible.

In *G (An Adult) (Mental Capacity: Court's Jurisdiction), Re* [2004] EWHC 2222 (Fam Div), an incapacitated young woman had been made the subject of interim declarations to protect her from the actions of her father. The evidence was that after a period of being subject to the interim declarations the daughter would regain her mental capacity and her mental health would improve, but that once the protection of the court was withdrawn the daughter's mental health would deteriorate and she would lose her mental capacity. Bennett J. held that in these circumstances he had jurisdiction to make declarations to ensure that the continuing protection of the court was not withdrawn simply because the daughter had regained her mental capacity, given the likely consequences if the court withdrew its protection. The judge said at para.104 that if the declarations sought were in the daughter's best interests, the court, by intervening, far from depriving her of her right to make decisions, will be ensuring that her now stable and improving mental health is sustained, that she has the best possible chance of continuing to be mentally capable, and of ensuring a quality of life that prior to the court's intervention she was unable to enjoy.

A declaration will not be used to require a doctor to act against his or her clinical judgment. In *National Health Service Trust v D* [2000] 2 F.L.R. 677, Cazalet J. said at 686:

"[I]t is well-established that there can be no question of the court directing a doctor to provide treatment which he or she is unwilling to give and which is contrary to that doctor's clinical judgment."

In recent years declarations have been made to regulate the care of mentally incapable adults in cases where there is a dispute about the care that the adult either is receiving or will receive in the future. It is now possible for the High Court to make declarations as to the lawfulness of proposed actions in relation to the adult in circumstances where the issue in question cannot be resolved by recourse to the Mental Health Act 1983. In *Local Authority v Health Authority (Disclosure: Restriction on Publication)* [2003] EWHC 2746 (Fam Div); [2004] 1 All E.R.480, Butler-Sloss P. said at para.96 that the granting of declarations is "a flexible remedy and adaptable to ensure the protection of a person who is under a disability". Caselaw has extended the jurisdiction to the extent that "in cases of controversy and cases involving momentous and irrevocable decisions, the courts have treated as justiciable any genuine question as to what the best interests of a patient require or justify" (*S (Hospital Patient: Court's Jurisdiction) (No.1), Re*), above, *per* Sir Thomas Bingham MR at 18). By using this jurisdiction the High Court is able to effectively resolve disputes such as who should have responsibility for the future care of the adult, who the adult should have contact with and under what circumstances, and the powers that staff can use when providing the adult with care, including the use of restraint and detention.

In *F (Adult: Court's Jurisdiction), Re* [2000] 2 F.L.R. 512, CA, the local authority was concerned that T, an 18 her old with an intellectual age of 5-8 years, who was being accommodated in one of the authority's specialist establishments contrary to her mother's wishes, would be at risk of neglect and exposure to sexual exploitation if she were to return to her home. As T was not mentally impaired within the meaning of s.1(2) of the Mental Health Act, 1983 the local authority was unable to protect T by making her the subject of a guardianship application. The authority therefore sought declarations from the High Court, the effect of which were to keep T in the accommodation and to restrict and supervise her contact with her family. In determining the question of the jurisdiction of the High Court to make such declarations, the Court held that:

i   the application of the common law doctrine of necessity (see *F v West Berkshire HA*, above), is not limited to medical and similar matters; it embraces the problems that arose in this case;

ii   the doctrine, which can be invoked by both an authority and an individual, may properly be invoked side by side with the 1983 Act (*R. v Bournewood Community and Mental Health NHS Trust Ex p. L* [1998] 3 All E.R. 289, HL);

iii   the jurisdiction of the High Court under its inherent jurisdiction to grant relief by way of declarations was therefore not excluded by the 1983 Act;

iv   the jurisdiction will only be invoked if there is a serious justiciable issue; and

v   in making a declaration the judge will be guided by the patient's best interests on an application of a welfare test analogous to that applied in wardship cases.

Sedley L.J. said at 529: "[N]either the mother nor the (imaginary) sister nor the local authority possesses by virtue of their status any power to detain T. Nor, however, does T have the capacity to choose one of them as an appropriate carer. If the role of carer is contested, it is the court alone which has the power - and in my judgment the duty - to make that choice in T's best interests. From the choice will follow the exercise of care; and from the exercise of care, if absolutely necessary, some restraint may follow."

The nature of the High Court's declaratory jurisdiction over mentally incompetent adults was reviewed by Munby J. in *A (A Patient) v A Health Authority* [2002] EWHC 18 (Fam Div/Admin); [2002] Fam 213. His Lordship held that:

i   the jurisdiction could be invoked by anyone whose past or present relationship with the incompetent adult, whether formal or informal, gave him or her a genuine and legitimate interest in obtaining a decision, rather than being a stranger or officious busybody. Thus proceedings can be brought by a relative, a carer, a local authority or a NHS Trust;

ii   the jurisdiction may regulate all that conduces to the incompetent adult's welfare and happiness,

including companionship and his or her domestic and social environment;
iii   the jurisdiction, which extended no further than the parens patriae jurisdiction in relation to children, extended not merely to declaratory relief but also to the grant of injunctive relief - at least interlocutory injunctive relief to preserve or regulate the status quo;
iv   cases which involved only issues of public law should be litigated by way of an application in the Administrative Court for judicial review. Private law cases about the best interests of the adult were to be litigated in the Family Division notwithstanding the fact that issues of public law might be involved; and
v   if the task facing the judge was to come to a decision for and on behalf of an incompetent adult then the welfare of that person had to be the paramount consideration. If the task of the judge was to review the decision of the public authority taken in the exercise of some statutory power then the governing principles were those of public law.

In *A Local Authority v BS* [2003] EWHC 1909 (Fam Div); [2003] 2 F.L.R. 1235, a case where it was alleged that a mentally incapacitated adult had been struck by her father, interim declarations were made on a without notice basis rendering it lawful for the local authority to (1) place the adult in a residential placement; (2) to prohibit her father from removing her from that placement; and (3) to limit the contact between the adult and her father to supervised contact. Wall J. said at para.21 that although in a field as complex as care for the mentally disabled, a high degree of pragmatism is inevitable, in each case there are four essential building blocks. First, is mental incapacity established? Secondly, is there a serious justiciable issue relating to welfare? Thirdly, what is it? Fourthly, with the welfare of the incapable adult as the court's paramount consideration, what are the balance sheet factors which must be drawn up to decide which course of action is in his or her best interests? His Lordship said at para.18 that in certain circumstances, the court will have to make findings of fact about disputed historical matters but that this would only be necessary if they are required to determine the identification of the incapable person's best interests. There will plainly be cases which are very fact specific. There will be others in which the principle concern is the future, and the relative suitability of the plans which each party can put forward for both the short term and the long term care of the mentally incapable adult.

The inherent jurisdiction was invoked in *A London Borough Council v T and T B*, November 1, 2001, where detailed declarations and injunctions were made by the court on the application of the local authority in a situation where there had been a breakdown of trust between a mentally incapacitated adult's mother and the authority which had led to the parties becoming polarised in their positions. The judge found that "there have been occasions where the mother has behaved either in an illogical fashion or in a fashion which can perhaps be most aptly described as not constructive". The relief was designed to provide for the care of the adult by the authority for the foreseeable future and for regulating contact between the mother and her daughter. Constant and relentless complaints by the mother resulted in the judge approving the appointment of an independent non-legal advocate for the client who would provide a channel "for the time to be investigated and dealt with". A penal notice was added to some of the orders because of the past breaches of the undertakings that the mother had given to the court.

In *S (Hospital Patient: Court's Jurisdiction) (No.1), Re)*, above, the jurisdiction was used to determine a dispute between the local authority and the father of a mentally incapacitated adult about the future place of residence of the adult. Munby J. described at para.6 the court's role in this case, a case which fell entirely within the confines of private law, as acting as "a surrogate decision maker on behalf of [the adult]". His Lordship said at para.20:

"[T]he doctrine of necessity enables [the parents of a mentally incapacitated adult] not merely to assume the responsibility for the day-to-day care of their child, with all the routine decision-making which that entails, but also to decide, no doubt, where appropriate, in conjunction with suitable professional advisors, more important matters such as where their child should live, who he should see, what services offered by public authorities he should make use of, what medication he should take and what nursing, dental and medical treatment he should receive. [Cases should only come before the court] if disputes erupt between those seeking to care for the patient".

His Lordship reminded himself of the following point made by Lord Goff in *F v West Berkshire HA*, above, at 566:

" officious intervention cannot be justified by the principle of necessity. So intervention cannot be justified when another more appropriate person is available and willing to act"

The jurisdiction was invoked in Re S. because there is no presumption of the right of contact between a parent and an adult child, even one under a disability (D-R (Adult: Contact), Re [1999] 1 F.L.R. 1161, *per* Butler-Sloss L.J. at 1165) and neither the local authority nor the father had the legal authority to decide where the adult should live. The judge had to weigh the father's rights under Art.8 of the European Convention on Human Rights against the son's Art.8 rights. Munby J. held at para.39 that where there is a conflict between these rights, the State, in the form of the local authority, may have a positive obligation to intervene, even at the risk of detriment to the father's family life, if such intervention is necessary to ensure respect for the son's Art.8 rights. His Lordship further held that in proceedings under the inherent jurisdiction concerning mentally incapable adults:

i   there is nothing analogous to the threshold requirements contained in ss.31 and 100 of the Children Act 1989 requiring the State to establish, before intervention takes place, either the risk of significant harm and/or parenting which falls short of the reasonable;

ii   although there is no presumption that mentally incapacitated adults are better off with their families, other things being equal, the parent, if he or she is willing and able, is the most appropriate person to look after such an adult; not some public authority, however well meaning and seemingly well equipped to do so; and

iii   the Court has jurisdiction to identify a third party (a "surrogate decision maker") as the most appropriate person to be responsible not merely for the adult's care but also for taking important decisions about his life.

A noteworthy feature arising from the cases noted above is that the threshold for removing a mentally incapable adult from the parental home is substantially lower than that required to remove a child in that there is no requirement to establish that the adult is either suffering, or is likely to suffer significant harm. All that is required is that the balance sheet exercise identified by Thorpe L.J. in *Re A*, above, indicates that removal is in the adult's best interests.

In *A Local Authority v Z* [2004] EWHC 2817 (Fam Div); [2005] H.R.L.R. 2, Hedley J. considered the extent of the duty owed by a local authority when the welfare of a vulnerable adult (who may or may not be mentally incapacitated) in their area is threatened by the criminal (or other wrongful) act of another. In this case a husband was intending to assist his severely disabled wife in her desire to commit suicide. Assisting the suicide of another is a crime (Suicide Act 1961 (c.60), s.2(1)). His Lordship held that in such a case the local authority incurred the following duties:

1   To investigate the position of a vulnerable adult to consider what was her true position and intention.

2   To consider whether she was legally competent to make and carry out her decision and intention;

3   To consider whether any other (and if so, what) influence may be operating on her position and intention and to ensure that she has all the relevant information and knows all the available options.

4   To consider whether to invoke the inherent jurisdiction of the High Court so that the question of competence could be judicially investigated and determined.

5   In the event of the adult not being competent to, provide all such assistance as may be reasonably required both to determine and give effect to her best interests.

6   In the event of the adult being competent to allow her in any lawful way to give effect to her decision although that should not preclude the giving of advice or assistance in accordance with what are perceived to be in her best interests.

7   Where there are reasonable grounds to suspect that the commission of a criminal offence may be involved, to draw that to the intention of the police;

8   In very exceptional circumstances, to invoke the jurisdiction of the court under s.222 of the Local Government Act 1972 (c.70) in order to seek an injunction to restrain a criminal act.

Although a local authority can invoke the inherent jurisdiction in order to determine whether a mentally vulnerable adult has the capacity to marry, the High Court has no jurisdiction to determine whether it is in the best interests of that adult to marry a particular person (*Sheffield City Council v E* [2004] EWHC 2808 (Fam Div)). The test for determining capacity to marry was laid down by the Court of Appeal in *Park, In the Estate of* [1954] P. 112.

Butler-Sloss P. has invoked the inherent jurisdiction to grant an injunction to prevent the publication of a report that had been prepared by a local authority subsequent to its decision to remove a number of foster children and vulnerable adults from the home of their foster mother (*Local Authority v Health Authority (Disclosure: Restriction on Publication)*), above). Her Ladyship found that the publication of the report would be "deeply damaging and detrimental" to the welfare of the mentally incapacitated adults.

In *NHS Trust v Bland*, above, Lord Goff at 864-865 reiterated his opinion that declaratory relief was justified, while recognising:

"that strong warnings have been given against the civil courts usurping the function of the criminal courts, and it has been authoritatively been stated that a declaration as to the lawfulness or otherwise of future conduct is 'no bar to criminal prosecutions, no matter the authority of the court which grants it': see *Imperial Tobacco Ltd v Attorney General* [1980] 1 All E.R. 866."

The wardship jurisdiction of the High Court should be invoked if the individual that needs protecting is a child and intervention under the Children Act 1989 is either not possible or inappropriate (*F (Mental Health Act: Guardianship), Re* [2000] 1 F.L.R. 192).

Subsection (1)

Capacity. In *Masterman-Lister v Brutton & Co* [2002] EWCA Civ 1889; [2003] 3 All E.R. 162, Kennedy L.J. said at para.29 that the "conclusion that in law capacity depends on time and context means that inevitably a decision as to capacity in one context does not bind a court which has to consider the same issue in a different context." This case is also authority for the proposition that although the final decision as to capacity rests with the court, in almost every case "the court will need medical evidence to guide it" (*ibid.*).

16. Powers to make decisions and appoint deputies: general

(1) This section applies if a person (P) lacks capacity in relation to a matter or matters concerning—

    (a) P's personal welfare, or

    (b) P's property and affairs.

(2) The court may—

    (a) by making an order, make the decision or decisions on P's behalf in relation to the matter or matters, or

    (b) appoint a person (a deputy) to make decisions on P's behalf in relation to the matter or matters.

(3) The powers of the court under this section are subject to the provisions of this Act and, in particular, to sections 1 (the principles) and 4 (best interests).

(4) When deciding whether it is in P's best interests to appoint a deputy, the court must have regard (in addition to the matters mentioned in section 4) to the principles that—

    (a) a decision by the court is to be preferred to the appointment of a deputy to make a decision, and

    (b) the powers conferred on a deputy should be as limited in scope and duration as is reasonably practicable in the circumstances.

(5) The court may make such further orders or give such directions, and confer on a deputy such powers or impose on him such duties, as it thinks necessary or expedient for giving effect to, or otherwise in connection with, an order or appointment made by it under subsection (2).

(6) Without prejudice to section 4, the court may make the order, give the directions or make the appointment on such terms as it considers are in P's best interests, even though no application is before the court for an order, directions or an appointment on those terms.

(7) An order of the court may be varied or discharged by a subsequent order.

(8) The court may, in particular, revoke the appointment of a deputy or vary the powers conferred on him if it is satisfied that the deputy—

    (a) has behaved, or is behaving, in a way that contravenes the authority conferred on him by the court or is not in P's best interests, or

    (b) proposes to behave in a way that would contravene that authority or would not be in P's best interests.

DEFINITIONS
  "property": s.64(1)
  "the court": s.64(1)

GENERAL NOTE

This section sets out the core jurisdiction of the Court of Protection, which is to make substitute decisions for persons lacking the required mental capacity to make decisions for themselves about either their personal welfare or their property and affairs, or to appoint a deputy to do so if this is in their best interests. The court does not have jurisdiction to supply consent to any matter on behalf of P. Sections 17 and 18 indicate to extent of the court's powers with regard to the personal welfare and the property and affairs of P. A decision of the court is to be preferred to the appointment of a deputy who, if appointed, should be granted powers as limited in scope and duration as is reasonable practicable (subs.(4)). This requirement is consistent with the least restrictive intervention principle set out in s.1(6). The deputy's appointment can be revoked or his or her powers varied if the court considers that the deputy's past, present or future actions will not serve P's best interests (subs.(8)). The court has power to act on its "own motion" to make whatever order is in P's best interests (subs.(6)), and can vary or discharge existing orders (subs.(7)). When exercising this jurisdiction, the court must make decisions which are in the best interests of the mentally incapacitated person (subs.(3)). The court can make any order or appointment which is in the best interests of P, regardless of the nature of the application made to it

The Public Guardian is required to establish and maintain a register of orders appointing deputies, and to supervise deputies (s.58(1)(b) and (c)), and will receive reports from deputies (s.58(1)(f)). The Public Guardian can investigate a complaint about the way in which a deputy is exercising his or her powers (s.58(1)(h)). Ultimately the matter could be referred to the court which has power to either discharge the order appointing the deputy or to vary the deputy's powers (subs.(7)). The supervision and investigatory functions of the Public Guardian can be discharged in co-operation with other persons who are involved in the care of treatment of P (s.58(2)).

Subsection (2)

Making an order. The draft Code of Practice at para.7.17 provides the following examples of the "types of cases when an application for a single order may be appropriate:

●   When there is a genuine doubt or disagreement about the existence, validity or applicability of an advance decision to refuse treatment.
●   Where there is a major dispute regarding a serious decision for example about where a person lacking capacity should live.
●   Where it is suspected that a person lacking capacity is at risk of harm or abuse from a named individual, the court could be asked for an order prohibiting that individual from having contact with the person who lacks capacity.
●   Where formal authority is needed to deal with significant one-off financial decisions for a person lacking capacity to manage financial affairs (such as paying a costly bill for house repairs or selling a valuable item of property), but there is no need for on-going financial powers, the court could be asked to make an order providing the necessary authority.
●   Where it is necessary to make a will, or amend an existing will, on behalf of a person lacking testamentary capacity, this can only be done by order of the court."

Appoint a person. See s.19. Where possible, the court will seek to make a single order (subs.(4)(a)). Given the terms of s.5, it is likely that the appointment of a deputy to make personal welfare decisions in relation to P will be made rarely. The Government said its response to recommendation 54 of the Joint Committee's Report (Cm.6121):

"We would only expect deputies to be given healthcare powers in rare cases, for example, where there is a dispute between family members as to who has the patient's best interests at heart and where the patient has chronic and/or degenerative health problems calling for repeated assessments and decisions by doctors and carers".

In these circumstances, the "court is unlikely to appoint as a deputy someone who is unknown to the person Appointing someone who has no particular insight into the person's wishes, feelings, values or healthcare needs would not be in the person's best interests. The court must appoint a deputy only if that appointment would be in the best interests of the person lacking capacity under [s.16(3)]", *per* the Parliamentary Under-Secretary of State, St. Comm. A, para.195.

The draft Code of Practice at para.7.28 provides the following examples of "circumstances which may require the appointment of a personal welfare deputy for a person lacking capacity:

- Where there is a history of acrimonious and serious family disputes which could have a detrimental effect on decisions about the person's future care.
- Where the person's best interests are best met by a deputy consulting with everybody concerned and having the final authority to make necessary decisions.
- In exceptional cases where the person is felt to be at risk of serious harm if left in the care of family members, a local authority officer or other independent person could be appointed as deputy to make personal care decisions - this could, for example, be combined with a court order prohibiting those family members from having contact with the person.
- When a series of linked welfare decisions need to be made over time, for which single orders of the court are not appropriate."

The need for a deputy to be appointed to manage the person's property and affairs is likely to arise in the same circumstances that governed the appointment of receivers under Pt VII of the Mental Health Act 1983, in particular when property needs to be sold or if the person has financial resources that the court considers requires management by a deputy. The Public Accounts Committee stated that for "a receivership to be successful [under the 1983] Act, it is crucial that the receiver appointed is trustworthy and reliable. It is also important that the receiver is competent to manage the patient's affairs and should take an active interest in the patient's welfare" (House of Commons, Session 1993-1994, Thirty-ninth Report, para.5). The following cases decided under the 1983 Act on the position of receivers are relevant to the position of deputies under this Act:

1   As well as establishing that the receiver acts as the patient's agent (see the note on s.19), the case of *EG, Re* [1914] 1 Ch. 927 established that a solicitor instructed by the receiver in connection with the patient's affairs is the solicitor of the patient and not that of the receiver.
2   The effect of an appointment of a receiver is not to create a liability to a third party that would not otherwise exist. A receiver's duty to satisfy a patient's legal liabilities is entirely dependent on there being such liabilities in existence (*Bell v Todd* [2002] Lloyd's L.R. 12 at para.22).
3   A person who has been rendered a patient as the result of the actions of a tortfeasor is entitled to require the tortfeasor to bear the costs of the receiver as part of the damages (*Cassel v Riverside HA* [1992] P.I.Q.R. Q168).

Subsection (4) para.(a)
See the General Note, above.

Subsection (4) para.(b)
Limited in scope and duration. This provision reflects the fact that many disabled people have capacity to take many day-to-day decisions and would only require the assistance of a deputy in relation to a limited range of matters.

Subsection (5)
If a deputy considers that the powers conferred by the court are insufficient to carry out the necessary duties toward the person lacking capacity, he or she should apply to the court either to vary the powers in the order of appointment, or for the court to make a particular decision itself. The court "will be able to grant powers to the deputy on condition that it first obtains the Public Guardian's consent for certain actions. It is important that deputies are, of course, properly supervised, but it would be disproportionately burdensome and costly to require them to apply to the court all the time for authority to act. That supervisory role should properly be undertaken by the Public Guardian", *per* the Parliamentary Under-Secretary of State (*Hansard*, HL Vol.670, col.1474).

Subsection (7)
See s.18(5).

Subsection (8)
This provides the court with similar powers to those it has with respect to donees: see s.22(3),(4).

17. Section 16 powers: personal welfare

(1) The powers under section 16 as respects P's personal welfare extend in particular to—

(a) deciding where P is to live;

(b) deciding what contact, if any, P is to have with any specified persons;

(c) making an order prohibiting a named person from having contact with P;

(d) giving or refusing consent to the carrying out or continuation of a treatment by a person providing health care for P;

(e) giving a direction that a person responsible for P's health care allow a different person to take over that responsibility.

(2) Subsection (1) is subject to section 20 (restrictions on deputies).

DEFINITIONS
"treatment": s.64(1)
"deputy": s.64(1)

GENERAL NOTE

This section sets out in subs.(1) the types of personal welfare matters that, under s.16, the Court of Protection may either determine itself or appoint a deputy to make decisions about on P's behalf. The power of deputies to make decisions is subject to the restrictions set out in s.20 (subs.(2)). The list in subs.(1) which is indicative, not exhaustive, is based on matters that have been dealt with by the High Court in the exercise of its inherent jurisdiction to make declarations: see the General Note to s.15. It is not a list of decisions that must always go the court for determination; rather it provides examples of decisions that could go to the court for determination if it would be appropriate to do so.

The court does not have the power to make an order which has the effect of depriving P of his or her liberty as the absence of a right to the regular review of the order means that the detention fails to meet the requirements of Art.5(4) of the European Convention on Human Rights as set out in *HL v United Kingdom* (2005) 40 E.H.R.R. 32, ECHR, at para.135.

Subsection (1) (a)

As the court only has power to make any decision that P could have made, this power cannot be used to override the provisions of either s.47 of the National Health Service and Community Care Act 1990 (c.19), which provides for the assessment by a local authority of a person's need for community care services (which includes the provision of accommodation), or the National Assistance Act (Choice of Accommodation) Directions 1992.

Subsection (1) (c)

A restraining order could be made where the named person presents a risk of abuse, or where continued contact with that person will harm or distress P. The power restrain a named person cannot extend to any interference with other rights of that person, such as the right to occupy property.

Subsection (1) (d)

In the consultation paper "*Who Decides*" (Cm.3803 at 7.26), the Government expressed its concern that a deputy "might have less prior knowledge of a patient's wishes regarding treatment than the patient's doctor". The fact that a deputy has the power to refuse treatment on behalf of P represents a significant change in the doctor patient relationship in that a non-medical deputy can override the doctor's clinical judgment as to what medical treatment his or her patient should receive; see further the General Note to s.11. This power is subject to the limitation set out in s.20(5).

The deputy does not have the power to direct that a different person should take over responsibility for P's health care (s.20(2)(b)). Neither does the deputy have the power to require a doctor to provide treatment which is not considered to be in P's best interests. This is because if P were capable, he or she would not have such a power.

Subsection (1) (e)

Subsection (1) (e)

This allows for the court to order that the responsibility for P's healthcare be transferred to another doctor where P's doctor has a conscientious or clinical objection to a treating P.

18. Section 16 powers: property and affairs

(1) The powers under section 16 as respects P's property and affairs extend in particular to—

(a) the control and management of P's property;

(b) the sale, exchange, charging, gift or other disposition of P's property;

(c) the acquisition of property in P's name or on P's behalf;

(d) the carrying on, on P's behalf, of any profession, trade or business;

(e) the taking of a decision which will have the effect of dissolving a partnership of which P is a member;

(f) the carrying out of any contract entered into by P;

(g) the discharge of P's debts and of any of P's obligations, whether legally enforceable or not;

(h) the settlement of any of P's property, whether for P's benefit or for the benefit of others;

(i) the execution for P of a will;

(j) the exercise of any power (including a power to consent) vested in P whether beneficially or as trustee or otherwise;

(k) the conduct of legal proceedings in P's name or on P's behalf.

(2) No will may be made under subsection (1)(i) at a time when P has not reached 18.

(3) The powers under section 16 as respects any other matter relating to P's property and affairs may be exercised even though P has not reached 16, if the court considers it likely that P will still lack capacity to make decisions in respect of that matter when he reaches 18.

(4) Schedule 2 supplements the provisions of this section.

(5) Section 16(7) (variation and discharge of court orders) is subject to paragraph 6 of Schedule 2.

(6) Subsection (1) is subject to section 20 (restrictions on deputies).

DEFINITIONS

"property": s.64(1)

GENERAL NOTE

This section, which is supplemented by Sch.2, provides a non-exhaustive, indicative list of the matters relating to P's property and affairs that come within the jurisdiction of the Court of Protection under s.16. The Court may either determine the matter itself or appoint a deputy to make decisions on P's behalf The power of deputies to make decisions is subject to the restrictions set out in s.20 (subs.(6)). Like s.17, subs.(1) does not contain a list of matters which must always be referred to the court; it provides an indication of the types of order the court might make if an application is made.

It is submitted that the court may make an order if the provisions of a financial LPA do not enable P's best interests to be satisfied: see *Re C* (9103771T), Rattee J., January 23, 1996.

Subsection (1)

This largely reproduces the list which applied to the Court of Protection under s.96 of the Mental Health Act 1983.

Paragraph (a)

Property. This includes papers held by the Official Solicitor in an action in which he acts as the patient's litigation friend (*E (Mental Health Patient), Re* [1985] 1 All E.R. 609, CA). In this case the court held that the parents of a patient had no absolute right to see such papers, although they were the patient's property, but must obtain the authority of the Court of Protection to order disclosure of them as necessary or expedient for the benefit of the patient.

Paragraph (b)

Gift. The court will adopt the stance that it takes to the making of wills: see *C, Re* and *S, Re,* noted under para.(i), below. Although it is proper to propose a gift where one of the objectives is to reduce liability for tax, this should not be the sole objective (*CWM, Re* [1951] 2 K.B. 714).

Any view expressed by the P about a gift can be taken into account by the court but cannot be regarded as determinative, even if P retains the capacity to make a gift. The court will be concerned to establish whether P has been subjected to the undue influence of the proposed recipient of the gift. The criteria for capacity to make a gift were set out in *Beaney (Deceased), Re* [1978] 2 All E.R.595 at 601:

"The degree or extent of understanding required in respect of any instrument is relative to the particular transaction which it is to effect Thus, at one extreme, if the subject-matter and value of a gift are trivial in relation to the donor's other assets, a low degree of understanding will suffice. But, at the other, if its effect is to dispose of the donor's only asset of value and thus, for practical purposes, to pre-empt the devolution of his estate under [the donor's] will or intestacy, then the degree of understanding required is as high as that required for a will, and the donor must understand the claims of all potential donees and the extent of the property to be disposed of."

Disposition of P's property. Provisions relating to the preservation of interests in property disposed of on behalf of P are contained in paras 8 and 9 of Sch.2.

Paragraph (h)

Paragraphs 5 and 6 of Sch.2 are concerned with the making of settlements on behalf of P. Settlements are likely to be created, with or without the appointment of a deputy, where P has been awarded substantial damages for personal injury.

In *L (WJG), Re* [1966] Ch. 135, at 144 and 145, Cross J. considered the approach to be adopted by a judge in determining whether and how he should exercise his discretion in regard to the making of a settlement where one of the objects of the exercise was to save death duties. His Lordship said: "As the state had maintained [P] free of charge for many years, it would be a little shabby to deprive it of the chance of recouping some of that expenditure by way of death duties."

Paragraph (i)

Paragraphs 2 to 4 of Sch.2 apply to the making of a will on behalf of P.

P must be an adult before a will can be made (subs.(2)). In *D (J), Re* [1982] 2 All E.R. 37 at 42 and 43, Megarry V-C. identified five considerations which the court should have in mind when deciding on what provisions should be inserted in a will. They are:

1   It is to be assumed that the patient is having a brief lucid interval at the time when the will was made.
2   During the lucid interval the patient has full knowledge of the past and a full realisation that as soon as the will is executed he will relapse into the actual mental state that previously existed, with the prognosis as it actually is.
3   It is the actual patient who has to be considered and not a hypothetical patient.
4   During the hypothetical lucid interval, the patient is to be envisaged as being advised by competent solicitors.
5   In all normal cases, the patient is to be envisaged as taking a broad brush to the claims on his bounty, rather than an accountant's pen.

In *C (Spinster and Mental Patient), Re* [1991] 3 All E.R. 866, Hoffmann J. held that in the case of a person who has never enjoyed a rational mind the court when called upon to interpret the phrase "the patient might be expected to provide" in s.95(1)(c) of the 1983 Act should assume that the patient would have been a normal decent person who would have acted in accordance with contemporary standards of morality. In appropriate cases this could result in the patient making charitable gifts and bequests. *Re C* was considered in *S (Gifts by Mental Patient), Re* [1997] 1 F.L.R. 96 at 99 where Ferris J. said on the question of dispositions to charity: "It seems to me that I ought not authorise the making of dispositions to charity except to the extent that I have a reasonable degree of confidence that not only is it objectively reasonable but that it is something which the patient herself would have wished to be done if she were of full capacity and aware of the circumstances."

The court will not make a new will under this provision unless it is satisfied that there are grounds for making a change. In *Re S*, above, Ferris J. said at 99:

"[M]y approach gives weight to the undesirability of the court exercising its jurisdiction in such a way as to change the existing position in circumstances where it is not fully satisfied that the change is something which the patient herself would have desired."

The court has no jurisdiction to determine the validity of an existing will and, in particular, whether P had the required mental capacity when he made it. The test for testamentary capacity (the capacity required to make a will) was set out by the Court of Appeal in *Banks v Goodfellow* (costs) (1870-71) L.R. 11 Eq. 472:

"It is essential that a testator shall understand the nature of the act and its effects; shall understand the extent of the property of which he is disposing; shall be able to comprehend and appreciate the claims to which he ought to give effect; and, with a view to the latter object, that no disorder of mind shall poison his affections, pervert his sense of right, or prevent the exercise of his natural faculties - that no insane delusion shall influence his will in disposing of his property and bring about a disposal of it which, if the mind had been sound, would not have been made."

Paragraph (k)

The conduct of legal proceedings need not be confined to proceedings relating either to P's personal welfare or his property and affairs (*W (EEM), Re* [1971] Ch. 123).

Subsection (3)

This provision enables the court to take a long term view where a brain damaged child has been awarded a large sum of damages and there is no prospect of the child ever gaining the capacity to manage that money.

19. Appointment of deputies

(1) A deputy appointed by the court must be—
  (a) an individual who has reached 18, or
  (b) as respects powers in relation to property and affairs, an individual who has reached 18 or a trust corporation.

(2) The court may appoint an individual by appointing the holder for the time being of a specified office or position.

(3) A person may not be appointed as a deputy without his consent.

(4) The court may appoint two or more deputies to act—
  (a) jointly,
  (b) jointly and severally, or
  (c) jointly in respect of some matters and jointly and severally in respect of others.

(5) When appointing a deputy or deputies, the court may at the same time appoint one or more other persons to succeed the existing deputy or those deputies—
  (a) in such circumstances, or on the happening of such events, as may be specified by the court;
  (b) for such period as may be so specified.

(6) A deputy is to be treated as P's agent in relation to anything done or decided by him within the scope of his appointment and in accordance with this Part.

(7) The deputy is entitled—
  (a) to be reimbursed out of P's property for his reasonable expenses in discharging his functions, and
  (b) if the court so directs when appointing him, to remuneration out of P's property for discharging them.

(8) The court may confer on a deputy powers to—

    (a) take possession or control of all or any specified part of P's property;

    (b) exercise all or any specified powers in respect of it, including such powers of investment as the court may determine.

(9) The court may require a deputy—

    (a) to give to the Public Guardian such security as the court thinks fit for the due discharge of his functions, and

    (b) to submit to the Public Guardian such reports at such times or at such intervals as the court may direct.

DEFINITIONS

"deputy": s.64(1)
"the court": s.64(1)
"property": s.64(1)
"trust corporation": s.64(1)
"Public Guardian": s.64(1)

GENERAL NOTE

A deputy appointed by the Court of Protection must be an adult who consents to the appointment, although a trust corporation can be appointed in respect of P's property and affairs (subss.(1) and (3)). Most deputies are likely to be a member of P's family. When appointing a deputy, the court will exercise its discretion so as to satisfy the best interests of P (s.1(5)). The spouse of P has no right to be appointed (*Davy (Laura), Re* [1892] 3 Ch. 38). The court will decide the extent of the powers to be conferred on the deputy (s.16(5)). The powers will be subject to the restrictions contained in s.20. The deputy's powers can be varied by the court, which can also revoke the appointment (s.16(8)). A deputy will be provided with protection by ss.5 and 6 for acts done outside the scope of the appointment. There is no time limit attached to the appointment.

Those applying to become deputies would need to demonstrate why an appointment is necessary. There is no requirement for the court to be satisfied as to the suitability of an individual for appointment by, for example, investigating any actual or potential conflict of interest, although the Public Guardian is required to supervise deputies (s.58(1)(c)). Unlike a donee under a lasting power of attorney, the deputy can be the holder of a specified office, such as a Director of Social Services (subs.(2)). Where there is more than one deputy, they can be appointed to act either jointly or jointly and severally, *i.e.* they must either act together with the agreement of all donees (jointly), or each donee can act independently of the other (severally). As an alternative, the donees can be appointed to act jointly in respect of some matters and jointly and severally in respect of others (subs.(4)). The donor therefore "has all possible options when wanting to appoint more than one donee", *per* the Parliamentary Under-Secretary of State (*Hansard*, HL Vol.670, col.1473). When making the appointment, the court has the power to appoint a successor or successors to the original appointee(s) and to specify the circumstances under which this could occur (subs.(5)). "This arrangement may be particularly helpful when the best candidate for appointment is already elderly and [the court] wishes to be sure that someone else will take over in the future" (Draft Code of Practice, para.7.31).

A deputy can claim reasonable expenses and, if the court directs, the deputy can be paid for his or her services. Both expenses and the payments will be made out of P's property (subs.(7)). The deputy can be provided with the power to deal with all matters concerning the control and management of P's property, including being able to invest (subs.(8)). The court will be able to require a deputy to give the Public Guardian security against misbehaviour and to direct the deputy to file reports with the Public Guardian at specified intervals (subs.(9)). Although case law has established that receivers appointed Court of Protection under Pt VII of the Mental Health Act 1983 are statutory agents of the person who lacks capacity (*EG, Re* [1914] 1 Ch. 927), it was considered "helpful to make statutory provision to that effect in relation to dputies" (Explanatory Notes, para.73). This is done in subs.(6). An act of an agent, done within the scope of his authority binds his principal, in this case P. As as agent the deputy is bound by a number of common law duties toward P, including the duty to act with due care and skill, to act within the scope of the authority granted by the court, to act in good faith, not to delegate his or her functions to another without authority, to keep the affairs of P confidential, to keep accounts of monies recieved and paid on P's behalf, and not to permit his own interests to conflict with his duties to P. In addition to these duties, the deputy is required to act in P's best interests (s.20(6)). *EG, Re* is authority for the propositions that the propert of P does not vest in the deputy (at 933), and that the deputy is not personally liablefor the costs of those he or she employs in the cours of acting for P (at 935). The deputy should notify any third party with whom he is dealing of the fact that he is acting as deputy for P, as it is a general principle of the law of agency that an agent is personally liable on any contract made in his own name on behalf of a principle where the name or existence of the principle (P) is undisclosed at the time of contracting. Also see the comment on the law of agency in the General Note to s.10.

Any concerns about the manner in which a deputy is performing his or her functions should be reported to the Public Guardian. The Public Guardian may decide to direct a Court of Protection Visitor to visit P and/or the deputy. Allegations of serious criminal conduct, such as physical or sexual abuse, should be reported directly to the police, and the Public Guardian informed. Also see the note on adult protection procedures in s.42.

In this Act references to making decisions, in relation to a deputy, include, where appropriate, acting on decisions made (s.64(2)).

Subsection (6)

"A key principle governing deputies is that they cannot do more than the person could do if he or she had capacity", *per* the Parliamentary Under-Secretary of State, St. Comm. A, para.191.

Subsection (9)

Security. "For example, deputies appointed to deal with property and affairs may be required to deposit an amount of money, or to purchase insurance such as a guarantee bond, to cover any loss to the person lacking capacity as a result of the deputy's misbehaviour in his role" (Draft Code of Practice, para.7.35).

20. Restrictions on deputies

(1) A deputy does not have power to make a decision on behalf of P in relation to a matter if he knows or has reasonable grounds for believing that P has capacity in relation to the matter.

(2) Nothing in section 16(5) or 17 permits a deputy to be given power—

    (a) to prohibit a named person from having contact with P;

    (b) to direct a person responsible for P's health care to allow a different person to take over that responsibility.

(3) A deputy may not be given powers with respect to—

    (a) the settlement of any of P's property, whether for P's benefit or for the benefit of others,

    (b) the execution for P of a will, or

    (c) the exercise of any power (including a power to consent) vested in P whether beneficially or as trustee or otherwise.

(4) A deputy may not be given power to make a decision on behalf of P which is inconsistent with a decision made, within the scope of his authority and in accordance with this Act, by the donee of a lasting power of attorney granted by P (or, if there is more than one donee, by any of them).

(5) A deputy may not refuse consent to the carrying out or continuation of life-sustaining treatment in relation to P.

(6) The authority conferred on a deputy is subject to the provisions of this Act and, in particular, sections 1 (the principles) and 4 (best interests).

(7) A deputy may not do an act that is intended to restrain P unless four conditions are satisfied.

(8) The first condition is that, in doing the act, the deputy is acting within the scope of an authority expressly conferred on him by the court.

(9) The second is that P lacks, or the deputy reasonably believes that P lacks, capacity in relation to the matter in question.

(10) The third is that the deputy reasonably believes that it is necessary to do the act in order to prevent harm to P.

(11) The fourth is that the act is a proportionate response to—

(a) the likelihood of P's suffering harm, or

(b) the seriousness of that harm.

(12) For the purposes of this section, a deputy restrains P if he—

(a) uses, or threatens to use, force to secure the doing of an act which P resists, or

(b) restricts P's liberty of movement, whether or not P resists,

or if he authorises another person to do any of those things.

(13) But a deputy does more than merely restrain P if he deprives P of his liberty within the meaning of Article 5(1) of the Human Rights Convention (whether or not the deputy is a public authority).

DEFINITIONS

"deputy": s.64(1)

"property": s.64(1)

"lasting power of attorney": s.64(1)

"life-sustaining treatment": s.64(1)

"the Human Rights Convention": s.64(1)

"public authority": s.6(1)

GENERAL NOTE

This section sets out a number of limitations on the powers of deputies, who must always act in P's best interests (subs.(6)).

Subsection (1) specifies that a deputy cannot act where P is able to act for himself. The Explanatory Notes state at para.75:

"In some cases the person may have fluctuating capacity, for example as a result of mental health problems, and it is not acceptable for a deputy to carry on making substitute decisions when the person concerned has in fact recovered."

As it is can be difficult to determine whether a person with fluctuating mental capacity is enjoying a lucid interval, the deputy should consider seeking professional assistance if he suspects that P is able to act for himself.

Subsections (2) and (3) list matters which must always be dealt with by the court, not a deputy.

Subsection (4) provides that a deputy cannot be given power to override a valid decision made by a donee under P's LPA. If there is concern or a dispute about the way the donee is carrying on his or her responsibilities under the LPA, the court must use its powers under ss.22 and 23 rather that seeking to appoint a deputy.

Subsection (5) prevents deputies from refusing consent to the carrying out or continuation of life-sustaining treatment.

Subsections (7)-(13) impose limitations on a deputy's power to restrain P. They match those imposed in relation to "section 5 acts" by s.6 and on donees by s.11, and reference should be made to the notes on s.6. The deputy will have to be acting within the scope of an authority expressly conferred on him by the court (subs.(8)).

Subsection (2)(a)

If a deputy is concerned about someone's conduct toward P, he or she can apply to the court for a relevant order to be made, or apply for a non-molestation order under Pt IV of the Family Law Act 1996 (c.27) as P's litigation friend.

Subsection (13)

See the notes to s.6(5).

21. Transfer of proceedings relating to people under 18

The Lord Chancellor may by order make provision as to the transfer of proceedings relating to a person under 18, in such circumstances as are specified in the order—

    (a) from the Court of Protection to a court having jurisdiction under the Children Act 1989 (c. 41), or

    (b) from a court having jurisdiction under that Act to the Court of Protection.

GENERAL NOTE

Generally speaking, this Act is concerned with people aged 16 and over who lack capacity (s.2(5); but see s.18(3)), while the Children Act 1989 is mainly concerned with people under the age of 18. This section deals with any overlap between the two jurisdictions by providing the Lord Chancellor with a power to make transfer of proceedings orders. The Parliamentary Under-Secretary of State gave the following example of the need for a transfer:

"[I]f the parents of a 17 year-old who has profound learning difficulties are in dispute with each other about residence or contact, it might be more appropriate for the Court of Protection to deal with that, since a s.8 order made under the Children Act 1989 would expire on the child's eighteenth birthday at the latest" (*Hansard*, HL Vol.668, col.1485).

Powers of the court in relation to lasting powers of attorney

22. Powers of court in relation to validity of lasting powers of attorney

    (1) This section and section 23 apply if—

      (a) a person (P) has executed or purported to execute an instrument with a view to creating a lasting power of attorney, or

      (b) an instrument has been registered as a lasting power of attorney conferred by P.

    (2) The court may determine any question relating to—

      (a) whether one or more of the requirements for the creation of a lasting power of attorney have been met;

      (b) whether the power has been revoked or has otherwise come to an end.

    (3) Subsection (4) applies if the court is satisfied—

      (a) that fraud or undue pressure was used to induce P—

         (i) to execute an instrument for the purpose of creating a lasting power of attorney, or

         (ii) to create a lasting power of attorney, or

      (b) that the donee (or, if more than one, any of them) of a lasting power of attorney—

         (i) has behaved, or is behaving, in a way that contravenes his authority or is not in P's best interests, or

         (ii) proposes to behave in a way that would contravene his authority or would not be in P's best interests.

    (4) The court may—

      (a) direct that an instrument purporting to create the lasting power of attorney is not to be registered, or

      (b) if P lacks capacity to do so, revoke the instrument or the lasting power of attorney.

    (5) If there is more than one donee, the court may under subsection (4)(b) revoke the instrument or the lasting power of attorney so far as it relates to any of them.

(6) "Donee" includes an intended donee.

GENERAL NOTE

This section and s.23 set out the powers of the Court of Protection where a person has drawn up a document (an "instrument") which is either intended to be registered as a lasting power of attorney (LPA) at some time in the future, or has already been registered as a LPA. The court is provided with a power to determine questions about the validity and revocation of LPAs (subs.(2)), and can direct that the instrument should not be registered, or where it has been registered and P lacks capacity, that it should be revoked if any of the grounds in subs.(3) are satisfied (subs.(4)). This section also provides that where there is more than one donee, the court may revoke the instrument or the LPA so far as it relates to any of them provided that P lacks capacity (subss.(5),(6)).

23. Powers of court in relation to operation of lasting powers of attorney

(1) The court may determine any question as to the meaning or effect of a lasting power of attorney or an instrument purporting to create one.

(2) The court may—

    (a) give directions with respect to decisions—

        (i) which the donee of a lasting power of attorney has authority to make, and

        (ii) which P lacks capacity to make;

    (b) give any consent or authorisation to act which the donee would have to obtain from P if P had capacity to give it.

(3) The court may, if P lacks capacity to do so—

    (a) give directions to the donee with respect to the rendering by him of reports or accounts and the production of records kept by him for that purpose;

    (b) require the donee to supply information or produce documents or things in his possession as donee;

    (c) give directions with respect to the remuneration or expenses of the donee;

    (d) relieve the donee wholly or partly from any liability which he has or may have incurred on account of a breach of his duties as donee.

(4) The court may authorise the making of gifts which are not within section 12(2) (permitted gifts).

(5) Where two or more donees are appointed under a lasting power of attorney, this section applies as if references to the donee were to all or any of them.

GENERAL NOTE

This section provides the Court of Protection with powers to decide any questions about the "meaning or effect" of a LPA or an instrument purporting to create one (subs.(1)), to give directions to donees where P lacks capacity (subs.(2)(a)), and to give any consent or authorisation which P might have given had he or she not lacked capacity (subs.(2)(b)). If P is incapacitated, the court also has power to give the donee directions in relation to producing reports, accounts, records and information, determining a donee's remuneration and expenses, and relieving a donee from some or all of the liabilities arising from a breach of his or her duties as donee (subs.(3)). The Court may also authorise the making of gifts beyond the scope of what is permitted by s.12(2) (subs.(4)).

Subsection (1)

Meaning or effect. This gives the court power to determine any point of construction arising on the LPA, and whether a donee has power to carry out a particular act.

Subsection (2)

The purpose of para.(b) was explained by the Parliamentary Under-Secretary of State:

"[Donees] are in law regarded as agents and are therefore affected by the law of agency as well as the provisions of the Bill. [Under the law of agency] it is sometimes necessary for the [donee] to give the consent or authorisation of the donor before they can act. The obvious example is where the donee would like to purchase the donor's property. The donor would make it a condition of the power of attorney that the [donee] must get their consent. In other words, if I wanted to buy the house of someone for whom I acted as [donee], I would need to get their consent to do so. However, if they lack capacity, I cannot get their consent. Yet, it would be wrong for me to purchase their house without consent. In those circumstances, the court would step in and give the consent. So, it is a protection, but a protection in circumstances where the law of agency applies" (*Hansard*, HL Vol.668, col.1426).

Subsection (3)

As, generally speaking, the court will not exercise any supervision over the conduct of a donee, the giving of directions relating to the production of reports *etc* is likely to be triggered by concerns being raised by persons who are in close contact with P.

Remuneration. The directions could override a provision for remuneration contained in the LPA.

Any liability. Note the breath of this power. Unlike the power to relive trustees from breaches of trust under s.61 of the Trustee Act 1925, there is no requirement for the donee to have acted "honestly and reasonably".

Subsection (4)

This provision could be used to authorise gifts for tax planning purposes.

Advance decisions to refuse treatment

24. Advance decisions to refuse treatment: general

(1) "Advance decision" means a decision made by a person (P), after he has reached 18 and when he has capacity to do so, that if—

(a) at a later time and in such circumstances as he may specify, a specified treatment is proposed to be carried out or continued by a person providing health care for him, and

(b) at that time he lacks capacity to consent to the carrying out or continuation of the treatment,

the specified treatment is not to be carried out or continued.

(2) For the purposes of subsection (1)(a), a decision may be regarded as specifying a treatment or circumstances even though expressed in layman's terms.

(3) P may withdraw or alter an advance decision at any time when he has capacity to do so.

(4) A withdrawal (including a partial withdrawal) need not be in writing.

(5) An alteration of an advance decision need not be in writing (unless section 25(5) applies in relation to the decision resulting from the alteration).

DEFINITIONS
"treatment": s.64(1)

GENERAL NOTE

Sections 24-26 deal with advance decisions to refuse medical treatment. As they broadly "seek to codify and clarify the current common law rules" relating to advance directives (Explanatory Notes, para.84), an account of these rules is set out below. The Government's cautious approach to legislating in this area is illustrated by the following extract from "*Who Decides? Making Decisions on Behalf of Mentally Incapacitated Adults*" (Cm.3803):

"The Government recognises the strength of feeling on this subject. This was the area of the Law Commission's work which aroused the greatest public concern, and it is clear that this is a matter on which many have deep rooted personal, moral, religious and ethical views. The Government does not believe that it would be appropriate to reach any conclusions in this area in the absence of fresh consultation - not just on the detailed plans put forward by the Law Commission, but also on the need for and the merits of legislation in this area generally" (para.4.2).

This caution was, to a certain extent, explained by the conclusion of the House of Lords Select Committee on Medical Ethics which had commended the development of advance directives, but decided that "it could well be impossible to give advance directives in general greater legal force without depriving patients of the benefit of the doctor's professional expertise and of new treatments and procedures which may have become available since the directive was signed" ((1993-4) HL Paper 21-1, para.185).

Advance Directives

The case of *C (Adult: Refusal of Medical Treatment), Re* [1994] 1 All E.R. 819, was the first occasion when an English Court had been invited to rule directly on the legal validity of an advance directive. Thorpe J. held that a refusal of treatment could take the form of a declaration of intention never to consent in the future or never to consent in some future circumstances. The effect of this ruling is that an advance refusal of treatment for either a physical or mental disorder made when the patient is mentally capable survives any supervening incapacity, even if the refusal leads to the patient's death. His Lordship accepted that a patient might have capacity to make a present refusal but lack the capacity to make an anticipatory refusal.

The criteria required for an advance directive to be valid were identified by Hughes J. in *AK (Adult Patient) (Medical Treatment: Consent), Re* [2001] 1 F.L.R. 129 (points 1 and 2), and by Munby J. in *HE v A Hospital NHS Trust* [2003] EWHC 1017 (Fam Div); [2003] 2 F.L.R. 408 (points 3-9). They are:

1   The treating doctor must be satisfied that the patient was mentally capable at the time when the patient made it known that he or she would not consent to the treatment in question.
2   All the circumstances in which the expression of wishes was given will have to be investigated. In particular, care must be taken to (a) ensure that the anticipatory declaration of wishes still represent the wishes of the patient; (b) investigate how long ago the expression of wishes was made; and (c) investigate with what knowledge the expression of wishes was made.
3   There are no formal requirements for a valid advance directive. An advance directive may be oral or in writing.
4   There are no formal requirements for the revocation of an advance directive. An advance directive, whether oral or in writing, may be revoked either orally or in writing. A written advance directive or an advance directive executed under seal can be revoked orally.
5   An advance directive is inherently revocable. Any condition in an advance directive purporting to make it irrevocable, any even self-imposed fetter on a patient's ability to revoke an advance directive, and any provision in an advance directive purporting to impose formal or other conditions upon its revocation, is contrary to public policy and void. So, a stipulation in an advance directive, even if in writing, that it shall be binding unless and until it is revoked in writing is void as being contrary to public policy.
6   The existence and continuing validity and applicability of an advance directive is a question of fact. Whether an advance directive has been revoked or has for some other reason ceased to be operative is a question of fact.
7   The burden of proof is on those who seek to establish the existence and continuing validity and applicability of an advance directive.
8   Where life is at stake the evidence must be scrutinised with especial care. Clear and convincing proof is required. The continuing validity and applicability of the advance directive must be clearly established by convincing and inherently reliable evidence.
9   If there is doubt that doubt falls to be resolved in favour of the preservation of life.

Before the decision of Munby J. in *R. (on the application of Burke) v General Medical Council* [2004] EWHC 1879 (Admin); [2004] 2 F.L.R. 1121, the legal position was that an advance directive could not be used to require that a particular treatment be given. In Burke, the mentally capable claimant was suffering from a degenerative brain illness that would eventually result in an inability to swallow. He would therefore require artificial nutrition and hydration ("ANH") in order to survive. He sought clarification of the circumstances when ANH may lawfully be withdrawn, contenting that the relevant GMC guidance "Withholding and Withdrawing Life Prolonging Treatments: Good Practice in Decision-Making" (1999) was incompatible with his rights under Arts 2,3,8, and 14 of the European Convention on Human Rights. In essence the claimant wanted recognition of his advance directive that ANH be instituted and continued at least while he remained conscious. This was delivered by Munby J. at para.171:

"Given what I have to assume would by then be his clearly expressed wishes, embodied in an advance directive both valid and relevant to the treatment in question (ANH), to withdraw ANH at any stage before the claimant finally lapses into a coma would in principle involve clear breaches of both Art.8 and Art.3; for it is clear that if ANH were to be withdrawn he would be exposed to acute mental and physical suffering".

His Lordship held at para.166 that the previous position that prohibited advance directives from being used to require treatment which is against the doctor's clinical judgment being given had to be modified in the light of Arts 3 and 8:

"[I]f the personal autonomy which is protected by Art.8 embraces such matters as how one chooses to pass the closing days and moments of one's life and how one manages one's death, and if Art.3 embraces, as in my judgment it does, the right to die with dignity and the right to be protected from treatment, or from a lack of treatment, which will result in one dying in avoidably distressing circumstances, then the personal autonomy protected by Art.8 means that in principle it is for the competent patient, not his doctor, to decide what treatment should or should not be given in order to achieve what the patient believes conduces to his dignity and in order what the patient would find distressing".

If a patient makes a valid advance directive to the effect that he or she is not to be resuscitated if he or she is found in an unconscious state after attempting suicide, the directive must be respected (*W (Adult: Refusal of Medical Treatment), Re* [2002] EWHC 901 (Fam Div)). A failure to respect a valid advance directive can result in a claim for battery being made against the clinician (*Airedale NHS Trust v Bland* [1993] 1 All E.R. 821, HL).

For advance directives and psychiatric treatment, see A. Halpern and G. Szmukler, "Psychiatric advance directives: reconciling autonomy and non-consensual treatment", Psychiatric Bulletin (1997), 21, 323-327. Dr A. Treloar identifies major potential problems with the use of advance directives in "Advance directives: limitations upon their application in elderly care", International Journal of Geriatric Psychiatry (1999), 14, 1039-1053. A study by T. Thompson, R. Barbour and L. Schwartz found that advance directives are open to widely varying interpretations ("Adherence to advance directives in critical care decision making: vignette study", British Medical Journal (2003), 327, 1011-1018).

Advance Decisions

This section defines an advance decision, sometimes referred to as a "living will". The person making the advance decision need not refer to it as such. An advance decision can only be made by a mentally capable person aged 18 or over and the decision must specify the treatment that is being refused. The decision could have been made a considerable time before the coming into force of this Act. The effect of an advance decision is to enable the person to refuse the specified treatment when that person loses the capacity to give or refuse consent to that treatment. In other words, an advance decision which is valid and applicable (s.25) is as effective as a contemporaneous decision made by a mentally capable person in that healthcare professionals are bound by it (s.26), even if they or the patient's relatives or carers disagree with it. As this section is only concerned with refusals of treatment (subs.(1)), it does not cover the situation in *R. (on the application of Burke) v General Medical Council*, above.

The advance decision can specify particular circumstances in which the refusal may apply. Both the treatment and the circumstances may be specified in lay (i.e. non-medical) terms. Section 25(5) and (6) comes into play if the person wishes the advance decision to apply to a refusal of life sustaining treatment. Disputes about the existence, validity or applicability of an advance decision can be referred to the Court of Protection (s.26(4)). An advance decision cannot be used to give effect to an unlawful act such as euthanasia, which is a deliberate intervention with the express aim of ending life (s.62).

The best interests criterion does not apply to the application of an advance decision as the person concerned has identified his or her best interests when making the advance decision: see the General Note to s.26.

An advance decision can be overridden by the provisions of ss.57, 58 and 63 of the Mental Health Act 1983 (see s.28), so that a decision that refuses a specific treatment for a mental disorder will be rendered ineffective if a person is detained under a section of the 1983 Act which comes within the scope of Pt IV of that Act.

Apart from an advance decision that relates to life-sustaining treatment (see s.25(5),(6)), this Act does not establish any procedures or formalities that must be followed for an advance decision to be made. The advance decision can be oral or written and there is no procedure that must be followed to establish that the person was mentally capable at the time when the advance decision is made. The advanced decision need not be witnessed and can be made without the benefit of professional advice. There is no provision requiring the advance decision to be reviewed over time, although this is clearly desirable. A written advance directive can be withdrawn or altered orally.

It may be very difficult for a treating doctor to be confident that a patient who is said to have made an oral advance decision during the course of a conversation with a relative satisfied the requirements of s.3, *i.e.* the person had the required mental capacity at the when the he or she was reported to have expressed his or her wishes (the person must be assumed to have had capacity unless it is established otherwise (s.1(2)). It might also be difficult to establish whether the person was subject to the undue influence of the relative at the relevant time (see the note on s.1(3)), or had subsequently revoked the advance decision. Indeed, it may be difficult to establish whether the reported conversation took place at all. In cases where there are doubts as to the applicability and/or validity of an advance decision, consideration should be given to invoking the declaratory jurisdiction of the Court of Protection (s.26(4)). In *HE v A Hospital NHS Trust*, above, Munby J. said at para.34:

"The absence of anything in writing goes only to the practicability of proof. For it may be difficult to establish the existence of a binding oral advance directive given, first, the need for clear and convincing proof founded on convincing and inherently reliable evidence and, secondly, the need to demonstrate that the patient's expressed views represented a firm and settled commitment and not merely an offhand remark or informally expressed reaction to other people's problems."

The Minister assured members of the Standing Committee which considered the Bill that "including oral decisions does not mean that any casual statement would count as an advance decision. There would be a world of difference between someone remarking casually to a friend that they would never like to be kept alive artificially and someone with Alzheimer's discussing with a doctor charged with their care how they might expect the condition to progress and making an oral decision to refuse certain interventions as their condition worsens. I remind the Committee that the Bill requires tough tests to be passed if an advance decision is to apply. The decision must be specific and made with capacity to be valid and applicable to the treatment in question. Where there is any doubt, a clinician can safely treat someone and receive protection from liability for a claim for damages, tort, criminal liability or assault [see s.26(2)]", *per* the Parliamentary Under-Secretary of State, St. Comm. A, para.225.

The Draft Code of Practice states at para.8.15 that it would be "helpful for the following information to be included in a written advance decision:

- Full details of the maker, including date of birth, home address, and any distinguishing features (so that an unconscious person, for example, might be identified).
- Name and address of General Practitioner and whether they have a copy.
- [Where relevant] information on where the advance decision is stored and list of people who are aware of its existence and should be contacted.
- A statement that the decision is intended to have effect if the maker lacks capacity to make treatment decisions.
- A clear statement of the decision, specifying the treatment to be refused and the circumstances in which the decision will apply or which will trigger a particular course of action.
- [Where relevant] a clear statement that the decision is intended to apply even if the treatment in question is necessary to sustain life.
- Date the document was written (or reviewed) and, if appropriate, the time interval between the creation and review.
- The signature of the witnesses who witnessed the maker's signature. Information on the independence of witnesses, including details of their relationship with the maker."

With regard to oral advance decisions made to a member of the patient's healthcare team, the Draft Code suggests at para.8.17 that the following information be included in the patient's medical notes:

- "A note that the decision is intended to have effect if the maker lacks capacity to make treatment decisions in the future.

- A clear note of the decision, specifying the treatment to be refused and the circumstances in which the decision will apply.
- Details of a witness to the decision. [Where relevant] a clear note that the decision is intended to apply even if the treatment in question is necessary to sustain life [this guidance is rendered redundant by the terms of s.25(5),(6)]".

If healthcare professionals are alerted to the possibility that a patient might have made an advance decision, reasonable efforts, such as contacting relatives of the patient and the patient's GP, should be made to establish whether this is the case. Treatment should not be delayed while attempts are made to establish whether an advance decision has been made if the delay would prejudice the patient's health.

Healthcare professionals who have a conscientious objection to respecting a patient's valid and applicable advance directive should ensure that the care of the patient is transferred to the care of another healthcare professional. The following extract from correspondence between the Parliamentary Under-Secretary of State for Health and the Opposition spokesperson on health was read into the record during the report stage of the Bill in the House of Lords at H.L. Vol.670, col.1306:

"I promised to check GMC and BMA guidance on provisions for when a doctor does not want to carry out treatment. Doctors are entitled to have their personal beliefs respected and will not be pressured to act contrary to those beliefs. As I stated during the Committee, where a doctor has a conscientious objection they may withdraw from the care of the patient. In doing so however they must ensure, without delay, that arrangements have been made for another suitably qualified colleague to take over their role, so that the patient's care does not suffer. The individual doctor does not necessarily have to arrange personally for a transfer of care, provided there are alternative means of doing so. However, the doctor must not abandon the patient or otherwise cause their care to suffer."

Also of relevance in this context is the following guidance given by Butler-Sloss P. in *B (Consent to Treatment: Capacity), Re* [2002] EWHC 429 (Fam Div); [2002] 2 All E.R. 499 at para.100(viii) and (ix):

"If the doctors are for any reason unable to carry out the wishes of the patient, their duty is to find other doctors who will do so.

If all appropriate steps to seek independent assistance from medical experts outside the hospital have failed, the NHS hospital trust should not hesitate to make an application to the High Court or seek the advice of the Official Solicitor."

Guidance on conscientious objection is given in the Draft Code at paras 8.43 and 8.44. Freedom of thought, conscience and religion is provided for in Art.9 of the European Convention on Human Rights.

As an alternative to making an advance decision, the person could either leave decision making in the hands of healthcare professionals, make an advance statement (see below), or appoint someone to act as their donee under a lasting power of attorney (see s.9). A personal welfare LPA does not take effect until the donor loses capacity (s.11(7)(a)).

The provisions of the Bill relating to advance decisions caused considerable controversy. The Joint Committee set out the opposing views in paras 195-200 of its Report:

"A very considerable number of written submissions were received expressing grave concern about this aspect of the draft Bill. Many argued from a standpoint of moral conviction that it was wrong to introduce a statute that could enable decisions that could effectively shorten life. Others argued that it was wrong to require a doctor not to give treatment that the doctor believed was in the patient's best clinical interests.

A considerable body of written evidence claimed that the inclusion of advance decisions meant that the Bill was introducing 'euthanasia by the back door'. We took evidence on this matter and considered the issues at length. For several faith organisations and the Guild of Catholic Doctors the omission of treatment that might prolong life even if for a short period of time was considered unacceptable unless such treatment was likely itself to result in undue suffering. We noted that there was nothing in the Bill that allowed for an act that had the clear intent to end a person's life. This was confirmed in oral evidence by the Parliamentary Under-Secretary of the Department for Constitutional Affairs, Lord Filkin.

Allied to these concerns numerous witnesses objected to the fact that the draft Bill allows life sustaining treatment (*e.g.* artificial ventilation) to be refused. They drew attention to the Court ruling in the case of Bland that the provision of hydration and nutrition by artificial means amounted to 'treatment'. They argued that withdrawal of nutrition and hydration would result in undue suffering and an unpleasant and undignified death. The BMA in their evidence suggested that, while the use of artificial means of nutrition and hydration amounted to treatment and could therefore be refused, the Bill should stipulate that basic care could not be refused.

Witnesses from the medical profession also put to us that: (a) people when capable could not foresee how they might wish to act if they were to become incapable and therefore could not commit themselves to a course of action from which they could not withdraw having become incapable; (b) unforeseen circumstances, such as the development of a new treatment the use of which would be in their best interests, could arise after the advance decision had been made; and (c) the course of action specified in the advance decision might prolong suffering rather than relieving it. We heard evidence from Professor the Baroness Finlay of the difficulties she and her medical and nursing colleagues faced working in palliative care services. She told us that her personal choice would be that advance decisions should be advisory 'but case law seems to have taken us beyond that point already'.

Those who believed that advance decisions should be included argued that this was a logical and appropriate continuation of respect for a patient's individual autonomy in matters of medical treatment. The law already recognises that a capable person can refuse treatment even if that refusal might end their life. But for a doctor to proceed with treatment under such circumstances would be unlawful. Thus it was argued that the draft Bill only proposed to regularise the existing status quo and that it was a logical extension of the established principle of autonomy. For these reasons the making Decisions Alliance, for example, strongly supported the inclusion of advance decisions to refuse treatment in the Bill. Several witnesses regretted that the draft Bill did not require advance decisions to be made in writing, witnessed or made with the benefit of professional advice. Other feared that people might make advance decisions while in a state of despair or depression that they would not have made under more normal circumstances. The risk of advance decisions being made under coercion was also raised."

Advance statements

Unlike an advance decision, an advance statement is a non-legally binding document which may identify a person's views and preferences on a large range of medical and other issues. Under s.4(6)(a), such a statement would need to be taken into account when decisions are made subsequent to the patient's mental incapacity even though it would not qualify as an advance decision. The Making Decisions Alliance briefing document on the second reading debate on the Bill states at p.19 that "advance statements would enable an individual to express their views and preferences on a large range of issues, including:

- domestic arrangements
- treatment preferences
- financial arrangements
- childcare arrangements
- clarification of who to disclose information to, and the limits of what can be discussed dietary requirements."

The literature is replete with examples of a failure to appreciate the distinction between directives and statements: see the studies cited by T. Exworthy in "Psychiatric advance decisions - an opportunity missed", Journal of Mental Health Law, September 2004, pp.129-141, at 132.

Subsection (1)

Aged 18. The 16 years of age cut off specified in s.2(4) is not used here as the refusal of a 16 or 17 year old to receive medical treatment may be overridden by a person with parental responsibility for the child, or by the court.

Capacity. The doctor should assume that the patient was capable in the absence of evidence to the contrary (s.1(2)).

Treatment. Is widely defined in s.64(1). It can include the provision of nutrition and hydration to the patient by artificial means (*Airedale NHS Trust v Bland* [1993] 1 All E.R.821, HL). The Joint Committee on Human Rights expressed its concern that the "classification of artificial nutrition and hydration as 'treatment' may not be well known to lay people" (23rd Report, para.2.46).

This Act distinguishes between "treatment" and "care": see, for example, s.5(1). The provision of "basic care" such as feeding and hydration which is not medically assisted, and care to maintain bodily cleanliness cannot be categorised as treatment and can therefore not be subject to an advance decision.

As an advance decision must relate to a specific treatment(s), a statement or a note which merely indicates a desire not to be treated would not qualify.

At that time he lacks capacity. Section 2(2) states that "it does not matter" if the patient's incapacity is temporary or permanent. This provision will cause difficulty in cases where P has made an advance decision refusing treatment, P becomes incapacitated and P's capacity could be restored if P was treated. It is likely that s.25(4)(c) would apply in such a situation.

Situations can arise when it will only become apparent that a seemingly incapable person is, in fact, perfectly capable of making the decision in question if considerable time and trouble is taken in an attempt to communicate with that person. In a powerful and moving speech on the second reading of the Bill (*Hansard*, HC Vol.425, cols.64-67), Mrs Claire Curtis-Thomas MP recounted how her mother, who had been hospitalised after having suffered a massive stoke which had left her paralysed, was considered to be mentally incapable and was not being fed. Mrs Curtis-Thomas's mother had made an advance directive subsequent to her recovery from a previous stoke. Mrs Curtis-Thomas's attempts to communicate with her mother, which lasted a number of weeks, eventually succeeded and her mother was able to blink out "I want to live". The advance directive was therefore revoked. Mrs Curtis-Thomas said: "If my mother had not had me, all I believe would have happened is that she would have starved to death. I do not think that anybody would have taken the time or known her well enough to realise that she was actually present and capable of making decisions." The principle contained in s.1(3) is applicable to the situation described by Mrs Curtis-Thomas.

Subsection (2)

The use of lay terms to specify a particular treatment should be avoided as they could result in the decision being ambiguous. It might be advisable for reference to be made to the objectives of the treatments, rather than to the treatments themselves.

Subsection (3)

There is no procedure for withdrawing or altering an advance decision. A simple statement such as, "I no longer wish my advance decision to stand", would be sufficient to withdraw a decision. An alteration has to be in writing, and the formalities set out in s.25(6) complied with, if the decision relates to a life-sustaining treatment (subs.(5)).

Subsection (4)

It is therefore possible for a capable patient to withdraw an advance decision immediately before an anaesthetic is administered.

25. Validity and applicability of advance decisions

(1) An advance decision does not affect the liability which a person may incur for carrying out or continuing a treatment in relation to P unless the decision is at the material time—
  (a) valid, and
  (b) applicable to the treatment.
(2) An advance decision is not valid if P—
  (a) has withdrawn the decision at a time when he had capacity to do so,
  (b) has, under a lasting power of attorney created after the advance decision was made, conferred authority on the donee (or, if more than one, any of them) to give or refuse consent to the treatment to which the advance decision relates, or
  (c) has done anything else clearly inconsistent with the advance decision remaining his fixed decision.
(3) An advance decision is not applicable to the treatment in question if at the material time P has capacity to give or refuse consent to it.
(4) An advance decision is not applicable to the treatment in question if—
  (a) that treatment is not the treatment specified in the advance decision,
  (b) any circumstances specified in the advance decision are absent, or
  (c) there are reasonable grounds for believing that circumstances exist which P did not anticipate at the time of the advance decision and which would have affected his decision had he anticipated them.

(5) An advance decision is not applicable to life-sustaining treatment unless—
    (a) the decision is verified by a statement by P to the effect that it is to apply to that treatment even if life is at risk, and
    (b) the decision and statement comply with subsection (6).
(6) A decision or statement complies with this subsection only if—
    (a) it is in writing,
    (b) it is signed by P or by another person in P's presence and by P's direction,
    (c) the signature is made or acknowledged by P in the presence of a witness, and
    (d) the witness signs it, or acknowledges his signature, in P's presence.
(7) The existence of any lasting power of attorney other than one of a description mentioned in subsection (2)(b) does not prevent the advance decision from being regarded as valid and applicable.

DEFINITIONS
"advance decision": s.64(1)
"treatment": s.64(1)
"lasting power of attorney": s.64(1)
"life-sustaining treatment": s.64(1)

GENERAL NOTE
This section states that a person shall not be legally liable for providing treatment to a patient who has made an advance decision unless the decision is both valid and applicable. It then proceeds to define both "valid" and "applicable". In *HE v A Hospital NHS Trust* [2003] EWHC 1017 (Fam Div); [2003] 2 F.L.R. 408, Munby J. said at para.24:

"Where life is at stake the evidence must be scrutinised with special care. Clear and convincing proof is required. The continuing validity and applicability of the advance directive must be clearly established by convincing and inherently reliable evidence."

Establishing whether an advance decision is both valid and applicable could lead to a significant increase in the workload of medical practitioners. As the Law Commission pointed out, the existence of a formal document is no guarantee of either validity of applicability, nor is the absence of such a document any guarantee that a valid and applicable advance decision has not been made (Law Com No.231, para.5.29).

An advance decision is not valid if P has withdrawn the decision while he or she had the mental capacity to do so, has made a subsequent lasting power of attorney (which has the effect of overriding the decision by enabling the donee to refuse consent to the treatment specified in the decision), or has acted in a manner which is clearly inconsistent with the terms of the decision (subs.(2)). In addition to these provisions, an advance decision will not be valid if it was made either by a child or by an adult who lacked capacity (s.24(1)). Although an adult should be assumed to have been mentally capable at the time when the decision was made (s1(2)), the medical practitioner should investigate any factors that suggest that this assumption could be rebutted.

An advance decision will not be applicable if P is capable of making the treatment decision at the time the treatment is proposed (subs.(3)). It will also not be applicable to treatments not specified in the decision, if the circumstances specified in the decision are absent, or if there are reasonable grounds for believing that that the current circumstances were not anticipated by P and, if they had been anticipated they would have affected P's decision (subs.(4)). Finally, an advance decision is not applicable to life-sustaining treatment unless P has specified in writing that it should be, and the decision is signed and witnessed (subss.(5) and (6)). A valid and applicable advance decision to refuse treatment will be as legally effective as a contemporaneous refusal of consent. It cannot be overridden by the Court of Protection, a deputy appointed by the court, the donee of a LPA made before the advance decision was made, or a person acting under s.5 (s.5(4)). Although the court may make declarations as to the existence, validity and applicability of an advance decision (s.15(1)(c)), it has no power to override a valid and applicable advance decision. Life sustaining treatment or action to prevent a serious deterioration of the patient's condition may be provided while a decision is being sought from the court (s.26(5)).

Subsection (1)

The healthcare professional must be aware of the existence of the advance decision if he or she is to incur legal liability for providing the treatment (s.26(2)). If the healthcare professional has knowledge of the advance directive, the treatment can proceed if the professional considers that it is either invalid and/or not applicable to the treatment.

Subsection (2) para. (a)

A written advance decision can be withdrawn orally. In the absence of evidence to the contrary, the doctor should assume that the patient was capable of withdrawing the decision (s.1(2)).

Patients can change their minds about having treatment at a very late stage. The difficulties of relying on an advance decision that has not been revoked can be seen from the following clinical example given by Baroness Finlay to the Joint Committee concerning a patient who had taken a massive overdose of paracetamol:

"He did not want to come to hospital but was persuaded to. He flatly refused any intervention or any treatment. Two psychiatrists spent a lot of time negotiating with him for several days and explained absolutely everything that might happen to him in graphic detail and he was adamant he wanted no treatment. They warned him of every scenario, including coughing up blood as he started to haemorrhage to death. When he started vomiting blood, he changed his mind and requested treatment. He ended up being transferred to King's [Hospital] for a liver transplant" (Oral and Written Evidence, Ev 131).

If this patient had lost capacity at the point where he started to vomit blood, the doctors would have been bound by his advance decision and the patient would have died. However, there must be a doubt as to whether a patient in this situation would have had the required capacity to make a valid advance decision. A high level of capacity would be required to make such a decision (*T (Adult: Refusal of Treatment), Re* [1992] 4 All E.R. 649, CA).

Subsection (2) para. (b)

It would be sensible for the advance decision to be withdrawn if a LPA of this nature is created as there could be a danger of the doctor being unaware of the LPA.

Subsection (2) para. (c)

The inconsistent behaviour would indicate that P has had a change of mind. An example of such inconsistent behaviour is to be found in *HE v A Hospital NHS Trust*, noted under s.24 above, where the patient, a Jehovah's Witness, had made an advance directive refusing blood. Subsequent to this she had become betrothed to a Muslim upon condition that she would revert to being a Muslim, and had ceased attending Jehovah's Witness meetings. The judge held that the advance directive was founded entirely on the patient's faith and could not survive the abandonment of that faith.

Subsection (4) para. (a)

As an advance decision is a refusal of a specific treatment, a suicide note written by a capable person which does not specify a treatment that should not be given in the event of a suicide attempt that leads to mental incapacity is not an advance decision. Neither is a general statement such as: "If I become mentally incapacitated I do not wish my life to be sustained."

Subsection (4) para. (b)

The advance decision should be specific about the circumstances where it is to apply as a generally written decision could give rise to a situation where the decision applies in unintended circumstances.

Subsection (4) para. (c)

It is anticipated that this paragraph will be frequently invoked as it is unlikely that patients will have been able to precisely predict the circumstances that they will be in subsequent to the onset of their mental incapacity. In order to determine whether the unanticipated circumstances "would", rather than "may" have affected P's decision, the health care professional will need to step into P's shoes by effectively making a substituted judgment on behalf of P. An obvious and relevant change of circumstances could be the development of new treatments that radically change the prognosis for a particular condition.

Patients' views about the medical treatment that they would wish to receive are not fixed; they adapt to circumstances. In particular, healthy patients tend not make the same choices as sick ones as they may not fully comprehend what the future might hold for them should they become mentally incapacitated. It has been argued that patients need to experience a situation to know how they would feel about it and hence how they wish to be treated (Dr David Kingsley, Oral and written evidence, Ev 322). The clinical experience is that many patients accept and benefit from treatment which they might not have anticipated when they were well. In *MB (Caesarean Section), Re* [1997] 2 F.L.R. 426, CA at 436 in a case concerning the mental capacity of a patient who was refusing to be anaesthetised in order to have a caesarean section, Butler-Sloss L.J. said that a "feature of some of the cases to which we have referred has been the favourable reaction of the patient who refused treatment to the subsequent medical intervention and successful outcome." A number of witnesses to the Joint Committee gave examples of patients who had made advance directives refusing life-prolonging treatment and had subsequently agreed to such treatment (see, for example, Dr Fiona Randall, Oral and written evidence, Ev 303). In her evidence to the Joint Committee, Baroness Finlay said:

"It is a feature of people who are suddenly facing the reality that they are dying that they could not preconceive how they would feel at the time. That is also a situation that one sees in people who are very seriously ill" (Oral and written Evidence, Ev 127).

These issues should be considered by those who make advance decisions and by those who advise them.

Subsection (5)

This provision and subs.(6) were moved by the Government at the committee stage in the House of Lords to meet concerns that had been raised by Parliamentarians, outside bodies, and the Joint Committee on Human Rights. They are aimed at tipping "the balance of advance decisions even further in favour of preserving life", *per* the Parliamentary Under-Secretary of State (*Hansard*, HL Vol.668, col.1486).

If there is a dispute about the validity and/or applicability of an advance decision that relates to life sustaining treatment, P can be treated until the issue is determined by the court (s.26(5)).

Life-sustaining treatment. The reference to "life" includes the life of an unborn child: see the note on s.4(10). It might be difficult to identify whether a treatment is a "life-sustaining treatment" in those cases where, for example, drugs do not have single, targeted effects. Treatments may be life-sustaining in some circumstances, and in others not. This concern has been addressed by the requirement that P must verify that the decision is to apply to the specified treatment "even if life is at risk".

"[T]here can be no doubt that ANH constitutes life-sustaining treatment. Thus, if a person has not specified that the refusal is still to apply where ANH is necessary to sustain life then ANH (if in the person's best interests) will have to be given" (Letter from the Parliamentary-Under Secretary of State to the Chair of the Joint Committee on Human Rights, December 16, 2004, Annex, para.28).

Subsection (6)

In writing. "I want to make it clear what 'in writing' can mean. It means that an advance decision can be written by a family member or recorded in medical notes by a doctor or healthcare professional, and it can include electronic records", *per* the Parliamentary Under-Secretary of State (*Hansard*, HL Vol.668, col.1487).

Is signed. The decision can be signed in P's presence and by his or her direction. This is to ensure that there is "no discrimination against people who, for whatever reason, are unable to write but have the capacity to make decisions", *ibid.*

26. Effect of advance decisions

    (1) If P has made an advance decision which is—

        (a) valid, and

        (b) applicable to a treatment,

the decision has effect as if he had made it, and had had capacity to make it, at the time when the question arises whether the treatment should be carried out or continued.

    (2) A person does not incur liability for carrying out or continuing the treatment unless, at the time, he is satisfied that an advance decision exists which is valid and applicable to the treatment.

(3) A person does not incur liability for the consequences of withholding or with-drawing a treatment from P if, at the time, he reasonably believes that an advance decision exists which is valid and applicable to the treatment.

(4) The court may make a declaration as to whether an advance decision—

(a) exists;

(b) is valid;

(c) is applicable to a treatment.

(5) Nothing in an apparent advance decision stops a person—

(a) providing life-sustaining treatment, or

(b) doing any act he reasonably believes to be necessary to prevent a serious deterioration in P's condition,

while a decision as respects any relevant issue is sought from the court.

DEFINITIONS

"advance decision": s.64(1)

"treatment": s.64(1)

"the court": s.64(1)

"life-sustaining treatment": s.64(1)

GENERAL NOTE

If an advance decision is both valid and applicable as defined in s.25, it has the same effect as a contem-poraneous refusal of treatment by a person with capacity (subs.(1)). Subject to subs.(5), this means that the treatment specified in the decision cannot lawfully be given. If the treatment is given, the patient would be able to claim damages for the tort of battery and the person who provided the treatment could face criminal liability for assault. However, a treatment provider will be protected from legal liability un-less satisfied that there is a valid and applicable advance decision (subs.(2)); and a treatment provider may safely withhold or withdraw treatment as long as he or she has reasonable grounds for believing that there is a valid and applicable advance decision (subs.(3)). The responsibility for determining whether an advance directive is both valid and applicable is that of the healthcare professional who would be re-sponsible for providing the treatment specified in the decision.

A clinician who follows a valid and applicable advance decision is not acting "for or on behalf of a per-son who lacks capacity" for the purposes of s.1(5); he or she is acting on the instructions of a capacitated individual. Such a decision must therefore be complied with even if it conflicts with an objective evalua-tion of the patient's best interests. This is the case even though complying with the decision would lead to the patient's death: the principle of the sanctity of human life must yield to the principle of patient self-determination as long as the terms of s.25(5) and (6) are satisfied.

Any dispute about the existence, validity or applicability of an advance decision can be determined by the court (subs.(4)). However, action may be taken to prevent the death of the person concerned, or a serious deterioration to his or her condition, whilst a ruling is sought (subs.(5)).

The draft Code of Practice states at para.8.42:

"There are some situations which may be sufficient to raise concerns about the existence, validity or applicability of an advance decision to refuse treatment, which might alert health professional to the need to make more careful enquiries. In cases where serious doubt remains, it will be possible to seek a declara-tion from the court. Grounds for concern might include:

- A disagreement between relatives and health professionals about whether the person's oral comments really amounted to a qualifying advance decision.
- Evidence about the person's state of mind at the time of making the advance decision that raised ques-tions about his/her capacity to have made the advance decision.
- Evidence of significant changes in the person's behaviour prior to lacking capacity that might indicate a change of mind since the advance decision was made."

Subsection (2)

Satisfied. If the clinician has a real doubt about the existence of a valid and applicable advance deci-sion, the treatment can be given.

Subsection (3)

   Reasonable believes. This is an objective standard. The belief must be supported by evidence.

Excluded decisions

27.   Family relationships etc

  (1) Nothing in this Act permits a decision on any of the following matters to be made on behalf of a person—

    (a) consenting to marriage or a civil partnership,

    (b) consenting to have sexual relations,

    (c) consenting to a decree of divorce being granted on the basis of two years' separation,

    (d) consenting to a dissolution order being made in relation to a civil partnership on the basis of two years' separation,

    (e) consenting to a child's being placed for adoption by an adoption agency,

    (f) consenting to the making of an adoption order,

    (g) discharging parental responsibilities in matters not relating to a child's property,

    (h) giving a consent under the Human Fertilisation and Embryology Act 1990 (c. 37).

  (2) "Adoption order" means—

    (a) an adoption order within the meaning of the Adoption and Children Act 2002 (c. 38) (including a future adoption order), and

    (b) an order under section 84 of that Act (parental responsibility prior to adoption abroad).

GENERAL NOTE

  This section lists decisions that can never be made by the Court of Protection or a donee on behalf of a person who lacks capacity.

28.   Mental Health Act matters

  (1) Nothing in this Act authorises anyone—

    (a) to give a patient medical treatment for mental disorder, or

    (b) to consent to a patient's being given medical treatment for mental disorder,

if, at the time when it is proposed to treat the patient, his treatment is regulated by Part 4 of the Mental Health Act.

  (2) "Medical treatment", "mental disorder" and "patient" have the same meaning as in that Act.

DEFINITIONS

  "Mental Health Act": s.64(1)

GENERAL NOTE

  If a mentally disordered patient who is also mentally incapacitated has been detained under the long term provisions of the Mental Health Act 1983, the patient is subject to the regulatory regime for the treatment of his or her mental disorder which is set out in Pt IV of that Act. This section ensures that the provisions of this Act do not apply to any treatment given to a patient which is provided under the authority of Pt IV of the 1983 Act. In other words, the consent to treatment provisions contained in Pt IV will "trump" the provisions of this Act. Treatment decisions falling outside the scope of Pt IV, such as decisions about whether the patient should receive treatment for a physical disorder and treatments given to patients detained under the emergency provisions of the 1983 Act, are governed by this Act.

The 1983 Act should be invoked in respect of a mentally incapacitated patient who needs to be hospitalised for treatment for his or her mental disorder in the following circumstances if the criteria for admission under that Act can be satisfied:

1   Where the patient is subjected to a deprivation of his or her liberty (*HL v United Kingdom (45508/ 99)* (2005) 40 E.H.R.R. 32, ECHR). The provisions in ss.5 and 6 of this Act cannot be used to deprive a patient of his or her liberty (see s.6(5)). The Department of Health has issued "*Advice on the decision of the European Court of Human Rights in the case of HL v UK (the "Bournewood"case)*" (December 10, 2004).

2   Where it is considered that the provisions of a valid and applicable advance decision refusing a particular treatment for the patient's mental disorder should be overridden.

In *HL v UK*, the patient, who was mentally incapacitated, alleged that he had been detained at the hospital as an informal patient in violation of Art.5(1) of the European Convention on Human Rights, and that the procedures available to him for a review of the legality of his detention did not satisfy the requirements of Art.5(4) which provides a person who has been deprived of his or her liberty with a right to a speedy independent legal review of the detention. The decision of the ECHR focussed on the finding of the House of Lords ([1998] 3 All E.R. 289) that the detention of a compliant mentally incapacitated patient could be justified under the doctrine of necessity. The ECHR held that:

1   In order to determine whether a person has been deprived of his or her liberty for the purposes of Art.5(1), the starting point must be the specific situation of the individual concerned and account must be taken of a whole range of factors arising in a particular case such as the type, duration, effects and manner of implementation of the measure in question. The distinction between a deprivation of, and a restriction upon, liberty is merely one of degree or intensity and not one of nature or substance (para.89).

2   The correspondence between HL's carers and his psychiatrist reflected both the carer's wish to have HL immediately released to their care and, equally, the clear intention of the health care professionals to exercise strict control over his assessment, treatment, contacts and, notably, movement and residence: HL would only be released from the hospital to the care of his carers as and when the professionals considered it appropriate. It followed that HL was being deprived of his liberty because he "was under continuous supervision and control and was not free to leave" (para.91). The fact that HL might have been on a ward which was not "locked" or "lockable" was not determinative (para.92).

3   The ECHR found "striking the lack of any fixed procedural rules by which the admission and detention of compliant incapacitated patients is conducted" when contrasted with "the extensive network of safeguards applicable to psychiatric committals covered by the 1983 Act" (para.120). This absence of procedural safeguards in the doctrine of necessity failed to protect HL against arbitrary deprivations of his liberty. His detention therefore violated Art.5(1).

4   There had also been a violation of Art.5(4) of the Convention as HL did not have the opportunity to have the lawfulness of his detention reviewed by a court as neither judicial review nor other judicial remedies cited by the Government satisfied the requirements of Art.5(4) (para.141).

The judgment of the ECHR is binding on those who provide care and treatment for mentally incapacitated persons in institutional settings as s.6 of the Human Rights Act 1998 (c.42) requires public authorities to act in a way which is compatible with a Convention right, unless they are prevented from doing so by primary legislation. A Mental Health Act assessment should therefore be made in respect of a mentally incapacitated patient who is being deprived of his or her liberty as the absence of a "section" will result in a violation of that person's rights under Art.5. As the decision of the ECHR also applies to mentally incapacitated persons who are being deprived of their liberty in care homes, local authorities should consider making a guardianship application in respect of such persons. Although guardianship does not provide authority to detain the person, it does provide a degree of procedural protection: see the General Note to s.6. A significant number of "*Bournewood*" patients will not fall into the category of a person who has been deprived of his or her liberty because the facts relating to their care and treatment will not be of a "degree" or "intensity" sufficiently serious to justify such a conclusion. Such a finding was made by the ECHR in *HM v Switzerland* (2004) 38 E.H.R.R. 17, where it was held that an elderly mentally disordered patient who was required to reside in a "foster home" was not being deprived of her liberty because the home was an open institution which allowed freedom of movement and encouraged contact with the outside world.

In Secretary of State for the *R. (on the application of Secretary of State for the Home Department) v Mental Health Review Tribunal (Conditions of Discharge)* [2002] EWCA Civ 1868, Keene L.J. identified the following principles which are applicable to the interpretation of Art.5(1):

1   A basic distinction is to be drawn between mere restrictions on liberty of movement and the deprivation of liberty.
2   The distinction is one merely of degree or intensity of restrictions, not of nature and substance.
3   The court must start with the concrete or actual situation of the individual concerned and take account of a range of criteria, such as type, duration, effects and manner of implementation of the measure in question.
4   Account must be taken of the cumulative effect of the various restrictions.
5   The purpose of any measures of restriction is a relevant consideration and if the measures are taken principally in the interests of the individual who is being restricted, they may well be regarded as not amounting to a deprivation of liberty.

The Royal College of Psychiatrists and Professor G. Richardson gave evidence to the Joint Committee expressing their concern that this provision, as it appeared in the draft Bill, could be interpreted to the effect that this Act "would not apply in any case in which treatment regulated under Pt IV may be required, i.e. when the Mental Health Act could potentially be applied". The Committee noted that the "effect of this would be to require the compulsory detention under the Mental Health Act of any person lacking capacity to consent to treatment for mental disorder, regardless of the circumstances" (para.218). As it is difficult to see how this provision could give rise to such an interpretation, the concern can be disregarded. This is also the view of the Government: see "*The Government Response to the Scrutiny Committee's Report on the draft Mental Incapacity Bill*" (Cm.6121).

Subsection (2)
Under s.145(1) of the 1983 Act, "medical treatment" is defined as including "nursing, and also includes care, habilitation and rehabilitation under medical supervision", and "patient" is defined as "a person suffering or appearing to be suffering from mental disorder". "Mental disorder" is defined in s.1 of that Act as meaning "mental illness, arrested or incomplete development of mind, psychopathic disorder and any other disorder or disability of mind."

29. Voting rights

(1) Nothing in this Act permits a decision on voting at an election for any public office, or at a referendum, to be made on behalf of a person.
(2) "Referendum" has the same meaning as in section 101 of the Political Parties, Elections and Referendums Act 2000 (c. 41).

GENERAL NOTE
This section excludes decisions on voting at an election for public office, or at a referendum, from the remit of this Act.

Research

30. Research

(1) Intrusive research carried out on, or in relation to, a person who lacks capacity to consent to it is unlawful unless it is carried out—
   (a) as part of a research project which is for the time being approved by the appropriate body for the purposes of this Act in accordance with section 31, and
   (b) in accordance with sections 32 and 33.

(2) Research is intrusive if it is of a kind that would be unlawful if it was carried out—

(a) on or in relation to a person who had capacity to consent to it, but

(b) without his consent.

(3) A clinical trial which is subject to the provisions of clinical trials regulations is not to be treated as research for the purposes of this section.

(4) "Appropriate body", in relation to a research project, means the person, committee or other body specified in regulations made by the appropriate authority as the appropriate body in relation to a project of the kind in question.

(5) "Clinical trials regulations" means—

(a) the Medicines for Human Use (Clinical Trials) Regulations 2004 (S.I. 2004/1031) and any other regulations replacing those regulations or amending them, and

(b) any other regulations relating to clinical trials and designated by the Secretary of State as clinical trials regulations for the purposes of this section.

(6) In this section, section 32 and section 34, "appropriate authority" means—

(a) in relation to the carrying out of research in England, the Secretary of State, and

(b) in relation to the carrying out of research in Wales, the National Assembly for Wales.

GENERAL NOTE

The Draft Mental Incapacity Bill made no provision to enable incapacitated adults to take part in medical research. While recognising that "this is an ethically difficult area", the Joint Committee concluded that a clause should be included in the Bill "to enable strictly-controlled medical research to explore the causes and consequences of mental incapacity and to develop effective treatment for such conditions. This clause must include rigorous protocols to protect incapacitated adults from being exploited or harmed" (para.288). In its response to the Joint Committee's report (Cm.6121), the Government accepted that the Bill "should include provision for strictly-controlled research to fill the gap that exists in the current law and the uncertainty and inequality this creates." The Joint Committee also recommended at para.289 that the Bill "should set out the key principles governing research, such as those enshrined by the World Medical Association [in the Helsinki Declaration]. Those key principles should include the following:

● research involving people who may be incapacitated must be reviewed by a properly established and independent ethics committee and can only proceed if ethical permission is granted.
● where a person has the capacity to consent then his decision whether or not to partake in research must be respected.
● considerable care should be taken to ensure that under these circumstances consent to participate was freely given and not a consequence of coercion.
● the inclusion of people in research, who lacked the capacity to consent, must only occur when such research has the potential for direct benefit to those with that particular problem and could not have been done through the involvement of those with capacity.
● those undertaking research involving people lacking the capacity to consent must respect any indications that a person did not wish to participate (*i.e.* was dissenting). any discomfort or risk involved in the research must be, at the most, minimal."

The Government agreed that "key principle are important" and stated that it would "explore the extent to which these need be in statute, or whether they are already covered by existing Good Practice Guidance".

This section, together with ss.31 to 34, make provision for "intrusive" research to be lawfully carried out on, or in relation to a person who lacks the capacity to consent to it, where the research is part of a research project which has been approved by the "appropriate body", as defined in subs.(4), and is carried out in accordance with the conditions set out in ss.32 and 33 (subs.(1)). Intrusive research is research that would require consent if it involved a person with capacity (subs.(2)). In addition to the obligations placed on them by this Act, researchers must also comply with their wider legal obligations such as their duties under the data protection and health and safety legislation.

If a person with capacity has consented to his involvement in research, the fact that he subsequently loses capacity does not mean that he has to be withdrawn from the research, in so far as it relates to the matter that he has consented to, because the fact that he given his consent means that the research is not intrusive (see subs.(2)). Baroness Andrews said "The Bill does not apply to research during temporary incapacity, such as general anaesthesia during surgery, providing that consent was obtained in advance. Consent endures the temporary loss of capacity" (*Hansard*, HL Vol.670, col.1521). However, if the research is a continuing project rather than a one-off event, any further research would be research undertaken without consent and would therefore be intrusive research that would trigger the procedures set out in ss.31-33. For example, if the person consents to a sample of blood being taken as part of a research project, the sample can be taken even if the person loses capacity before that point. The taking of any further samples would constitute intrusive research because of the absence of the person's consent. Transitional provisions are contained in s.34.

Clinical trials that are regulated by the clinical trials regulations are excluded (subss.(3) and (5)) because the regulations already make provision for trials involving participants who lack capacity.

The ethical and legal issues arising from medical research on mentally incompetent adults are considered by M.J.Gunn, J.G Wong, I.C.H. Clare and A.J. Holland in "Medical Research and Incompetent Adults", (2000), J. of Mental Health Law, 60-72.

Subsection (4)
The appropriate body is likely to be the Research Ethics Committee, although "in some social care research projects it can be a different type of body", *per* the Minister of State, St. Comm. A, col.268.

Subsection (6)
The 2004 Regulations, which came into force on May 1st, 2004, implement European Clinical Trials Directive 2001/20/EC on "the approximation of the laws, regulations and administrative provisions of the Member States relating to the implementation of good clinical practice in the conduct of clinical trials on medicinal products for human use."

31. Requirements for approval

(1) The appropriate body may not approve a research project for the purposes of this Act unless satisfied that the following requirements will be met in relation to research carried out as part of the project on, or in relation to, a person who lacks capacity to consent to taking part in the project (P).

(2) The research must be connected with—
   (a) an impairing condition affecting P, or
   (b) its treatment.

(3) "Impairing condition" means a condition which is (or may be) attributable to, or which causes or contributes to (or may cause or contribute to), the impairment of, or disturbance in the functioning of, the mind or brain.

(4) There must be reasonable grounds for believing that research of comparable effectiveness cannot be carried out if the project has to be confined to, or relate only to, persons who have capacity to consent to taking part in it.

(5) The research must—
   (a) have the potential to benefit P without imposing on P a burden that is disproportionate to the potential benefit to P, or
   (b) be intended to provide knowledge of the causes or treatment of, or of the care of persons affected by, the same or a similar condition.

(6) If the research falls within paragraph (b) of subsection (5) but not within paragraph (a), there must be reasonable grounds for believing—
   (a) that the risk to P from taking part in the project is likely to be negligible, and

(b) that anything done to, or in relation to, P will not—

  (i) interfere with P's freedom of action or privacy in a significant way, or

  (ii) be unduly invasive or restrictive.

(7) There must be reasonable arrangements in place for ensuring that the requirements of sections 32 and 33 will be met.

DEFINITIONS

"appropriate body": s.30(4)

GENERAL NOTE

This section sets out the requirements that must be satisfied before the Secretary of State and the National Assembly for Wales can approve a research project involving people who lack capacity. It does not preclude either observational or epidemiological research being undertaken. Paragraph 12.5 of the Draft Code states:

"Research has been defined as an activity that attempts to derive new knowledge by addressing clearly defined questions (hypotheses) using systematic and rigorous methods. The knowledge gained may provide information that can be generalised to the particular illness, disorder, or circumstances under investigation. Such knowledge may inform further research, may lead directly to the use of new medical treatments or other interventions (*e.g.* surgical procedure, psychological treatments), or may have wider implications, such as informing health or social care policy and practice (*e.g.* investigating factors that influence or maximise a potentially incapacitated person's decision-making capacity)."

There is a clear tension between the nature of some research contemplated by this section and the best interests principle established in s.1(5). The Parliamentary Under-Secretary of State said that "the research procedures provide an alternative to a best interests determination" (*Hansard*, HL Vol.669, col.135). The Minister of State described the application of the best interests principle to research as being "difficult" (St. Comm. A, col.278), and that the principle is "interpreted slightly differently" when applied to research (*Hansard*, HC Vol.428, col.1604). At the third reading of the Bill, she said:

"[I]t is always difficult to prove that [research] can be in someone's best interests. We can only say that it is of potential benefit to that person, or might benefit him or her in the longer term, or might benefit him or her indirectly once more research has been done, or might benefit others with the same condition now or in the future" (*Hansard*, HC Vol.428, col.1603).

The Parliamentary Under-Secretary of State said:

"The purpose of [sections] 30 to 33 is to make provision for acts in connection with research that cannot necessarily be shown precisely to coincide with the person's best interests. It may be that the research procedure involves different or additional approaches to a person's care, which might not meet a narrow assessment of best interest" (*Hansard*, HL Vol.669, col.135).

Although the provisions of this Act relating to research are partly based on the Council of Europe Convention on Human Rights and Biomedicine (ETS No.164) (the Oviedo Convention), the UK Government has not ratified the Convention. The Convention was supplemented by an Additional Protocol concerning Biomedical Research, which was opened for signature by the signatories to the Convention on January 25, 2005.

The Joint Committee on Human Rights concluded that the "nature of the benefit from the research required in [subs.(5)] has the effect of lowering the threshold of when research will be permissible compared with the standards contained in the Convention" (23rd Report, para.2.60). The Government responded to this comment as follows:

"We have taken careful note of the Oviedo Convention, but are conscious that it does not appear to extend across the breadth of research activities that we wish to cover. For example, Arts.15-17 of the Oviedo Convention are concerned with research 'on a person', which is further clarified in the Explanatory memorandum as 'research on human beings' and in the Additional Protocol which refers to 'research activities in the health field involving interventions on human beings'. We wished to cover wider aspects of research that would not normally require consent from a person with incapacity, including research into medical records, or observation of P in a social care setting. We hope that this helps to explain why, in some cases, we have departed from the language used in the Oviedo Convention" ("Memorandum submitted to the Joint Committee on Human Rights in response to their letter of 18 November 2004 as published in their 23rd Report", paras 59 and 60).

Subsection (1)
    Appropriate body. See s.30(4).

Subsections (2) and (3)
    These provisions, which were the subject of amendments in both Houses, identify the scope of the provisions relating to research. Baroness Andrews explained:
    "The emphasis is now more clearly on the requirement that the research must be connected to an impairing condition that the person has. It concedes that the relationship between the impairing condition and the impairment of, or disturbance in, the functioning of the mind or brain is sometimes not perfectly understood. It makes it clearer that it may be valid to conduct properly designed research to see whether the condition and the impairment or the disturbance are linked.
    The amendment makes it clear that research, for example, to prevent kidney failure in a person in a coma following a car accident or heart attack would be permissible if the other safeguards are met. The impairing condition would be the trauma or shock following the sudden crash or heart attack. The research ethics committee would have to be satisfied that there was a good case for believing that the research into kidney failure was connected to the impairing condition, or its treatment" (*Hansard*, HL Vol.670, col.1500).
    Impairment of, or disturbance in the functioning of the mind or brain. See the note to s.2(1).

Subsection (4)
    This provision was subject to a Government amendment to bring it closer to the wording of Art.17.1 iii of the Oviedo Convention which states that "research of comparable effectiveness cannot be carried out on individuals capable of giving consent".

Subsection (5) para. (a)
    Potential to benefit P. If something is done which is intended to be of direct benefit to P, it would constitute treatment rather than research.
    Burden that is disproportionate. "By 'burden' we mean the risk or inconvenience of a trial. For example, researchers might submit a proposal to use an MRI scanner to understand the brain structures of people with dementia or schizophrenia. It might be of potential benefit to their treatment. But if the use of an MRI scanner required long confinement - we know that people with mental capacity or those suffering from cancer or claustrophobia can be very vulnerable to extreme worry in these situations - or perhaps regular and frequent scans, an ethics committee might decide that the research would simply not bring enough benefit to justify the extra scans or trauma that might be involved", *per* Baroness Andrews, (*Hansard* HL Vol.669, col.154).

Subsection (5) para. (b)
    The Explanatory Notes state at para.98 that this category or research "might include indirect research on medical notes, or on tissue already taken for other purposes. It may also include interviews or questionnaires with carers about health or social-care services received by the person or limited observation of the person. And it could include taking samples from the person, *e.g.* blood samples, specifiacally for the research project". It would also include research into how the incapacity, and the medical and other complications that are associated with it, might impact upon the care regime for the mentally incapacitated.
    Treatment. This provision allows for research into diagnostic procedures (s.64(1)).

32. Consulting carers etc

(1) This section applies if a person (R)—
    (a) is conducting an approved research project, and
    (b) wishes to carry out research, as part of the project, on or in relation to a person (P) who lacks capacity to consent to taking part in the project.
(2) R must take reasonable steps to identify a person who—
    (a) otherwise than in a professional capacity or for remuneration, is engaged in caring for P or is interested in P's welfare, and
    (b) is prepared to be consulted by R under this section.

(3) If R is unable to identify such a person he must, in accordance with guidance issued by the appropriate authority, nominate a person who—
   (a) is prepared to be consulted by R under this section, but
   (b) has no connection with the project.

(4) R must provide the person identified under subsection (2), or nominated under subsection (3), with information about the project and ask him—
   (a) for advice as to whether P should take part in the project, and
   (b) what, in his opinion, P's wishes and feelings about taking part in the project would be likely to be if P had capacity in relation to the matter.

(5) If, at any time, the person consulted advises R that in his opinion P's wishes and feelings would be likely to lead him to decline to take part in the project (or to wish to withdraw from it) if he had capacity in relation to the matter, R must ensure—
   (a) if P is not already taking part in the project, that he does not take part in it;
   (b) if P is taking part in the project, that he is withdrawn from it.

(6) But subsection (5)(b) does not require treatment that P has been receiving as part of the project to be discontinued if R has reasonable grounds for believing that there would be a significant risk to P's health if it were discontinued.

(7) The fact that a person is the donee of a lasting power of attorney given by P, or is P's deputy, does not prevent him from being the person consulted under this section.

(8) Subsection (9) applies if treatment is being, or is about to be, provided for P as a matter of urgency and R considers that, having regard to the nature of the research and of the particular circumstances of the case—
   (a) it is also necessary to take action for the purposes of the research as a matter of urgency, but
   (b) it is not reasonably practicable to consult under the previous provisions of this section.

(9) R may take the action if—
   (a) he has the agreement of a registered medical practitioner who is not involved in the organisation or conduct of the research project, or
   (b) where it is not reasonably practicable in the time available to obtain that agreement, he acts in accordance with a procedure approved by the appropriate body at the time when the research project was approved under section 31.

(10) But R may not continue to act in reliance on subsection (9) if he has reasonable grounds for believing that it is no longer necessary to take the action as a matter of urgency.

DEFINITIONS
   "appropriate authority": s.30(6)
   "lasting power of attorney": s.64(1)
   "deputy": s.64(1)
   "appropriate body": s.30(4)

GENERAL NOTE
   This section provides that before any decision is taken to involve P in approved research, the researcher (R) must take reasonable steps to identify either an unpaid carer or a person who is interested in P's welfare in a non-professional capacity who is prepared to be consulted about P's involvement in the research (subss.(1),(2)). This person could be a deputy or donee (subs.(7)). If there is no such person, R must nomi-

nate (in accordance with guidance issued by the appropriate authority) a person who is willing to be consulted, but has no connection with the project (subs.(3)).

Subsection (4) identifies the purpose of the consultation. If the consultee advises R that, in his or her opinion, P would have been likely to decline to take part if he or she had capacity, P cannot be involved in the research, or if it is already underway P must be withdrawn from it (subs.(5)). However, if P has been receiving treatment as part of the research it should not be withdrawn if to do so would place P's health at significant risk (subs.(6)).

Subsections (8) and (9) allow for cases where P is being, or is about to be, provided with urgent treatment, research into that treatment must also be undertaken as a matter of urgency, and it is not reasonable practicable for R to consult. R may proceed to involve P in the research if he has the agreement of a doctor who is not concerned in the organisation or conduct of the research project, or, if there is no time to do this, he follows an approved procedure. R cannot continue to use these provisions if there is no longer an urgent need to act (subs.(10)). The Explanatory Notes, at para.104, state that examples of this type of research "may involve action by a paramedic or doctor to make measurements in the first few minutes following a serious head injury or stroke."

Subsection (2)

A person. Such as a family member, advocate or friend.

Subsection (3)

Appropriate authority. See s.30(6).

No connection with the project. This phrase "would certainly include someone involved with, or connected to, either the study itself or a member of the research team. It would also cover wider connections, such as someone with a direct link to funding decisions for the study, for example, or who was involved with the research ethics committee" *per* Baroness Andrews (*Hansard*, HL Vol.670, col.1515).

Subsection (5)

If P is withdrawn part way through the project, this provision does not provide that information collected with respect to P up to that point must be disregarded for the purposes of the project.

Subsection (7)

Deputy. "[W]e will amend the Code of Practice to make it clear that if a deputy has no relationship to, or knowledge of, P before their appointment, they should not be consulted on the question of P's participation in research", *per* the Minister of State (*Hansard*, HC Vol.428, col.1605).

Subsection (9)

Registered medical practitioner. The doctor to be consulted may be involved in the treatment of P. Baroness Andrews said:

"We want provide that a doctor who can be consulted may well be a consultant surgeon or even a GP whose patient suffers a sudden cardiac arrest or goes into septic shock, for example.

If the emergency happens in the community - outside the hospital - it is perfectly possible that a person's GP can be involved and give approval for research to be initiated by, for example, a paramedic attending the person at home. It is important to think that research in such a case may simply be the taking of a blood sample. As I hope is clear, those doctors are usually best placed to advise the researcher, as they are familiar with the patient's medical history" (*Hansard*, HL Vol.670, col.1501).

Appropriate body. See s.30(4).

33. Additional safeguards

(1) This section applies in relation to a person who is taking part in an approved research project even though he lacks capacity to consent to taking part.

(2) Nothing may be done to, or in relation to, him in the course of the research—

(a) to which he appears to object (whether by showing signs of resistance or otherwise) except where what is being done is intended to protect him from harm or to reduce or prevent pain or discomfort, or

(b) which would be contrary to—

    (i) an advance decision of his which has effect, or

    (ii) any other form of statement made by him and not subsequently withdrawn,

of which R is aware.

(3) The interests of the person must be assumed to outweigh those of science and society.

(4) If he indicates (in any way) that he wishes to be withdrawn from the project he must be withdrawn without delay.

(5) P must be withdrawn from the project, without delay, if at any time the person conducting the research has reasonable grounds for believing that one or more of the requirements set out in section 31(2) to (7) is no longer met in relation to research being carried out on, or in relation to, P.

(6) But neither subsection (4) nor subsection (5) requires treatment that P has been receiving as part of the project to be discontinued if R has reasonable grounds for believing that there would be a significant risk to P's health if it were discontinued.

DEFINITIONS
   "advance decision": s.64(1)

GENERAL NOTE
   This section provides that P's involvement in research must cease without delay if it appears that he objects to what is being done (this requirement is subject to the exceptions contained in subs.(2)(a)), if what is being done is contrary to either an advance decision made by P or to some other statement made by P, or if P indicates that he wishes to be withdrawn from the research (subss.(2),(4)). These provisions are subject to the principle that the interests of P must be assumed to outweigh those of science and society (subs.(3)). P must also be withdrawn from the research if the person conducting the research believes that one or more of requirements for approval is no longer met (subs.(5)). Subsection (6) makes it clear that any withdrawal from research does not require beneficial treatment to be halted.
   Researchers have a duty to have regard to the guidance contained in the Code of Practice (s.42(4)(c)).

Subsection (3)
   This principle is taken from section A.5 of the World Medical Association's Declaration of Helsinki on Ethical Principles for Medical Research Involving Human Subjects.

34. Loss of capacity during research project

(1) This section applies where a person (P)—

(a) has consented to take part in a research project begun before the commencement of section 30, but

(b) before the conclusion of the project, loses capacity to consent to continue to take part in it.

(2) The appropriate authority may by regulations provide that, despite P's loss of capacity, research of a prescribed kind may be carried out on, or in relation to, P if—

(a) the project satisfies prescribed requirements,

(b) any information or material relating to P which is used in the research is of a prescribed description and was obtained before P's loss of capacity, and

(c) the person conducting the project takes in relation to P such steps as may be prescribed for the purpose of protecting him.

(3) The regulations may, in particular,—

(a) make provision about when, for the purposes of the regulations, a project is to be treated as having begun;

(b) include provision similar to any made by section 31, 32 or 33.

DEFINITIONS
"appropriate authority": s.30(6)
"prescribed": s.64(1)

GENERAL NOTE
The purpose of this section was explained by the Baroness Andrews:

"[This section establishes] a transitional regulation-making power to cover ongoing research and provides for the necessary flexibility in the provisions for approval of research by a research ethics committee, with consultation of carers and additional safeguards. Why do we need transitional regulations? Primarily because it is necessary to smooth the transition for researchers from the current common law position to the new statutory safeguards for research involving those who lose capacity. We need them to avoid stopping ongoing and essential research

We already have the flexibility to cater for the majority of those in the ordinary powers for making transitional provisions in [s.65], but we need to provide for more comprehensive regulation-making powers to cover projects that enrol people with capacity who go on to lose capacity during the research projects

Our aim is to ensure that a research project can continue in relation to samples or data obtained from people before they lost capacity, subject to certain specified safeguards" (*Hansard*, HL Vol.670, cols 1520-1522).

Subsection (2)
Appropriate authority. See s.30(6).
Regulations. Regulations made under this power are subject to the affirmative resolution procedure (s.65(4)).

Independent mental capacity advocate service

35. Appointment of independent mental capacity advocates

(1) The appropriate authority must make such arrangements as it considers reasonable to enable persons (independent mental capacity advocates) to be available to represent and support persons to whom acts or decisions proposed under sections 37, 38 and 39 relate.

(2) The appropriate authority may make regulations as to the appointment of independent mental capacity advocates.

(3) The regulations may, in particular, provide—

(a) that a person may act as an independent mental capacity advocate only in such circumstances, or only subject to such conditions, as may be prescribed;

(b) for the appointment of a person as an independent mental capacity advocate to be subject to approval in accordance with the regulations.

(4) In making arrangements under subsection (1), the appropriate authority must have regard to the principle that a person to whom a proposed act or

decision relates should, so far as practicable, be represented and supported by a person who is independent of any person who will be responsible for the act or decision.

(5) The arrangements may include provision for payments to be made to, or in relation to, persons carrying out functions in accordance with the arrangements.

(6) For the purpose of enabling him to carry out his functions, an independent mental capacity advocate—

  (a) may interview in private the person whom he has been instructed to represent, and

  (b) may, at all reasonable times, examine and take copies of—

    (i) any health record,

    (ii) any record of, or held by, a local authority and compiled in connection with a social services function, and

    (iii) any record held by a person registered under Part 2 of the Care Standards Act 2000 (c. 14),

  which the person holding the record considers may be relevant to the independent mental capacity advocate's investigation.

(7) In this section, section 36 and section 37, "the appropriate authority" means—

  (a) in relation to the provision of the services of independent mental capacity advocates in England, the Secretary of State, and

  (b) in relation to the provision of the services of independent mental capacity advocates in Wales, the National Assembly for Wales.

GENERAL NOTE

In *R. v Bournewood Community and Mental Health NHS Trust Ex p. L* [1998] 3 All E.R. 289, the House of Lords held that mentally disordered patients who are admitted to hospital without the formalities necessary for detention under the Mental Health Act 1983, fall into two categories: those who, having the capacity to consent to the admission, do consent ("voluntary patients") and those who, though lacking capacity to consent to the admission, do not object ("informal patients"). Their Lordships held that the treatment and care of patients of patients who fall into the latter category is justified under the common law doctrine of necessity. Concern about relying on this doctrine (now see ss.5 and 6), which does not provide any procedural safeguards for the patient, was expressed by their Lordships. Sections 35-41 represent a partial attempt to address these concerns by creating a scheme designed to provide the input of an independent mental capacity advocate ("IMCA") who will act as a representative and supporter of particularly vulnerable persons who lacks capacity where certain decisions need to be taken. Such people "may include older people with dementia who have lost contact with all friends and family, or people with severe learning disabilities or long term mental health problems who have been in residential institutions for long periods and lack outside contacts" (Explanatory Notes, para.109). The IMCA will become involved where there is no person, such as a family member or an unremunerated carer, to be consulted with about P's best interests. The application of the IMCA scheme is far wider than the situation that obtained in *Bournewood* as it is not confined to situations where the mentally incapacitated person is hospitalised. The Minister of State said:

"We estimate that about 20 per cent of people in England and Wales who lack capacity when major decisions are being taken about their living arrangements, care or treatment, have no friends or family to consult. The [independent mental capacity advocate] safeguard will provide the person with someone who is on their side so that there is never a closed relationship between the decision maker and the person lacking capacity

...The [independent mental capacity advocate] will clearly have the right to talk to the person lacking capacity and a right of access to relevant records. They will find out as much as they possibly can about the likely wishes of the person and explore a range of possible outcomes that may be open to that individual. We want to give the person those powers so that they can take a broad view of what will eventually be in the best interests of the individual, which they can then recommend to the decision maker" (St. Comm. A, cols 314 and 315).

This section places a duty on the Secretary of State for Health and the National Assembly for Wales to make arrangements for the provision of an IMCA service (subss.(1)-(4) and (7)) and provides the IMCA with the power to interview P in private and to examine relevant records (subs.(6)). The IMCA, who could be remunerated for his or her services (subs.(5)), will act in P's best interests (ss.l(5) and 4). However, as the role of the IMCA is to support and represent the person lacking capacity and not the decision-maker, he or she will not make the best interests judgment. The particular functions of IMCAs will be set in regulations (s.36). The time taken to abide by these requirements will need to be tailored to the urgency of the issue under consideration. If the decision maker decides not to accept the advice proffered, the IMCA will need to consider whether take the matter further by, for example, using the NHS or local authority complaints procedure or, if the matter is particularly serious, seek permission to refer the matter to the Court of Protection. The Government estimates that "about 64,000 decisions a year will require the support of [an IMCA]", *per* the Minister of State, St. Comm. A, col.320.

Subsection (1)
  Appropriate authority. See subs.(7).

36.   Functions of independent mental capacity advocates

(1) The appropriate authority may make regulations as to the functions of independent mental capacity advocates.

(2) The regulations may, in particular, make provision requiring an advocate to take such steps as may be prescribed for the purpose of—

  (a) providing support to the person whom he has been instructed to represent (P) so that P may participate as fully as possible in any relevant decision;

  (b) obtaining and evaluating relevant information;

  (c) ascertaining what P's wishes and feelings would be likely to be, and the beliefs and values that would be likely to influence P, if he had capacity;

  (d) ascertaining what alternative courses of action are available in relation to P;

  (e) obtaining a further medical opinion where treatment is proposed and the advocate thinks that one should be obtained.

(3) The regulations may also make provision as to circumstances in which the advocate may challenge, or provide assistance for the purpose of challenging, any relevant decision.

DEFINITIONS
  "appropriate authority": s.35(7)
  "independent mental capacity advocate": s.64(1)
  "prescribed": s.64(1)

GENERAL NOTE
  This section enables the Secretary of State and the National Assembly for Wales to make regulations as to the functions of independent mental capacity advocates.

37.   Provision of serious medical treatment by NHS body

(1) This section applies if an NHS body—

  (a) is proposing to provide, or secure the provision of, serious medical treatment for a person (P) who lacks capacity to consent to the treatment, and

  (b) is satisfied that there is no person, other than one engaged in providing care or treatment for P in a professional capacity or for remuneration, whom it would be appropriate to consult in determining what would be in P's best interests.

(2) But this section does not apply if P's treatment is regulated by Part 4 of the Mental Health Act.

(3) Before the treatment is provided, the NHS body must instruct an independent mental capacity advocate to represent P.

(4) If the treatment needs to be provided as a matter of urgency, it may be provided even though the NHS body has not been able to comply with subsection (3).

(5) The NHS body must, in providing or securing the provision of treatment for P, take into account any information given, or submissions made, by the independent mental capacity advocate.

(6) "Serious medical treatment" means treatment which involves providing, withholding or withdrawing treatment of a kind prescribed by regulations made by the appropriate authority.

(7) "NHS body" has such meaning as may be prescribed by regulations made for the purposes of this section by—

(a) the Secretary of State, in relation to bodies in England, or

(b) the National Assembly for Wales, in relation to bodies in Wales.

DEFINITIONS
  "treatment": s.64(1)
  "Mental Health Act": s.64(1)
  "independent mental capacity advocate": s.64(1)

GENERAL NOTE

This section applies where "serious medical treatment" (apart from treatment regulated under Pt 4 of the Mental Health Act 1983 (subs.(2)) is to be provided by the NHS for a person who lacks capacity and there is no-one apart from a professional or paid carer for the treatment-provider to consult in determining what would be in P's best interests (subs.(1)). In this situation the treatment-provider must instruct an IMCA to represent P and any information given, or submissions made, by the IMCA must be taken into account when decisions are made about treating P (subs.(3),(5)). Such consultation is not required if the need for the treatment is urgent (subs.(4)). The particular types of treatment that will trigger the involvement of an IMCA will be prescribed in regulations.

Proper records should be taken by the treatment-provider of how the IMCA's representations has been taken into account and, where relevant, the reasons for disagreeing with or ignoring those representations. Where a disagreement arises, every effort must be made to resolve the disagreement at the earliest possible stage, where necessary using the authority's dispute resolution or complaint's procedure.

Subsection (1)
  NHS body. See subs.(7).

Subsection (1) para. (a)
  Serious medical treatment. See subs.(6).
  Secure the provision of. The duty under this section will arise if the NHS is funding P's treatment in the private sector.

Subsection (1) para. (b)
  No person. See the list set out in s.4(7).

Subsection (3)
  This provision does not apply if a person listed in s.40 is available to be consulted.

38. Provision of accommodation by NHS body

(1) This section applies if an NHS body proposes to make arrangements—

    (a) for the provision of accommodation in a hospital or care home for a person (P) who lacks capacity to agree to the arrangements, or

    (b) for a change in P's accommodation to another hospital or care home,

and is satisfied that there is no person, other than one engaged in providing care or treatment for P in a professional capacity or for remuneration, whom it would be appropriate for it to consult in determining what would be in P's best interests.

(2) But this section does not apply if P is accommodated as a result of an obligation imposed on him under the Mental Health Act.

(3) Before making the arrangements, the NHS body must instruct an independent mental capacity advocate to represent P unless it is satisfied that—

    (a) the accommodation is likely to be provided for a continuous period which is less than the applicable period, or

    (b) the arrangements need to be made as a matter of urgency.

(4) If the NHS body—

    (a) did not instruct an independent mental capacity advocate to represent P before making the arrangements because it was satisfied that subsection (3)(a) or (b) applied, but

    (b) subsequently has reason to believe that the accommodation is likely to be provided for a continuous period—

        (i) beginning with the day on which accommodation was first provided in accordance with the arrangements, and

        (ii) ending on or after the expiry of the applicable period,

it must instruct an independent mental capacity advocate to represent P.

(5) The NHS body must, in deciding what arrangements to make for P, take into account any information given, or submissions made, by the independent mental capacity advocate.

(6) "Care home" has the meaning given in section 3 of the Care Standards Act 2000 (c. 14).

(7) "Hospital" means—

    (a) a health service hospital as defined by section 128 of the National Health Service Act 1977 (c. 49), or

    (b) an independent hospital as defined by section 2 of the Care Standards Act 2000.

(8) "NHS body" has such meaning as may be prescribed by regulations made for the purposes of this section by—

    (a) the Secretary of State, in relation to bodies in England, or

    (b) the National Assembly for Wales, in relation to bodies in Wales.

(9) "Applicable period" means—

    (a) in relation to accommodation in a hospital, 28 days, and

    (b) in relation to accommodation in a care home, 8 weeks.

DEFINITIONS

"Mental Health Act": s.64(1)

"independent mental capacity act advocate": s.64(1)

GENERAL NOTE

This section applies if a NHS body intends to arrange for P to be accommodated in a hospital (either NHS or private) or a care home for a period likely to exceed 28 days (for a hospital) or eight weeks (for a care home), or for P to be moved between such accommodation, and there is no-one apart from a professional or paid carer for the NHS body to consult in determining what would be in P's best interests (subss.(1) and (9)). In this situation the NHS body must instruct an IMCA to represent P and must take into account any information given, or submissions made, by the IMCA when a decision is made about what arrangements to make for P (subss.(3) and (5)). Such consultation need not take place if the P is likely to stay in the accommodation for less than the applicable period or if the need for the move is urgent, for example, where P requires an emergency hospital admission, or where a care home place will be lost if P is not moved immediately (subs.(3)). However, the consultation must take place after the arrangements have been made if the NHS body subsequently believes that P will be accommodated at the hospital or care home for the applicable period (subs.(4)). The section does not apply if P is accommodated in the hospital or the care home as a result of an obligation imposed on him or her under the Mental Health Act 1983 (subs.(2)), as that Act contains its own safeguards. It will apply to decisions about providing accommodation for P if P is about to be discharged from the requirements of the 1983 Act.

Proper records should be taken by the responsible authority of how the IMCA's representations have been taken into account and, where relevant, the reasons for disagreeing with or ignoring the representations. Where a disagreement arises, every effort must be made to resolve the disagreement at the earliest possible stage, where necessary using the authority's dispute resolution or complaint's procedure.

Subsection (1)
    NHS body. See subs.(8).
    Hospital. See subs.(7).
    Care home. See subs.(6).
    No person. See the list set out in s.4(7).

Subsection (3)
    This provision does not apply if a person listed in s.40 is available to be consulted.
    Applicable period. See subs.(9).

Subsection (4)
    Beginning with. Including the day on which the accommodation was first provided (*Zoan v Rouamba* [2000] 2 All E.R. 620, CA).

39.   Provision of accommodation by local authority

(1) This section applies if a local authority propose to make arrangements—
    (a) for the provision of residential accommodation for a person (P) who lacks capacity to agree to the arrangements, or
    (b) for a change in P's residential accommodation,
and are satisfied that there is no person, other than one engaged in providing care or treatment for P in a professional capacity or for remuneration, whom it would be appropriate for them to consult in determining what would be in P's best interests.

(2) But this section applies only if the accommodation is to be provided in accordance with—
    (a) section 21 or 29 of the National Assistance Act 1948 (c. 29), or
    (b) section 117 of the Mental Health Act,
as the result of a decision taken by the local authority under section 47 of the National Health Service and Community Care Act 1990 (c. 19).

(3) This section does not apply if P is accommodated as a result of an obligation imposed on him under the Mental Health Act.

(4) Before making the arrangements, the local authority must instruct an independent mental capacity advocate to represent P unless they are satisfied that—
    (a) the accommodation is likely to be provided for a continuous period of less than 8 weeks, or
    (b) the arrangements need to be made as a matter of urgency.

(5) If the local authority—

(a) did not instruct an independent mental capacity advocate to represent P before making the arrangements because they were satisfied that subsection (4)(a) or (b) applied, but

(b) subsequently have reason to believe that the accommodation is likely to be provided for a continuous period that will end 8 weeks or more after the day on which accommodation was first provided in accordance with the arrangements,

they must instruct an independent mental capacity advocate to represent P.

(6) The local authority must, in deciding what arrangements to make for P, take into account any information given, or submissions made, by the independent mental capacity advocate.

DEFINITIONS

"local authority": s.64(1)
"treatment": s.64(1)
"Mental Health Act": s.64(1)
"independent mental capacity act advocate": s.64(1)

GENERAL NOTE

This section applies if a local authority intends to arrange for P to be provided with long-stay residential accommodation provided under s.21 of the National Assistance Act 1948 (c.29) or s.117 of the Mental Health Act 1983, or for the accommodation to be changed, and there is no-one apart from a professional or paid carer for the authority to consult in determining what would be in P's best interests (subss.(1) and (2)). In this situation the authority must instruct an IMCA to represent P and any information given, or submissions made, by the IMCA must be taken into account when a decision is made about what arrangements to make for P (subss.(4) and (6)). Such consultation need not take place if the P is likely to stay in the accommodation for less than eight weeks or if the need for the accommodation is urgent (subs.(4)). However, the consultation must take place after the placement has been effected if the authority subsequently believes that the accommodation will be provided for P for at least eight weeks (subs.(5)). This section does not apply if the accommodation is provided as a result of an obligation imposed on P under the 1983 Act (subs.(2)).

Proper records should be taken by the responsible authority of how the IMCA's submissions have been taken into account and, where relevant, the reasons for disagreeing with or ignoring the submissions. Where a disagreement arises, every effort must be made to resolve the disagreement at the earliest possible stage, where necessary using the authority's dispute resolution or complaint's procedure.

Subsection (1)

No person. See the list set out in s.4(7).

Subsection (2)

A local authority may itself provide accommodation under s.21 or it can make arrangements under s.29 of the National Assistance Act 1948 for the accommodation to be provided by a third party. In *R. (on the application of Batantu) v Islington LBC* (2001) 4 C.C.L. Rep. 445, Henriques J. said that the meaning of accommodation under the 1948 Act is wide and flexible and embraces care homes, ordinary and sheltered housing, housing association and other registered social housing, and private sector housing which may have been purchased by the local authority. It would also include hostel accommodation.

Section 117 of the 1983 Act places a duty on the relevant NHS Trust and local authority to provide after-care services to patients who have been discharged from non-emergency detention under that Act. The after-care services can include accommodation that is required to meet the mental health needs of P.

Section 47 of the 1990 Act places a duty on local social services authorities to assess the care needs of any person who appears to be in need of community care services and decide in the light of the assessment whether services should be provided to that person.

Subsection (4)
Subsection (4)
This provision does not apply if a person listed in s.40 is available to be consulted.

40. Exceptions

Sections 37(3), 38(3) and (4) and 39(4) and (5) do not apply if there is—
(a) a person nominated by P (in whatever manner) as a person to be consulted in matters affecting his interests,
(b) a donee of a lasting power of attorney created by P,
(c) a deputy appointed by the court for P, or
(d) a donee of an enduring power of attorney (within the meaning of Schedule 4) created by P.

DEFINITIONS
"lasting power of attorney": s.64(1)
"deputy": s.64(1)

GENERAL NOTE
This section confirms that the independent mental advocacy scheme does not apply where there is a suitable person who can be consulted about P's best interests.

Paragraph (a)
The nomination may be written or oral. The decision-maker must be satisfied that the nomination was made when P was mentally capable and that the nominee is willing to be consulted.

Paragraph (b)
The donee is to be consulted about a personal welfare matter even though the LPA relates to P's financial affairs.

Paragraph (c)
The deputy is to be consulted about a personal welfare matter even though he or she has been appointed to manage P's financial affairs.

41. Power to adjust role of independent mental capacity advocate

(1) The appropriate authority may make regulations—
(a) expanding the role of independent mental capacity advocates in relation to persons who lack capacity, and
(b) adjusting the obligation to make arrangements imposed by section 35.
(2) The regulations may, in particular—
(a) prescribe circumstances (different to those set out in sections 37, 38 and 39) in which an independent mental capacity advocate must, or circumstances in which one may, be instructed by a person of a prescribed description to represent a person who lacks capacity, and
(b) include provision similar to any made by section 37, 38, 39 or 40.
(3) "Appropriate authority" has the same meaning as in section 35.

DEFINITIONS
"independent mental capacity advocate": s.64(1)

GENERAL NOTE
This section provides that scope of the independent mental advocacy scheme can be extended by regulations made by the Secretary of State or the National Assembly for Wales.

Subsection (1)

Regulations. Regulations made under this power are subject to the affirmative resolution procedure (s.65(4)).

Subsection (2) para. (a)

Must, or ... may. This phrase was substituted for "must" at the report stage in the House of Lords "for two reasons. First, concerns have been expressed about extending the [scheme] compulsorily to situations where there are family members. We agree that that it is not necessarily desirable or helpful. It is fair to say that family carers are at the heart of decision-making in many circumstances. We would not wish to get in the middle of that relationship, particularly when we know what a critical and crucial role family members play in supporting their loved ones. We will ensure that the Code of Practice refers to the central role at the heart that unpaid carers play, and makes it clear that they will often be the best people to speak up for the person lacking capacity. In addition, we believe that where people have successful, loving and supportive relationships, the obligatory use of an independent mental advocacy scheme would neither be helpful, nor an effective use of resources, frankly. Also, we want to ensure the maximum flexibility to enable us to accommodate all possible outcomes of the consultation on extending the service. Following the consultation, consensus may or may not favour the use of a discretionary power. By tabling the amendment, we are simply allowing for that possibility", *per* the Parliamentary Under-Secretary of State (*Hansard*, HL Vol.670, col.1528).

Miscellaneous and supplementary

42. Codes of practice

(1) The Lord Chancellor must prepare and issue one or more codes of practice—

  (a) for the guidance of persons assessing whether a person has capacity in relation to any matter,

  (b) for the guidance of persons acting in connection with the care or treatment of another person (see section 5),

  (c) for the guidance of donees of lasting powers of attorney,

  (d) for the guidance of deputies appointed by the court,

  (e) for the guidance of persons carrying out research in reliance on any provision made by or under this Act (and otherwise with respect to sections 30 to 34),

  (f) for the guidance of independent mental capacity advocates,

  (g) with respect to the provisions of sections 24 to 26 (advance decisions and apparent advance decisions), and

  (h) with respect to such other matters concerned with this Act as he thinks fit.

(2) The Lord Chancellor may from time to time revise a code.

(3) The Lord Chancellor may delegate the preparation or revision of the whole or any part of a code so far as he considers expedient.

(4) It is the duty of a person to have regard to any relevant code if he is acting in relation to a person who lacks capacity and is doing so in one or more of the following ways—

  (a) as the donee of a lasting power of attorney,

  (b) as a deputy appointed by the court,

  (c) as a person carrying out research in reliance on any provision made by or under this Act (see sections 30 to 34),

  (d) as an independent mental capacity advocate,

  (e) in a professional capacity,

  (f) for remuneration.

(5) If it appears to a court or tribunal conducting any criminal or civil proceedings that—
  (a) a provision of a code, or
  (b) a failure to comply with a code,
is relevant to a question arising in the proceedings, the provision or failure must be taken into account in deciding the question.

(6) A code under subsection (1)(d) may contain separate guidance for deputies appointed by virtue of paragraph 1(2) of Schedule 5 (functions of deputy conferred on receiver appointed under the Mental Health Act).

(7) In this section and in section 43, "code" means a code prepared or revised under this section.

DEFINITIONS

"treatment": s.64(1)
"lasting power of attorney": s.64(1)
"deputy": s.64(1)
"the court": s.64(1)
"independent mental capacity advocate": s.64(1)
"advance decision": s.64(1)
"Mental Health Act": s.64(1)

GENERAL NOTE

This section requires the Lord Chancellor to publish one or more codes of practice to address the issues set out in subs.(1). The codes can be revised (subs.(2)). These responsibilities may be delegated (subs.(3)). The code(s) will set out how the legal rules contained in this Act and the associated regulations will work in practice. Donees, deputies, professionals, researchers, independent mental capacity advocates and paid workers acting on behalf of a person who lacks capacity must have regard to the code(s) (subs.(4)) The code(s) can be used as evidence in court or tribunal proceedings and, if relevant, will be taken into account in the determination (subs.(5)).

The Department of Constitutional Affairs published a draft Code of Practice on September 9, 2004. It is available online at www.dca.gov.uk/menincap/mcbdraftcode.pdf.

Subsection (1)

Guidance. In *R. v Secretary of State for the Environment Ex p. Lancashire* CC 93 L.G.R. 29 at 39, Jowitt J. said:

"The concept of guidance goes beyond simply providing a checklist of factors which should be taken into account. To guide someone is to lead, steer or point someone in a particular direction."

Subsection (1) para. (b)

Note the scope of this category, which includes informal and family carers. It will surely be the case that many who fall into this category will not be familiar with either this Act or the code(s).

Subsection (2)

The code(s) will "be revised fairly frequently", *per* the Parliamentary Under-Secretary of State (*Hansard*, HL Vol.669, col.758).

Subsection (4)

Have regard to. There is a duty to consider the guidance contained in relevant parts of the code(s); not a duty to abide by it (*De Falco v Crawley BC* [1980] 1 All E.R. 913). Where a person's rights under Arts 3, 5 or 8 of the European Convention on Human Rights are engaged, the guidance in the code should be followed unless there is a good reason to depart from it (*R. (on the application of Munjaz) v Mersey Care NHS Trust* [2003] EWCA Civ 1036). It is suggested that the following would constitute a good reason for justifying a departure from the guidance in the code:

1 The particular clinical or social care needs of P (or a group of persons who share particular well-defined characteristics) would not be satisfied if the guidance was followed.

2　There has been a determination of the High Court that a particular aspect of the guidance is not legally accurate.
3　Legal advice has been received which casts a significant doubt on the legal correctness of an aspect of the guidance.
4　Following the guidance would involve breaching P's Convention rights.
5　A judgment is taken that a particular aspect of the guidance should not be followed for safety or other legitimate reason.

If a person fails to comply with the guidance contained in the Code, he or she must be prepared to give reasons to explain the non-compliance. It would be sensible for a contemporaneous record of the reasons to be made.

Subsection (4) para. (f)
　For remuneration. For example, a care assistant who works in a care home where the residents lack capacity.

43.　Codes of practice: procedure

(1)　Before preparing or revising a code, the Lord Chancellor must consult—
　(a)　the National Assembly for Wales, and
　(b)　such other persons as he considers appropriate.
(2)　The Lord Chancellor may not issue a code unless—
　(a)　a draft of the code has been laid by him before both Houses of Parliament, and
　(b)　the 40 day period has elapsed without either House resolving not to approve the draft.
(3)　The Lord Chancellor must arrange for any code that he has issued to be published in such a way as he considers appropriate for bringing it to the attention of persons likely to be concerned with its provisions.
(4)　"40 day period", in relation to the draft of a proposed code, means—
　(a)　if the draft is laid before one House on a day later than the day on which it is laid before the other House, the period of 40 days beginning with the later of the two days;
　(b)　in any other case, the period of 40 days beginning with the day on which it is laid before each House.
(5)　In calculating the period of 40 days, no account is to be taken of any period during which Parliament is dissolved or prorogued or during which both Houses are adjourned for more than 4 days.

GENERAL NOTE
　This section sets out the procedure for issuing and revising the code(s) of practice and requires the Lord Chancellor to publish the code(s) in an appropriate format.

44.　Ill-treatment or neglect

(1)　Subsection (2) applies if a person (D)—
　(a)　has the care of a person (P) who lacks, or whom D reasonably believes to lack, capacity,
　(b)　is the donee of a lasting power of attorney, or an enduring power of attorney (within the meaning of Schedule 4), created by P, or
　(c)　is a deputy appointed by the court for P.
(2)　D is guilty of an offence if he ill-treats or wilfully neglects P.
(3)　A person guilty of an offence under this section is liable—

(a) on summary conviction, to imprisonment for a term not exceeding 12 months or a fine not exceeding the statutory maximum or both;

(b) on conviction on indictment, to imprisonment for a term not exceeding 5 years or a fine or both.

DEFINITIONS

"lasting power of attorney": s.64(1)

"deputy": s.64(1)

"the court": s.64(1)

GENERAL NOTE

This section creates the offence of ill-treatment or wilful neglect of a person who lacks capacity or is believed to lack capacity. It is "aimed at capturing those individuals who are in a position of trust, care or power over people who are then ill-treated or neglected. That could be a donee of a lasting power of attorney, a deputy appointed by the court or a person who has the care of someone who lacks capacity, such as a member of staff in a hospital or care home or a family member", *per* the Parliamentary Under-Secretary of State, St. Comm. A, col.383. In *R. v Newington (Susan)* (1990) 91 Cr. App. R. 247, a case under s.127 of the Mental Health Act 1983, the Court of Appeal said that "ill-treatment" could not be equated with "wilfully to neglect". The court therefore advised the Crown Prosecution Service that, when proceedings were brought, charges of "ill-treatment" and of "wilfully to neglect" should be put in separate counts in the indictment.

The Government rejected recommendation 80 of the Joint Committee that this section be "extended to include the misappropriation of the person's property and financial assets" on the ground that a person who uses the funds of someone who lacks capacity for his own benefit may be prosecuted for the offence of theft and that a new offence of "misappropriation" would be very similar to that offence (The Government Response to the Scrutiny Committee's Report on the Draft Mental Incapacity Bill, Cm 6121). The English "No Secrets" and the Welsh "In Safe Hands" guidance set out the multi-agency procedures to be followed when a vulnerable adult is believed to be suffering abuse. Abuse is defined as "a violation of an individual's human and civil rights by any other person or persons" (No Secrets, para.2.5). The Government rejected the Joint Committee's recommendation at para.266 that the statutory authorities should be given additional powers of investigation and intervention in cases of alleged physical, sexual or financial abuse of people lacking the capacity to protect themselves from the risk of abuse:

"The Committee recommended that the draft Bill should go further in the protection it offers against abuse and exploitation of those lacking capacity. However, the Government is already taking action to protect vulnerable adults against abuse. In particular, the 'No Secrets' guidance requires Councils to liaise with other public authorities and other agencies in their area and to produce written and agreed local procedures for handling incidents of abuse concerning vulnerable adults. The new Public Guardian under the Bill would have a role working with Councils and other agencies. The new criminal offence of ill-treatment or wilful neglect would also be another valuable tool in tackling potential abuse" (Cm.6121).

This section is drafted in broader terms than s.127 of the Mental Health Act 1983. Section 127 creates three separate offences that could apply to incapacitated people who are also suffering from a mental disorder within the meaning of s.1 of that Act at the time when the offence was committed. Firstly, under subs.(1) it is an offence for an employee or manager of a hospital, independent hospital or care home to ill-treat or wilfully to neglect an in-patient or out-patient of that hospital or home. Secondly, under subs.(2) it is an offence for a guardian appointed under the 1983 Act or some other person who has the custody or care of a mentally disordered person who is living in the community to ill-treat or wilfully to neglect that person. Thirdly, under subs.(2A) it is an offence for any person to ill-treat of wilfully to neglect a person who is subject to the supervised discharge provisions of the 1983 Act.

Subsection (2)

Ill-treats. There is Crown Court authority to support the proposition that it is not necessary to establish a course of conduct as a single act, such as slapping a person's face on one occasion, could constitute ill-treatment (*R. v Holmes* [1979] Crim. L.R. 52, Crown Court (Bodmin)). As it is likely that there is no need for the prosecution to show that the treatment in question caused actual injury to the victim, "ill-treatment" encompasses a wide range of conduct.

It is submitted that for the offence of ill-treatment to be proved, the prosecution would have to prove: (1) deliberate conduct by the accused which could properly be described as ill-treatment irrespective of whether it damaged or threatened to damage the victims health; (2) a guilty mind involving either an appreciation by the accused that he was inexcusably ill-treating a person or that he was reckless as to whether he was inexcusably acting in that way; and (3) that the victim was a person without capacity (*R. v Newington (Susan)*, above). In Newington the court disapproved of a direction given by the trial judge "that violence would inevitably amount to ill-treatment" on the ground that violence necessarily used for the reasonable control of a patient would not amount to ill-treatment.

Wilfully neglects. The meaning to be attributed to the expression "wilful neglect" may vary according to the context but generally the expression should be taken to mean that there has been an intentional or purposive omission to do something that the person in question knows he or she has a duty to do (*De Maroussem v Commissioner of Income Tax [2004]* UKPC 43, para.41).

The leading case on the term "wilfully" is *R. v Sheppard (James Martin)* [1981] A.C. 394, HL, a case brought under s.1(1) of the Children and Young Persons Act 1933 (c.12). Lord Keith said at 418:

"It is used here to describe the mental element, which, in addition to the fact of neglect, must be proved The primary meaning of 'wilful' is 'deliberate'. So a parent who knows that his child needs medical care and deliberately, that is by conscious decision, refrains from calling a doctor, is guilty under the sub-section. As a matter of general principle, recklessness is to be equiparated with deliberation. A parent who fails to provide medical care which his child needs because he does not care whether it is needed or not is reckless of his child's welfare. He too is guilty of an offence. But a parent who has genuinely failed to appreciate that his child needs medical care, through personal inadequacy or stupidity or both, is not guilty."

A direction of the kind suggested by Lord Keith's reasoning, suitably tailored to the facts of the case, should be given by the trial judge hearing a case under this section (*R. v Morrell (Karen Victoria)* [2002] EWCA Crim 2547).

PART 2

PART 2   THE COURT OF PROTECTION AND THE PUBLIC GUARDIAN

The Court of Protection

45.   The Court of Protection

(1) There is to be a superior court of record known as the Court of Protection.

(2) The court is to have an official seal.

(3) The court may sit at any place in England and Wales, on any day and at any time.

(4) The court is to have a central office and registry at a place appointed by the Lord Chancellor.

(5) The Lord Chancellor may designate as additional registries of the court any district registry of the High Court and any county court office.

(6) The office of the Supreme Court called the Court of Protection ceases to exist.

GENERAL NOTE

This section establishes a new superior court of record called the Court of Protection which will have a comprehensive jurisdiction over the health, welfare and financial affairs of people who lack capacity. The court will have the same powers, rights, privileges and authority as the High Court (s.47(1)). The former Court of Protection, which was an office of the Supreme Court dealing only with the patient's "property and affairs", is abolished (subs.(6). The new court will be able to sit anywhere in England and Wales (subs.(3)). The Explanatory Notes state at para.130 that it "is intended that the Court of Protection will have a regional presence but will have a central office and registry as designated by the Lord Chancellor. Additional registries (being High Court district registries or county courts) may also be designated."

In addition to the powers contained in s.16 to make an order and to appoint a deputy and the powers contained in ss.22 and 23 relating to lasting powers of attorney, the court also has the power under s.15 to make declarations on whether a person has capacity to make a particular decision, and whether an act done, or proposed to be done, in relation to a person who lacks capacity is lawful. Provision for applications to be made to the court is It is prima facie a contempt of court to publish information relating to proceedings which are brought under this Act and which are heard in private (Administration of Justice Act 1960 (c.65), s.12).

Subsection (3)

The Law Commission anticipated a need for there to be at least one venue for each of the six court circuits in England and Wales (Law Com No.231, para.10.16).

46. The judges of the Court of Protection

(1) Subject to Court of Protection Rules under section 51(2)(d), the jurisdiction of the court is exercisable by a judge nominated for that purpose by—

    (a) the Lord Chancellor, or

    (b) a person acting on the Lord Chancellor's behalf.

(2) To be nominated, a judge must be—

    (a) the President of the Family Division,

    (b) the Vice-Chancellor,

    (c) a puisne judge of the High Court,

    (d) a circuit judge, or

    (e) a district judge.

(3) The Lord Chancellor must—

    (a) appoint one of the judges nominated by virtue of subsection (2)(a) to (c) to be President of the Court of Protection, and

    (b) appoint another of those judges to be Vice-President of the Court of Protection.

(4) The Lord Chancellor must appoint one of the judges nominated by virtue of subsection (2)(d) or (e) to be Senior Judge of the Court of Protection, having such administrative functions in relation to the court as the Lord Chancellor may direct.

DEFINITIONS

  "the court": s.64(1)

GENERAL NOTE

The jurisdiction of the Court of Protection will be exercised by judges nominated by the Lord Chancellor, or a person acting on his behalf, from the list set out in subs.(2). One of the nominated judges must be appointed as President of the Court of Protection and another to be Vice-President (subs.(3)). A judge must also be appointed to be Senior Judge of the Court of Protection (subs.(4)). He or she will have various administrative responsibilities.

Supplementary powers

47. General powers and effect of orders etc

(1) The court has in connection with its jurisdiction the same powers, rights, privileges and authority as the High Court.

(2) Section 204 of the Law of Property Act 1925 (c. 20) (orders of High Court conclusive in favour of purchasers) applies in relation to orders and directions of the court as it applies to orders of the High Court.

(3) Office copies of orders made, directions given or other instruments issued by the court and sealed with its official seal are admissible in all legal proceedings as evidence of the originals without any further proof.

DEFINITIONS
"the court": s.64(1)
"purchaser": s.64(1)

GENERAL NOTE

Subsection (1)
This gives the Court of Protection the same powers as the High Court, for example in relation to witnesses, contempt, and enforcement.

Subsection (2)
Section 204 of the 1925 Act reads:

1   "An order of the court under any statutory or other jurisdiction shall not, as against a purchaser, be invalidated on the ground of want of jurisdiction, or of want of any concurrence, consent, notice, or service, whether the purchaser has notice of any such want or not.
2   This section has effect with respect to any lease, sale, or other act under the authority of the court, and purporting to be in pursuance of any statutory power notwithstanding any exception in such statute.
3   This section applies to all orders made before or after the commencement of this Act."

48.   Interim orders and directions

The court may, pending the determination of an application to it in relation to a person (P), make an order or give directions in respect of any matter if—
(a) there is reason to believe that P lacks capacity in relation to the matter,
(b) the matter is one to which its powers under this Act extend, and
(c) it is in P's best interests to make the order, or give the directions, without delay.

DEFINITIONS
"the court": s.64(1)

GENERAL NOTE
This section enables the court to make interim orders even if evidence of lack of capacity is not yet available, where there is reason for the court to believe that the person lacks capacity in respect of a particular matter within the jurisdiction of the court and it is in the best interests of the person for the court to act without delay.

49.   Power to call for reports

(1) This section applies where, in proceedings brought in respect of a person (P) under Part 1, the court is considering a question relating to P.
(2) The court may require a report to be made to it by the Public Guardian or by a Court of Protection Visitor.
(3) The court may require a local authority, or an NHS body, to arrange for a report to be made—

(a) by one of its officers or employees, or

(b) by such other person (other than the Public Guardian or a Court of Protection Visitor) as the authority, or the NHS body, considers appropriate.

(4) The report must deal with such matters relating to P as the court may direct.

(5) Court of Protection Rules may specify matters which, unless the court directs otherwise, must also be dealt with in the report.

(6) The report may be made in writing or orally, as the court may direct.

(7) In complying with a requirement, the Public Guardian or a Court of Protection Visitor may, at all reasonable times, examine and take copies of—

(a) any health record,

(b) any record of, or held by, a local authority and compiled in connection with a social services function, and

(c) any record held by a person registered under Part 2 of the Care Standards Act 2000 (c. 14),

so far as the record relates to P.

(8) If the Public Guardian or a Court of Protection Visitor is making a visit in the course of complying with a requirement, he may interview P in private.

(9) If a Court of Protection Visitor who is a Special Visitor is making a visit in the course of complying with a requirement, he may if the court so directs carry out in private a medical, psychiatric or psychological examination of P's capacity and condition.

(10) "NHS body" has the meaning given in section 148 of the Health and Social Care (Community Health and Standards) Act 2003 (c. 43).

(11) "Requirement" means a requirement imposed under subsection (2) or (3).

DEFINITIONS
"the court": s.64(1)
"Court of Protection Visitor": s.64(1)
"local authority": s.64(1)
"Court of Protection Rules": s.64(1)
"social services function": s.64(1)

GENERAL NOTE
This section makes provision for reports to be made to assist the Court of Protection in determining a case relating to P. The court can require either written or oral reports to be made by the Public Guardian, a Court of Protection Visitor, a local authority or a NHS body (subss.(2), (3) and (6)). The report must deal with such matters as the court and/or the Court of Protection Rules direct (subss.(4) and (5)). The Public Guardian and a Court of Protection Visitor are given power to examine and take copies of relevant records and to interview P in private (subss.(7) and (8)). Where a Court of Protection Visitor is a Special Visitor (see s.61(2)), he or she may, on the directions of the court, carry out in private medical, psychiatric or psychological examinations of P's capacity and condition (subs.(9)).

Subsection (2)
A case heard under the Mental Health Act 1959 (c.2) suggests that in initial applications for the appointment of a deputy and in applications to determine proceedings, where the ultimate issue is whether an individual should either become or remain subject to the court's jurisdiction, the court should lean towards disclosing the Visitor's report, and the individual should be permitted to test the report by putting questions to the Visitor. The court should only withhold disclosure where this is deemed to be in the person's best interests. In all other cases, the judge should only direct disclosure if he sees a positive advantage in doing so, either in the interests of the person generally, or because he feels it would assist the judge in the exercise of his functions (*WLW, Re* [1972] Ch 456 at 457, *per* Goff J.)

It is a contempt of court to interfere with the discharge of a Visitor's duties (*Anon, Re* (1875-90) 18 Ch.D 26, *per* James L.J. at 27).

Subsection (3)
Paragraph (b) covers the situation where the local authority or NHS body has subcontracted its work to someone else.
NHS body. See subs.(10).

Subsections (7), (8) and (9)
Requirement. See subs.(11)

Subsection (10)
Under s.148 of the 2003 Act, an English NHS body means a Primary Care Trust, a Strategic Health Authority, an English NHS trust and a NHS foundation trust. A Welsh NHS body means a Local Health Board, a Welsh NHS trust and a Special Health Authority performing functions only or mainly in respect of Wales. A "NHS body" also includes a cross-border Special Health Authority which means a SHA not performing functions only or mainly in respect of England or only or mainly in respect of Wales.

Practice and procedure

50. Applications to the Court of Protection

(1) No permission is required for an application to the court for the exercise of any of its powers under this Act—
   (a) by a person who lacks, or is alleged to lack, capacity,
   (b) if such a person has not reached 18, by anyone with parental responsibility for him,
   (c) by the donor or a donee of a lasting power of attorney to which the application relates,
   (d) by a deputy appointed by the court for a person to whom the application relates, or
   (e) by a person named in an existing order of the court, if the application relates to the order.
(2) But, subject to Court of Protection Rules and to paragraph 20(2) of Schedule 3 (declarations relating to private international law), permission is required for any other application to the court.
(3) In deciding whether to grant permission the court must, in particular, have regard to—
   (a) the applicant's connection with the person to whom the application relates,
   (b) the reasons for the application,
   (c) the benefit to the person to whom the application relates of a proposed order or directions, and
   (d) whether the benefit can be achieved in any other way.
(4) "Parental responsibility" has the same meaning as in the Children Act 1989 (c. 41).

DEFINITIONS
"the court": s.64(1)
"lasting power of attorney": s.64(1)
"deputy": s.64(1)
"Court of Protection Rules": s.64(1)

GENERAL NOTE

This section provides that persons listed in subs.(1) can make as application to the Court of Protection as of right. Others potential applicants will have to obtain the permission of the court, although the Court of Protection Rules might provide that certain types of application will not require permission. The factors that the court must have regard to when considering whether to grant permission are set out in subs.(3). They "are designed to ensure that any proposed application will promote the interests of the person concerned, rather than causing unnecessary distress or difficulty for him" (Explanatory Notes, para.136).

The draft Code of Practice deals with the identity of the applicant at para.7.5:

"The Act makes flexible provision as to who can make an application to the Court, since this will depend on the type and circumstances of the case under consideration. For example, in relation to disputes between family members, it will be a decision for the aggrieved family member as to whether court action is warranted, bearing in mind the need in most cases to obtain permission beforehand. Where the dispute relates to the provision of medical treatment, the NHS Trust or other body responsible for the patient's care should in most cases make the application to the Court. A local authority wishing to intervene in decisions affecting the personal welfare of a person lacking capacity should make the application. Regardless of who makes the application, the person lacking capacity in relation to the matter in question should in most cases be a party to the proceedings. The Court may appoint the Official Solicitor to act for the person lacking capacity."

The Joint Committee, at para.173, sought assurances from the Government that public funds will be made available to ensure that the Court of Protection is sufficiently accessible for those with limited assets. The Government responded as follows:

"We acknowledge that public funding for legal help and advice will need to be made available, as now, to enable those with limited assets to have access to the Court of Protection. Legal Representation will continue to be available, if necessary, for serious health or welfare issues which are currently heard in the High Court but will transfer to the Court of Protection. The detail remains to be resolved regarding provision in individual cases. We are undertaking further work on the provision of legal advice and envisage that the Public Guardian will offer a telephone information line" (*The Government Response to the Scrutiny Committee's Report on the draft Mental Incapacity Bill* (Cm.6121)).

Subsection (1) (a)

The Court of Protection Rules will enable the court to appoint someone to act for this person (s.51(2)(e)).

51. Court of Protection Rules

(1) The Lord Chancellor may make rules of court (to be called "Court of Protection Rules") with respect to the practice and procedure of the court.

(2) Court of Protection Rules may, in particular, make provision—

    (a) as to the manner and form in which proceedings are to be commenced;

    (b) as to the persons entitled to be notified of, and be made parties to, the proceedings;

    (c) for the allocation, in such circumstances as may be specified, of any specified description of proceedings to a specified judge or to specified descriptions of judges;

    (d) for the exercise of the jurisdiction of the court, in such circumstances as may be specified, by its officers or other staff;

    (e) for enabling the court to appoint a suitable person (who may, with his consent, be the Official Solicitor) to act in the name of, or on behalf of, or to represent the person to whom the proceedings relate;

    (f) for enabling an application to the court to be disposed of without a hearing;

    (g) for enabling the court to proceed with, or with any part of, a hearing in the absence of the person to whom the proceedings relate;

(h) for enabling or requiring the proceedings or any part of them to be conducted in private and for enabling the court to determine who is to be admitted when the court sits in private and to exclude specified persons when it sits in public;

(i) as to what may be received as evidence (whether or not admissible apart from the rules) and the manner in which it is to be presented;

(j) for the enforcement of orders made and directions given in the proceedings.

(3) Court of Protection Rules may, instead of providing for any matter, refer to provision made or to be made about that matter by directions.

(4) Court of Protection Rules may make different provision for different areas.

DEFINITIONS
"the court": s.64(1)

52. Practice directions

(1) The President of the Court of Protection may, with the concurrence of the Lord Chancellor, give directions as to the practice and procedure of the court.

(2) Directions as to the practice and procedure of the court may not be given by anyone other than the President of the Court of Protection without the approval of the President of the Court of Protection and the Lord Chancellor.

(3) Nothing in this section prevents the President of the Court of Protection, without the concurrence of the Lord Chancellor, giving directions which contain guidance as to law or making judicial decisions.

DEFINITIONS
"the court": s.64(1)

GENERAL NOTE

This section gives power to the President of the Court of Protection to make practice directions about the court's practice and procedure. Section 51(3) enables the Court of Protection Rules, instead of providing for any matter, to refer to provision made by a practice direction. The "intention is to make rules accompanied by practice directions, on the model of the Civil Procedure Rules 1998" (Explanatory Notes, para.138).

53. Rights of appeal

(1) Subject to the provisions of this section, an appeal lies to the Court of Appeal from any decision of the court.

(2) Court of Protection Rules may provide that where a decision of the court is made by—

(a) a person exercising the jurisdiction of the court by virtue of rules made under section 51(2)(d),

(b) a district judge, or

(c) a circuit judge,

an appeal from that decision lies to a prescribed higher judge of the court and not to the Court of Appeal.

(3) For the purposes of this section the higher judges of the court are—

(a) in relation to a person mentioned in subsection (2)(a), a circuit judge or a district judge;

(b) in relation to a person mentioned in subsection (2)(b), a circuit judge;

    (c) in relation to any person mentioned in subsection (2), one of the judges nominated by virtue of section 46(2)(a) to (c).

(4) Court of Protection Rules may make provision—

    (a) that, in such cases as may be specified, an appeal from a decision of the court may not be made without permission;

    (b) as to the person or persons entitled to grant permission to appeal;

    (c) as to any requirements to be satisfied before permission is granted;

    (d) that where a higher judge of the court makes a decision on an appeal, no appeal may be made to the Court of Appeal from that decision unless the Court of Appeal considers that—

        (i) the appeal would raise an important point of principle or practice, or

        (ii) there is some other compelling reason for the Court of Appeal to hear it;

    (e) as to any considerations to be taken into account in relation to granting or refusing permission to appeal.

DEFINITIONS
  "the court": s.64(1)

GENERAL NOTE
  This section, which will be supplemented by the Court of Protection Rules, is concerned with appeals from decisions of the Court of Protection. The appeal will either be to the Court of Appeal or, if the decision was made by a judge at a lower level in the judicial hierarchy of the court, to a higher judge within the court (subss.(1) and (2)).

Fees and costs

54. Fees

(1) The Lord Chancellor may with the consent of the Treasury by order prescribe fees payable in respect of anything dealt with by the court.

(2) An order under this section may in particular contain provision as to—

    (a) scales or rates of fees;

    (b) exemptions from and reductions in fees;

    (c) remission of fees in whole or in part.

(3) Before making an order under this section, the Lord Chancellor must consult—

    (a) the President of the Court of Protection,

    (b) the Vice-President of the Court of Protection, and

    (c) the Senior Judge of the Court of Protection.

(4) The Lord Chancellor must take such steps as are reasonably practicable to bring information about fees to the attention of persons likely to have to pay them.

(5) Fees payable under this section are recoverable summarily as a civil debt.

DEFINITIONS
  "the court": s.64(1)

GENERAL NOTE

Subsection (1)
  By order. See s.65(2).

Subsection (2)
  The principle underpinning this provision was explained by the Parliamentary Under-Secretary of State: "[W]e believe that it is right that people should pay a fair price for the court's work on their behalf, but it is also right that fee reduction and remission arrangements exist so that no one is prevented from going to court if paying the fees would cause them financial hardship, or if there are other exceptional circumstances" (*Hansard*, HL Vol. 669, col.754).

55. Costs

  (1) Subject to Court of Protection Rules, the costs of and incidental to all proceedings in the court are in its discretion.
  (2) The rules may in particular make provision for regulating matters relating to the costs of those proceedings, including prescribing scales of costs to be paid to legal or other representatives.
  (3) The court has full power to determine by whom and to what extent the costs are to be paid.
  (4) The court may, in any proceedings—
    (a) disallow, or
    (b) order the legal or other representatives concerned to meet,
the whole of any wasted costs or such part of them as may be determined in accordance with the rules.
  (5) "Legal or other representative", in relation to a party to proceedings, means any person exercising a right of audience or right to conduct litigation on his behalf.
  (6) "Wasted costs" means any costs incurred by a party—
    (a) as a result of any improper, unreasonable or negligent act or omission on the part of any legal or other representative or any employee of such a representative, or
    (b) which, in the light of any such act or omission occurring after they were incurred, the court considers it is unreasonable to expect that party to pay.

DEFINITIONS
  "Court of Protection Rules": s.64(1)
  "the court": s.64(1)

56. Fees and costs: supplementary

  (1) Court of Protection Rules may make provision—
    (a) as to the way in which, and funds from which, fees and costs are to be paid;
    (b) for charging fees and costs upon the estate of the person to whom the proceedings relate;
    (c) for the payment of fees and costs within a specified time of the death of the person to whom the proceedings relate or the conclusion of the proceedings.
  (2) A charge on the estate of a person created by virtue of subsection (1)(b) does not cause any interest of the person in any property to fail or determine or to be prevented from recommencing.

DEFINITIONS
"Court of Protection Rules": s.64(1)

The Public Guardian

57. The Public Guardian

(1) For the purposes of this Act, there is to be an officer, to be known as the Public Guardian.

(2) The Public Guardian is to be appointed by the Lord Chancellor.

(3) There is to be paid to the Public Guardian out of money provided by Parliament such salary as the Lord Chancellor may determine.

(4) The Lord Chancellor may, after consulting the Public Guardian—

(a) provide him with such officers and staff, or

(b) enter into such contracts with other persons for the provision (by them or their sub-contractors) of officers, staff or services,

as the Lord Chancellor thinks necessary for the proper discharge of the Public Guardian's functions.

(5) Any functions of the Public Guardian may, to the extent authorised by him, be performed by any of his officers.

GENERAL NOTE

This section provides for a new public official, the Public Guardian, to be appointed by the Lord Chancellor, and for the Lord Chancellor either to provide the Public Guardian with officers and staff and/or to enter into contacts with other persons for the provision of officers, staff or services for the discharge of the Public Guardian's functions. The Public Guardian, who replaces the Public Guardianship Office, will have both administrative and supervisory functions. These are set out in s.58. The Public Guardian, who will be subject to the scrutiny of the Public Guardian Board (s.59), is required to produce annual reports (s.60).

58. Functions of the Public Guardian

(1) The Public Guardian has the following functions—

(a) establishing and maintaining a register of lasting powers of attorney,

(b) establishing and maintaining a register of orders appointing deputies,

(c) supervising deputies appointed by the court,

(d) directing a Court of Protection Visitor to visit—

(i) a donee of a lasting power of attorney,

(ii) a deputy appointed by the court, or

(iii) the person granting the power of attorney or for whom the deputy is appointed (P),

and to make a report to the Public Guardian on such matters as he may direct,

(e) receiving security which the court requires a person to give for the discharge of his functions,

(f) receiving reports from donees of lasting powers of attorney and deputies appointed by the court,

(g) reporting to the court on such matters relating to proceedings under this Act as the court requires,

(h) dealing with representations (including complaints) about the way in which a donee of a lasting power of attorney or a deputy appointed by the court is exercising his powers,

    (i) publishing, in any manner the Public Guardian thinks appropriate, any information he thinks appropriate about the discharge of his functions.

  (2) The functions conferred by subsection (1)(c) and (h) may be discharged in co-operation with any other person who has functions in relation to the care or treatment of P.

  (3) The Lord Chancellor may by regulations make provision—

    (a) conferring on the Public Guardian other functions in connection with this Act;

    (b) in connection with the discharge by the Public Guardian of his functions.

  (4) Regulations made under subsection (3)(b) may in particular make provision as to—

    (a) the giving of security by deputies appointed by the court and the enforcement and discharge of security so given;

    (b) the fees which may be charged by the Public Guardian;

    (c) the way in which, and funds from which, such fees are to be paid;

    (d) exemptions from and reductions in such fees;

    (e) remission of such fees in whole or in part;

    (f) the making of reports to the Public Guardian by deputies appointed by the court and others who are directed by the court to carry out any transaction for a person who lacks capacity.

  (5) For the purpose of enabling him to carry out his functions, the Public Guardian may, at all reasonable times, examine and take copies of—

    (a) any health record,

    (b) any record of, or held by, a local authority and compiled in connection with a social services function, and

    (c) any record held by a person registered under Part 2 of the Care Standards Act 2000 (c. 14),

so far as the record relates to P.

  (6) The Public Guardian may also for that purpose interview P in private.

DEFINITIONS

  "lasting power of attorney": s.64(1)
  "deputy": s.64(1)
  "the court": s.64(1)
  "Court of Protection Visitor": s.64(1)
  "health record": s.64(1)
  "local authority": s.64(1)
  "social services function": s.64(1)

GENERAL NOTE

  The functions of the Public Guardian listed in subs.(1) may be supplemented by regulations made by the Lord Chancellor (subs.(3)). The Public Guardian is given power to examine and take copies of relevant health or social services records, and also interview P in private (subss.(5) and (6)). Similar rights are provided for when the Public Guardian is reporting to the Court of Protection (s.49(7)-(8)).

Subsection (1) (h)

  The Public Guardian might wish to refer a complaint concerning the personal welfare of P to the relevant health or social care agency. If the complaint suggests that a criminal offence has been committed, this will be referred to the police.

Subsection (2)

  It "is intended that the Public Guardian will work closely with organisations such as local authorities and NHS bodies" (Explanatory Notes, para.146). Although the Public Guardian's supervisory function will be mainly focused on financial affairs, it "would have a role in identifying and tackling possible abuse with other agencies by providing a focus for concerns and fielding them to the appropriate agency" (Department of Constitutional Affairs, Oral and written evidence, Ev 265).

59. Public Guardian Board

(1) There is to be a body, to be known as the Public Guardian Board.

(2) The Board's duty is to scrutinise and review the way in which the Public Guardian discharges his functions and to make such recommendations to the Lord Chancellor about that matter as it thinks appropriate.

(3) The Lord Chancellor must, in discharging his functions under sections 57 and 58, give due consideration to recommendations made by the Board.

(4) The members of the Board are to be appointed by the Lord Chancellor.

(5) The Board must have—

    (a) at least one member who is a judge of the court, and

    (b) at least four members who are persons appearing to the Lord Chancellor to have appropriate knowledge or experience of the work of the Public Guardian.

(6) The Lord Chancellor may by regulations make provision as to—

    (a) the appointment of members of the Board (and, in particular, the procedures to be followed in connection with appointments);

    (b) the selection of one of the members to be the chairman;

    (c) the term of office of the chairman and members;

    (d) their resignation, suspension or removal;

    (e) the procedure of the Board (including quorum);

    (f) the validation of proceedings in the event of a vacancy among the members or a defect in the appointment of a member.

(7) Subject to any provision made in reliance on subsection (6)(c) or (d), a person is to hold and vacate office as a member of the Board in accordance with the terms of the instrument appointing him.

(8) The Lord Chancellor may make such payments to or in respect of members of the Board by way of reimbursement of expenses, allowances and remuneration as he may determine.

(9) The Board must make an annual report to the Lord Chancellor about the discharge of its functions.

GENERAL NOTE

This section provides for the establishment of the Public Guardian Board which is charged with the duty of scrutinising and reviewing the manner in which the Public Guardian discharges his or her functions. The Board may make recommendations to the Lord Chancellor who must, in discharging his or her functions under ss.57 and 58, give them due consideration.

60. Annual report

(1) The Public Guardian must make an annual report to the Lord Chancellor about the discharge of his functions.

(2) The Lord Chancellor must, within one month of receiving the report, lay a copy of it before Parliament.

DEFINITIONS

"Public Guardian": s.64(1)

Court of Protection Visitors

61. Court of Protection Visitors

(1) A Court of Protection Visitor is a person who is appointed by the Lord Chancellor to—

    (a) a panel of Special Visitors, or

    (b) a panel of General Visitors.

(2) A person is not qualified to be a Special Visitor unless he—

    (a) is a registered medical practitioner or appears to the Lord Chancellor to have other suitable qualifications or training, and

    (b) appears to the Lord Chancellor to have special knowledge of and experience in cases of impairment of or disturbance in the functioning of the mind or brain.

(3) A General Visitor need not have a medical qualification.

(4) A Court of Protection Visitor—

    (a) may be appointed for such term and subject to such conditions, and

    (b) may be paid such remuneration and allowances,

as the Lord Chancellor may determine.

(5) For the purpose of carrying out his functions under this Act in relation to a person who lacks capacity (P), a Court of Protection Visitor may, at all reasonable times, examine and take copies of—

    (a) any health record,

    (b) any record of, or held by, a local authority and compiled in connection with a social services function, and

    (c) any record held by a person registered under Part 2 of the Care Standards Act 2000 (c. 14),

so far as the record relates to P.

(6) A Court of Protection Visitor may also for that purpose interview P in private.

DEFINITIONS

"health record": s.64(1)

"local authority": s.64(1)

"social services function": s.64(1)

GENERAL NOTE

This section provides for the Lord Chancellor to appoint Special Visitors, who will be clinicians, and General Visitors. Their role is to carry out visits and produce independent reports on matters relating to the exercise of powers under this Act as directed by the Court of Protection (s.49(2)) or the Public Guardian (s.58(1)(d)). The Visitors have the power to examine and take copies of relevant records, and to interview P in private.

Subsection (1)

General Visitors. Under the 1983 Act a "patient" would receive a visit from a General Visitor if they "are a minor, if they are living in their own home or with a relative, if they are in a nursing home, other than a NHS hospital and are not being regularly visited by relatives or friends, or if their receiver is a local authority" (35th report of the Public Accounts Committee for Session 1998-1999, p.15, n.13).

PART 3

PART 3   MISCELLANEOUS AND GENERAL

Declaratory provision

62.   Scope of the Act

For the avoidance of doubt, it is hereby declared that nothing in this Act is to be taken to affect the law relating to murder or manslaughter or the operation of section 2 of the Suicide Act 1961 (c. 60) (assisting suicide).

GENERAL NOTE

This section, which was inserted following representations from the Catholic Bishops' Conference of England and Wales, seeks to address the concerns that were expressed to the Joint Committee that this legislation might pave the way for "euthanasia by the backdoor" (see para.196). Euthanasia, which is "a deliberate intervention with the express aim of ending life", is illegal ("Who Decides: Making Decisions on Behalf of Mentally Incapacitated Adults", Cm.3803, para.1.8). Notwithstanding the declaration made in this section, it is the case that both a valid and applicable written advance decision to refuse life-sustaining treatment (see ss.24-26) and a refusal of such treatment by a donee under a lasting power of attorney, if such power is granted to the donee (see s.11(8)), are lawful and must be obeyed by healthcare professionals. A mentally capable patient can therefore use either of these mechanisms to bring about his or her death during a subsequent mental incapacity by refusing either the provision of nutrition and hydration by artificial means or other potentially life saving medical interventions in specified circumstances. In such an eventuality there can be no question of the person having committed suicide, nor therefore of the doctor having aided and abetted him or her in doing so (*Airedale NHS Trust v Bland* [1993] 1 All E.R. 821, HL, *per* Lord Goff at 866). However, if a donee "wanted to refuse consent to treatment and the doctors thought that this was with the intention of murder or manslaughter then the doctor could continue to treat", *per* the Parliamentary Under-Secretary of State in correspondence quoted at (*Hansard*, HL Vol.688, col.1150.

Whether a decision to discontinue treatment that would inevitably lead to the patient's death constitutes euthanasia was considered by Lord Goff in Bland at 867:

"[T]he law draws a crucial distinction between cases in which a doctor decides not to provide, or continue to provide, for his patient treatment or care which could or might prolong his life and those in which he decides, for example by administering a lethal drug, actively to bring his patient's life to an end. As I have already indicated, the former may be lawful, either because the doctor is giving effect to his patient's wishes by withholding the treatment or care, even in certain circumstances in which the patient is incapacitated from stating whether or not he gives his consent. But it is not lawful for a doctor to administer a drug to his patient to bring about his death, even though that course is prompted by a humanitarian desire to end his suffering, however great that suffering may be: see *R v Cox* (September 18, 1992, unreported) *per* Ognall J in the Crown Court at Winchester. So to act is to cross the Rubicon which runs between on the one hand the care of the living patient and on the other hand euthanasia - actively causing his death to avoid or to end his suffering. Euthanasia is not lawful at common law. It is, of course well known that there are many responsible members of our society who believe that euthanasia should be made lawful; but that result could I believe, only be achieved by legislation which expresses the democratic will that so fundamental a change should be made in our law, and can, if enacted, ensure that such legalised killing can only be carried out subject to appropriate supervision and control. It is true that the drawing of this distinction may lead to a charge of hypocrisy, because it can be asked why, if the doctor, by discontinuing treatment, is entitled in consequence to let his patient die, it should not be lawful to put him out of his misery straight away, in a more humane manner, by a lethal injection, rather than to let him linger on in pain until he dies. But the law does not feel able to authorise euthanasia, even in circumstances such as these, for, once euthanasia is recognised as lawful in these circumstances, it is difficult to see any logical basis for excluding it in others."

In *Bland* the House of Lords held that treatment, including the provision of nutrition and hydration to the patient by artificial means, could be withheld from a mentally incapacitated patient who had no hope of recovery when it was known that the patient would shortly thereafter die, provided that responsible and competent medical opinion was of the view that it would be in the patient's best interests not to prolong his life by continuing the treatment because such treatment would be futile and would not confer any benefit on him.

Private international law

63. International protection of adults

Schedule 3—

   (a) gives effect in England and Wales to the Convention on the International Protection of Adults signed at the Hague on 13th January 2000 (Cm. 5881) (in so far as this Act does not otherwise do so), and

   (b) makes related provision as to the private international law of England and Wales.

GENERAL NOTE

   Schedule 3 makes provision as to the private international law of England and Wales in relation to persons who cannot protect their interests. In particular, it gives effect in England and Wales to the Convention on the International Protection of Adults (Cm.5881) which was signed at the Hague on January 13, 2000. The text of the Convention is available at: www.hcch.net/e/conventions/menu35e.html. For the purposes of the Convention, England and Wales, Scotland and Northern Ireland are treated separately because they constitute separate jurisdictions. The provisions of Sch.3 are intended to be compatible with the provisions of Sch.3 to the Adults with Incapacity (Scotland) Act 2000 (asp 4) which provides for the private international law of Scotland in this field, and implemented the Convention in Scotland. The Explanatory Memorandum states at para.170:

   "Scotland is as yet, the only country to have ratified the Convention, which will enter into force only once it has been ratified by three states. However, Sch.3 provides private international law rules to govern jurisdictional issues between Scotland and England/Wales, irrespective of whether the Convention is in force."

   The aims of the Convention are set out in Art.1. They are to:

●   provide for the protection in international situations of adults who, by reason of impairment or insufficiency in their personal faculties, are not in a position to defend their interests

●   establish rules on jurisdiction, applicable law, international recognition and enforcement of protective measures which are to be respected by all Contracting States, and co-operation between Contracting States.

General

64. Interpretation

   (1) In this Act—

      "the 1985 Act" means the Enduring Powers of Attorney Act 1985 (c. 29),

      "advance decision" has the meaning given in section 24(1),

      "the court" means the Court of Protection established by section 45,

      "Court of Protection Rules" has the meaning given in section 51(1),

      "Court of Protection Visitor" has the meaning given in section 61,

      "deputy" has the meaning given in section 16(2)(b),

      "enactment" includes a provision of subordinate legislation (within the meaning of the Interpretation Act 1978 (c. 30)),

      "health record" has the meaning given in section 68 of the Data Protection Act 1998 (c. 29) (as read with section 69 of that Act),

      "the Human Rights Convention" has the same meaning as "the Convention" in the Human Rights Act 1998 (c. 42), "independent mental capacity advocate" has the meaning given in section 35(1),

"lasting power of attorney" has the meaning given in section 9,

"life-sustaining treatment" has the meaning given in section 4(10),

"local authority" means—

    (a) the council of a county in England in which there are no district councils,

    (b) the council of a district in England,

    (c) the council of a county or county borough in Wales,

    (d) the council of a London borough,

    (e) the Common Council of the City of London, or

    (f) the Council of the Isles of Scilly,

"Mental Health Act" means the Mental Health Act 1983 (c. 20),

"prescribed", in relation to regulations made under this Act, means prescribed by those regulations,

"property" includes any thing in action and any interest in real or personal property,

"public authority" has the same meaning as in the Human Rights Act 1998,

"Public Guardian" has the meaning given in section 57,

"purchaser" and "purchase" have the meaning given in section 205(1) of the Law of Property Act 1925 (c. 20),

"social services function" has the meaning given in section 1A of the Local Authority Social Services Act 1970 (c. 42),

"treatment" includes a diagnostic or other procedure,

"trust corporation" has the meaning given in section 68(1) of the Trustee Act 1925 (c. 19), and

"will" includes codicil.

(2) In this Act, references to making decisions, in relation to a donee of a lasting power of attorney or a deputy appointed by the court, include, where appropriate, acting on decisions made.

(3) In this Act, references to the bankruptcy of an individual include a case where a bankruptcy restrictions order under the Insolvency Act 1986 (c. 45) has effect in respect of him.

(4) "Bankruptcy restrictions order" includes an interim bankruptcy restrictions order.

GENERAL NOTE

Subsection (1)

  Treatment. The provision of nutrition and hydration to a patient which involves the application of a medical technique is "medical treatment" (*Airedale NHS Trust v Bland* [1993] 1 All E.R. 821, HL).

65. Rules, regulations and orders

(1) Any power to make rules, regulations or orders under this Act—

    (a) is exercisable by statutory instrument;

    (b) includes power to make supplementary, incidental, consequential, transitional or saving provision;

    (c) includes power to make different provision for different cases.

(2) Any statutory instrument containing rules, regulations or orders made by the Lord Chancellor or the Secretary of State under this Act, other than—

(a) regulations under section 34 (loss of capacity during research project),
(b) regulations under section 41 (adjusting role of independent mental capacity advocacy service),
(c) regulations under paragraph 32(1)(b) of Schedule 3 (private international law relating to the protection of adults),
(d) an order of the kind mentioned in section 67(6) (consequential amendments of primary legislation), or
(e) an order under section 68 (commencement),

is subject to annulment in pursuance of a resolution of either House of Parliament.

(3) A statutory instrument containing an Order in Council under paragraph 31 of Schedule 3 (provision to give further effect to Hague Convention) is subject to annulment in pursuance of a resolution of either House of Parliament.
(4) A statutory instrument containing regulations made by the Secretary of State under section 34 or 41 or by the Lord Chancellor under paragraph 32(1)(b) of Schedule 3 may not be made unless a draft has been laid before and approved by resolution of each House of Parliament.

66. Existing receivers and enduring powers of attorney etc

(1) The following provisions cease to have effect—
 (a) Part 7 of the Mental Health Act,
 (b) the Enduring Powers of Attorney Act 1985 (c. 29).
(2) No enduring power of attorney within the meaning of the 1985 Act is to be created after the commencement of subsection (1)(b).
(3) Schedule 4 has effect in place of the 1985 Act in relation to any enduring power of attorney created before the commencement of subsection (1)(b).
(4) Schedule 5 contains transitional provisions and savings in relation to Part 7 of the Mental Health Act and the 1985 Act.

GENERAL NOTE

This section repeals Pt VII of the Mental Health Act 1983 and the whole of the Enduring Powers of Attorney Act 1985, but provides through transitional provisions contained in Schs 4 and 5 that those with valid powers as attorneys under the 1985 Act or receivers appointed under the 1983 Act do not lose their powers on the implementation of the repeals. It will no longer be possible to create an enduring power of attorney once the repeal of the 1985 Act has taken effect

67. Minor and consequential amendments and repeals

(1) Schedule 6 contains minor and consequential amendments.
(2) Schedule 7 contains repeals.
(3) The Lord Chancellor may by order make supplementary, incidental, consequential, transitional or saving provision for the purposes of, in consequence of, or for giving full effect to a provision of this Act.
(4) An order under subsection (3) may, in particular—
 (a) provide for a provision of this Act which comes into force before another provision of this Act has come into force to have effect, until the other provision has come into force, with specified modifications;
 (b) amend, repeal or revoke an enactment, other than one contained in an Act or Measure passed in a Session after the one in which this Act is passed.

(5) The amendments that may be made under subsection (4)(b) are in addition to those made by or under any other provision of this Act.

(6) An order under subsection (3) which amends or repeals a provision of an Act or Measure may not be made unless a draft has been laid before and approved by resolution of each House of Parliament.

68. Commencement and extent

(1) This Act, other than sections 30 to 41, comes into force in accordance with provision made by order by the Lord Chancellor.

(2) Sections 30 to 41 come into force in accordance with provision made by order by—
   (a) the Secretary of State, in relation to England, and
   (b) the National Assembly for Wales, in relation to Wales.

(3) An order under this section may appoint different days for different provisions and different purposes.

(4) Subject to subsections (5) and (6), this Act extends to England and Wales only.

(5) The following provisions extend to the United Kingdom—
   (a) paragraph 16(1) of Schedule 1 (evidence of instruments and of registration of lasting powers of attorney),
   (b) paragraph 15(3) of Schedule 4 (evidence of instruments and of registration of enduring powers of attorney).

(6) Subject to any provision made in Schedule 6, the amendments and repeals made by Schedules 6 and 7 have the same extent as the enactments to which they relate.

69. Short title

This Act may be cited as the Mental Capacity Act 2005.

SCHEDULES

SCHEDULE 1 - Section 9

LASTING POWERS OF ATTORNEY: FORMALITIES

PART I

MAKING INSTRUMENTS

1. General requirements as to making instruments

(1) An instrument is not made in accordance with this Schedule unless—
   (a) it is in the prescribed form,
   (b) it complies with paragraph 2, and
   (c) any prescribed requirements in connection with its execution are satisfied.

(2) Regulations may make different provision according to whether—
   (a) the instrument relates to personal welfare or to property and affairs (or to both);
   (b) only one or more than one donee is to be appointed (and if more than one, whether jointly or jointly and severally).

(3) In this Schedule—
   (a) "prescribed" means prescribed by regulations, and

(b) "regulations" means regulations made for the purposes of this Schedule by the Lord Chancellor.

2. Requirements as to content of instruments

(1) The instrument must include—

    (a) the prescribed information about the purpose of the instrument and the effect of a lasting power of attorney,

    (b) a statement by the donor to the effect that he—

        (i) has read the prescribed information or a prescribed part of it (or has had it read to him), and

        (ii) intends the authority conferred under the instrument to include authority to make decisions on his behalf in circumstances where he no longer has capacity,

    (c) a statement by the donor—

        (i) naming a person or persons whom the donor wishes to be notified of any application for the registration of the instrument, or

        (ii) stating that there are no persons whom he wishes to be notified of any such application,

    (d) a statement by the donee (or, if more than one, each of them) to the effect that he—

        (i) has read the prescribed information or a prescribed part of it (or has had it read to him), and

        (ii) understands the duties imposed on a donee of a lasting power of attorney under sections 1 (the principles) and 4 (best interests), and

    (e) a certificate by a person of a prescribed description that, in his opinion, at the time when the donor executes the instrument—

        (i) the donor understands the purpose of the instrument and the scope of the authority conferred under it,

        (ii) no fraud or undue pressure is being used to induce the donor to create a lasting power of attorney, and

        (iii) there is nothing else which would prevent a lasting power of attorney from being created by the instrument.

(2) Regulations may—

    (a) prescribe a maximum number of named persons;

    (b) provide that, where the instrument includes a statement under sub-paragraph (1)(c)(ii), two persons of a prescribed description must each give a certificate under sub-paragraph (1)(e).

(3) The persons who may be named persons do not include a person who is appointed as donee under the instrument.

(4) In this Schedule, "named person" means a person named under sub-paragraph (1)(c).

(5) A certificate under sub-paragraph (1)(e)—

    (a) must be made in the prescribed form, and

    (b) must include any prescribed information.

(6) The certificate may not be given by a person appointed as donee under the instrument.

3. Failure to comply with prescribed form

(1) If an instrument differs in an immaterial respect in form or mode of expression from the prescribed form, it is to be treated by the Public Guardian as sufficient in point of form and expression.

(2) The court may declare that an instrument which is not in the prescribed form is to be treated as if it were, if it is satisfied that the persons executing the instrument intended it to create a lasting power of attorney.

PART 2

REGISTRATION

4.

(1) An application to the Public Guardian for the registration of an instrument intended to create a lasting power of attorney—

    (a) must be made in the prescribed form, and

    (b) must include any prescribed information.

(2) The application may be made—

    (a) by the donor,

(b) by the donee or donees, or

(c) if the instrument appoints two or more donees to act jointly and severally in respect of any matter, by any of the donees.

(3) The application must be accompanied by—

(a) the instrument, and

(b) any fee provided for under section 58(4)(b).

(4) A person who, in an application for registration, makes a statement which he knows to be false in a material particular is guilty of an offence and is liable—

(a) on summary conviction, to imprisonment for a term not exceeding 12 months or a fine not exceeding the statutory maximum or both;

(b) on conviction on indictment, to imprisonment for a term not exceeding 2 years or a fine or both.

5. Subject to paragraphs 11 to 14, the Public Guardian must register the instrument as a lasting power of attorney at the end of the prescribed period.

6.

(1) A donor about to make an application under paragraph 4(2)(a) must notify any named persons that he is about to do so.

(2) The donee (or donees) about to make an application under paragraph 4(2)(b) or (c) must notify any named persons that he is (or they are) about to do so.

7. As soon as is practicable after receiving an application by the donor under paragraph 4(2)(a), the Public Guardian must notify the donee (or donees) that the application has been received.

8.

(1) As soon as is practicable after receiving an application by a donee (or donees) under paragraph 4(2)(b), the Public Guardian must notify the donor that the application has been received.

(2) As soon as is practicable after receiving an application by a donee under paragraph 4(2)(c), the Public Guardian must notify—

(a) the donor, and

(b) the donee or donees who did not join in making the application,

that the application has been received.

9.

(1) A notice under paragraph 6 must be made in the prescribed form.

(2) A notice under paragraph 6, 7 or 8 must include such information, if any, as may be prescribed.

10. The court may—

(a) on the application of the donor, dispense with the requirement to notify under paragraph 6(1), or

(b) on the application of the donee or donees concerned, dispense with the requirement to notify under paragraph 6(2),

if satisfied that no useful purpose would be served by giving the notice.

11.

(1) If it appears to the Public Guardian that an instrument accompanying an application under paragraph 4 is not made in accordance with this Schedule, he must not register the instrument unless the court directs him to do so.

(2) Sub-paragraph (3) applies if it appears to the Public Guardian that the instrument contains a provision which—

(a) would be ineffective as part of a lasting power of attorney, or

(b) would prevent the instrument from operating as a valid lasting power of attorney.

(3) The Public Guardian—

(a) must apply to the court for it to determine the matter under section 23(1), and

(b) pending the determination by the court, must not register the instrument.

(4) Sub-paragraph (5) applies if the court determines under section 23(1) (whether or not on an application by the Public Guardian) that the instrument contains a provision which—

(a) would be ineffective as part of a lasting power of attorney, or

(b) would prevent the instrument from operating as a valid lasting power of attorney.

(5) The court must—

(a) notify the Public Guardian that it has severed the provision, or

(b) direct him not to register the instrument.

(6) Where the court notifies the Public Guardian that it has severed a provision, he must register the instrument with a note to that effect attached to it.

12.

(1) Sub-paragraph (2) applies if it appears to the Public Guardian that—

    (a) there is a deputy appointed by the court for the donor, and

    (b) the powers conferred on the deputy would, if the instrument were registered, to any extent conflict with the powers conferred on the attorney.

(2) The Public Guardian must not register the instrument unless the court directs him to do so.

13.

(1) Sub-paragraph (2) applies if a donee or a named person—

    (a) receives a notice under paragraph 6, 7 or 8 of an application for the registration of an instrument, and

    (b) before the end of the prescribed period, gives notice to the Public Guardian of an objection to the registration on the ground that an event mentioned in section 13(3) or (6)(a) to (d) has occurred which has revoked the instrument.

(2) If the Public Guardian is satisfied that the ground for making the objection is established, he must not register the instrument unless the court, on the application of the person applying for the registration—

    (a) is satisfied that the ground is not established, and

    (b) directs the Public Guardian to register the instrument.

(3) Sub-paragraph (4) applies if a donee or a named person—

    (a) receives a notice under paragraph 6, 7 or 8 of an application for the registration of an instrument, and

    (b) before the end of the prescribed period—

        (i) makes an application to the court objecting to the registration on a prescribed ground, and

        (ii) notifies the Public Guardian of the application.

(4) The Public Guardian must not register the instrument unless the court directs him to do so.

14.

(1) This paragraph applies if the donor—

    (a) receives a notice under paragraph 8 of an application for the registration of an instrument, and

    (b) before the end of the prescribed period, gives notice to the Public Guardian of an objection to the registration.

(2) The Public Guardian must not register the instrument unless the court, on the application of the donee or, if more than one, any of them—

    (a) is satisfied that the donor lacks capacity to object to the registration, and

    (b) directs the Public Guardian to register the instrument.

15. Where an instrument is registered under this Schedule, the Public Guardian must give notice of the fact in the prescribed form to—

    (a) the donor, and

    (b) the donee or, if more than one, each of them.

16.

(1) A document purporting to be an office copy of an instrument registered under this Schedule is, in any part of the United Kingdom, evidence of—

    (a) the contents of the instrument, and

    (b) the fact that it has been registered.

(2) Sub-paragraph (1) is without prejudice to—

    (a) section 3 of the Powers of Attorney Act 1971 (c. 27) (proof by certified copy), and

    (b) any other method of proof authorised by law.

PART 3

CANCELLATION OF REGISTRATION AND NOTIFICATION OF SEVERANCE

17.

(1) The Public Guardian must cancel the registration of an instrument as a lasting power of attorney on being satisfied that the power has been revoked—

    (a) as a result of the donor's bankruptcy, or

    (b) on the occurrence of an event mentioned in section 13(6)(a) to (d).

(2) If the Public Guardian cancels the registration of an instrument he must notify—

(a) the donor, and

(b) the donee or, if more than one, each of them.

18. The court must direct the Public Guardian to cancel the registration of an instrument as a lasting power of attorney if it—

(a) determines under section 22(2)(a) that a requirement for creating the power was not met,

(b) determines under section 22(2)(b) that the power has been revoked or has otherwise come to an end, or

(c) revokes the power under section 22(4)(b) (fraud etc.).

19.

(1) Sub-paragraph (2) applies if the court determines under section 23(1) that a lasting power of attorney contains a provision which—

(a) is ineffective as part of a lasting power of attorney, or

(b) prevents the instrument from operating as a valid lasting power of attorney.

(2) The court must—

(a) notify the Public Guardian that it has severed the provision, or

(b) direct him to cancel the registration of the instrument as a lasting power of attorney.

20. On the cancellation of the registration of an instrument, the instrument and any office copies of it must be delivered up to the Public Guardian to be cancelled.

PART 4

RECORDS OF ALTERATIONS IN REGISTERED POWERS

21. Partial revocation or suspension of power as a result of bankruptcy

If in the case of a registered instrument it appears to the Public Guardian that under section 13 a lasting power of attorney is revoked, or suspended, in relation to the donor's property and affairs (but not in relation to other matters), the Public Guardian must attach to the instrument a note to that effect.

22. Termination of appointment of donee which does not revoke power

If in the case of a registered instrument it appears to the Public Guardian that an event has occurred—

(a) which has terminated the appointment of the donee, but

(b) which has not revoked the instrument,

the Public Guardian must attach to the instrument a note to that effect.

23. Replacement of donee

If in the case of a registered instrument it appears to the Public Guardian that the donee has been replaced under the terms of the instrument the Public Guardian must attach to the instrument a note to that effect.

24. Severance of ineffective provisions

If in the case of a registered instrument the court notifies the Public Guardian under paragraph 19(2)(a) that it has severed a provision of the instrument, the Public Guardian must attach to it a note to that effect.

25. Notification of alterations

If the Public Guardian attaches a note to an instrument under paragraph 21, 22, 23 or 24 he must give notice of the note to the donee or donees of the power (or, as the case may be, to the other donee or donees of the power).

DEFINITIONS

"lasting power of attorney": s.64(1)

"Public Guardian": s.64(1)

"the court": s.64(1)

"deputy": s.64(1)

"bankruptcy": s.64(3)

GENERAL NOTE

This Schedule sets out the requirements with regard to the formalities of a LPA. A LPA is not created unless it is made and registered in accordance with the provisions s.9(2).

In summary, the requirements are:

Making instruments

● The LPA must be in the prescribed form.
● The form must contain statements by both the donor and donee to the effect that they have read (or in the case of the donor, had read to them) prescribed information.
● The LPA must include the names of any persons (a "named person"), not being a donee, whom the donor wishes to be notified of any application to register the LPA or a statement that there are no such persons.
● The form must include a certificate by a person of a prescribed description that, in his or her opinion, at the time when the donor executes the instrument the donor understands the purpose of the instrument and the scope of the authority conferred, that no fraud or undue pressure is being used to induce the donor to create a LPA, and that there is nothing else that would prevent a LPA being created.
● The Public Guardian may treat a LPA differing in an immaterial respect from the prescribed form as sufficient to create a LPA.
● The Court of Protection has the power to declare that an instrument not in the prescribed form is to be treated as if it were.

Registration

● The powers given in a LPA to the donee cannot be exercised until the document has been registered with the Public Guardian.
● The application, which must be in the prescribed form, can be made by the donor or donee.
● The named person must be notified of the pending registration by the donor or donee.
● The Public Guardian must notify the applicant that the application has been received unless the court has dispensed with this requirement.
● The donee or the named person may object to the LPA within a prescribed period.
● The objection is made to the either the Public Guardian or the court, depending upon the nature of the objection.
● If the LPA is registered, the Public Guardian must notify the donor and donee.

Cancellation of registration

● The Public Guardian will cancel the LPA if satisfied that the power has been revoked on the basis of the donor's bankruptcy, the donee disclaiming the appointment, the death or bankruptcy of the donee, the dissolution or annulment of a marriage or civil partnership between the donor and donee, and the lack of capacity of the donee.
● The court must direct the Public Guardian to cancel the registration of a LPA if the court decides that a requirement for creating the LPA was not met, decides that the LPA has been revoked or otherwise come to an end, or it revokes the power on fraud or undue pressure grounds.
● On cancellation the Public Guardian will notify both the donor and donee.

Records of alterations in registered powers

● The Public Guardian must attach a note to the LPA in the circumstances set out in paras 21-24.
● The Public Guardian must give the donor and donee notice of any notes attached.

Paragraph 2(1) (e)

"The relevant person would interview the donor without the presence of the proposed [donee] and immediately before the signing of the LPA", *per* the Parliamentary Under-Secretary of State, St.Comm.A, para.142.

SCHEDULE 2 - **Section 18(4)**

PROPERTY AND AFFAIRS: SUPPLEMENTARY PROVISIONS

1. Paragraphs 2 to 4 apply in relation to the execution of a will, by virtue of section 18, on behalf of P.

2. The will may make any provision (whether by disposing of property or exercising a power or otherwise) which could be made by a will executed by P if he had capacity to make it.

3.

(1) Sub-paragraph (2) applies if under section 16 the court makes an order or gives directions requiring or authorising a person (the authorised person) to execute a will on behalf of P.

(2) Any will executed in pursuance of the order or direction—

  (a) must state that it is signed by P acting by the authorised person,

  (b) must be signed by the authorised person with the name of P and his own name, in the presence of two or more witnesses present at the same time,

  (c) must be attested and subscribed by those witnesses in the presence of the authorised person, and

  (d) must be sealed with the official seal of the court.

4.

(1) This paragraph applies where a will is executed in accordance with paragraph 3.

(2) The Wills Act 1837 (c. 26) has effect in relation to the will as if it were signed by P by his own hand, except that—

  (a) section 9 of the 1837 Act (requirements as to signing and attestation) does not apply, and

  (b) in the subsequent provisions of the 1837 Act any reference to execution in the manner required by the previous provisions is to be read as a reference to execution in accordance with paragraph 3.

(3) The will has the same effect for all purposes as if—

  (a) P had had the capacity to make a valid will, and

  (b) the will had been executed by him in the manner required by the 1837 Act.

(4) But sub-paragraph (3) does not have effect in relation to the will—

  (a) in so far as it disposes of immovable property outside England and Wales, or

  (b) in so far as it relates to any other property or matter if, when the will is executed—

    (i) P is domiciled outside England and Wales, and

    (ii) the condition in sub-paragraph (5) is met.

(5) The condition is that, under the law of P's domicile, any question of his testamentary capacity would fall to be determined in accordance with the law of a place outside England and Wales.

5.

(1) If provision is made by virtue of section 18 for—

  (a) the settlement of any property of P, or

  (b) the exercise of a power vested in him of appointing trustees or retiring from a trust,

the court may also make as respects the property settled or the trust property such consequential vesting or other orders as the case may require.

(2) The power under sub-paragraph (1) includes, in the case of the exercise of such a power, any order which could have been made in such a case under Part 4 of the Trustee Act 1925 (c. 19).

6.

(1) If a settlement has been made by virtue of section 18, the court may by order vary or revoke the settlement if—

  (a) the settlement makes provision for its variation or revocation,

  (b) the court is satisfied that a material fact was not disclosed when the settlement was made, or

  (c) the court is satisfied that there has been a substantial change of circumstances.

(2) Any such order may give such consequential directions as the court thinks fit.

7.

(1) Sub-paragraph (2) applies if the court is satisfied—

  (a) that under the law prevailing in a place outside England and Wales a person (M) has been appointed to exercise powers in respect of the property or affairs of P on the ground (however formulated) that P lacks capacity to make decisions with respect to the management and administration of his property and affairs, and

  (b) that, having regard to the nature of the appointment and to the circumstances of the case, it is expedient that the court should exercise its powers under this paragraph.

(2) The court may direct—

  (a) any stocks standing in the name of P, or

  (b) the right to receive dividends from the stocks,

to be transferred into M's name or otherwise dealt with as required by M, and may give such directions as the court thinks fit for dealing with accrued dividends from the stocks.

(3) "Stocks" includes—

  (a) shares, and

(b) any funds, annuity or security transferable in the books kept by any body corporate or unincorporated company or society or by an instrument of transfer either alone or accompanied by other formalities,

and "dividends" is to be construed accordingly.

8.

(1) Sub-paragraphs (2) and (3) apply if—
    (a) P's property has been disposed of by virtue of section 18,
    (b) under P's will or intestacy, or by a gift perfected or nomination taking effect on his death, any other person would have taken an interest in the property but for the disposal, and
    (c) on P's death, any property belonging to P's estate represents the property disposed of.

(2) The person takes the same interest, if and so far as circumstances allow, in the property representing the property disposed of.

(3) If the property disposed of was real property, any property representing it is to be treated, so long as it remains part of P's estate, as if it were real property.

(4) The court may direct that, on a disposal of P's property—
    (a) which is made by virtue of section 18, and
    (b) which would apart from this paragraph result in the conversion of personal property into real property,

property representing the property disposed of is to be treated, so long as it remains P's property or forms part of P's estate, as if it were personal property.

(5) References in sub-paragraphs (1) to (4) to the disposal of property are to—
    (a) the sale, exchange, charging of or other dealing (otherwise than by will) with property other than money;
    (b) the removal of property from one place to another;
    (c) the application of money in acquiring property;
    (d) the transfer of money from one account to another;

and references to property representing property disposed of are to be construed accordingly and as including the result of successive disposals.

(6) The court may give such directions as appear to it necessary or expedient for the purpose of facilitating the operation of sub-paragraphs (1) to (3), including the carrying of money to a separate account and the transfer of property other than money.

9.

(1) Sub-paragraph (2) applies if the court has ordered or directed the expenditure of money—
    (a) for carrying out permanent improvements on any of P's property, or
    (b) otherwise for the permanent benefit of any of P's property.

(2) The court may order that—
    (a) the whole of the money expended or to be expended, or
    (b) any part of it,

is to be a charge on the property either without interest or with interest at a specified rate.

(3) An order under sub-paragraph (2) may provide for excluding or restricting the operation of paragraph 8(1) to (3).

(4) A charge under sub-paragraph (2) may be made in favour of such person as may be just and, in particular, where the money charged is paid out of P's general estate, may be made in favour of a person as trustee for P.

(5) No charge under sub-paragraph (2) may confer any right of sale or foreclosure during P's lifetime.

10.

(1) Any functions which P has as patron of a benefice may be discharged only by a person (R) appointed by the court.

(2) R must be an individual capable of appointment under section 8(1)(b) of the 1986 Measure (which provides for an individual able to make a declaration of communicant status, a clerk in Holy Orders, etc. to be appointed to discharge a registered patron's functions).

(3) The 1986 Measure applies to R as it applies to an individual appointed by the registered patron of the benefice under section 8(1)(b) or (3) of that Measure to discharge his functions as patron.

(4) "The 1986 Measure" means the Patronage (Benefices) Measure 1986 (No. 3).

DEFINITIONS
"will": s.64(1) "property": s.64(1)
"the court": s.64(1)

GENERAL NOTE

This Schedule contains detailed provisions relating to the court's powers in relation to property and affairs, in particular the making of wills and settlements.

Paragraph 3(2)(b)

As the authorised person is not a witness, he or she would not be precluded from benefiting under s.15 of the Wills Act 1837 (c.26).

Paragraph 3(2)(d)

"The benefit of a court seal is that it provides authentication as to the originality of a document. It helps prevent fraud, and it reassures the financial institutions that they are dealing with the right person", *per* the Parliamentary Under-Secretary of State, St.Comm.A, para.188.

Paragraph 4(3)

A statutory will has the same effect as a will made by a competent testator.

Paragraph 7

The purpose of this provision is to enable the court to recognise judicially the operation of foreign law, whereby some form of curatorship has been constituted for a patient, without itself having to go into questions of mental status and capacity.

Paragraph 8

This ensures that those who have an interest in property that has been disposed of by virtue this Act should preserve that interest.

Paragraph 10

A "benefice" is a freehold office of the Church of England, such as the vicar of a parish. The patron of a benefice has the right to appoint a cleric to that office. The representative of P "will have to be an individual who is a communicant of the Church of England or a church in communion with it or a clerk in holy orders. The representative will fulfil the patron's role not only in presenting a priest to a vacant benefice under the Patronage Benefices Measure 1986 (m.3) but also in performing the other functions of a patron such as acting as a consultee when there is a proposal to suspend presentation under s.67 of the Pastoral Measure 1983 (m.1). In discharging his or her functions the representative will be subject to the provisions of the 1986 Measure in the same way that a registered patron would be", *per* the Under-Secretary of State (*Hansard*, HL Vol.670, col.1496).

SCHEDULE 3 - **Section 63**

INTERNATIONAL PROTECTION OF ADULTS

PART I

PRELIMINARY

1. Introduction

This Part applies for the purposes of this Schedule.

2. The Convention

(1) "Convention" means the Convention referred to in section 63.

(2) "Convention country" means a country in which the Convention is in force.

(3) A reference to an Article or Chapter is to an Article or Chapter of the Convention.

(4) An expression which appears in this Schedule and in the Convention is to be construed in accordance with the Convention.

3. Countries, territories and nationals

(1) "Country" includes a territory which has its own system of law.

(2) Where a country has more than one territory with its own system of law, a reference to the country, in relation to one of its nationals, is to the territory with which the national has the closer, or the closest, connection.

4. Adults with incapacity

"Adult" means a person who—

    (a) as a result of an impairment or insufficiency of his personal faculties, cannot protect his interests, and

    (b) has reached 16.

5. Protective measures

(1) "Protective measure" means a measure directed to the protection of the person or property of an adult; and it may deal in particular with any of the following—

    (a) the determination of incapacity and the institution of a protective regime,

    (b) placing the adult under the protection of an appropriate authority,

    (c) guardianship, curatorship or any corresponding system,

    (d) the designation and functions of a person having charge of the adult's person or property, or representing or otherwise helping him,

    (e) placing the adult in a place where protection can be provided,

    (f) administering, conserving or disposing of the adult's property,

    (g) authorising a specific intervention for the protection of the person or property of the adult.

(2) Where a measure of like effect to a protective measure has been taken in relation to a person before he reaches 16, this Schedule applies to the measure in so far as it has effect in relation to him once he has reached 16.

6. Central Authority

(1) Any function under the Convention of a Central Authority is exercisable in England and Wales by the Lord Chancellor.

(2) A communication may be sent to the Central Authority in relation to England and Wales by sending it to the Lord Chancellor.

PART 2

JURISDICTION OF COMPETENT AUTHORITY

7.

(1) The court may exercise its functions under this Act (in so far as it cannot otherwise do so) in relation to—

    (a) an adult habitually resident in England and Wales,

    (b) an adult's property in England and Wales,

    (c) an adult present in England and Wales or who has property there, if the matter is urgent, or

    (d) an adult present in England and Wales, if a protective measure which is temporary and limited in its effect to England and Wales is proposed in relation to him.

(2) An adult present in England and Wales is to be treated for the purposes of this paragraph as habitually resident there if—

    (a) his habitual residence cannot be ascertained,

    (b) he is a refugee, or

    (c) he has been displaced as a result of disturbance in the country of his habitual residence.

8.

(1) The court may also exercise its functions under this Act (in so far as it cannot otherwise do so) in relation to an adult if sub-paragraph (2) or (3) applies in relation to him.

(2) This sub-paragraph applies in relation to an adult if—

    (a) he is a British citizen,

    (b) he has a closer connection with England and Wales than with Scotland or Northern Ireland, and

    (c) Article 7 has, in relation to the matter concerned, been complied with.

(3) This sub-paragraph applies in relation to an adult if the Lord Chancellor, having consulted such persons as he considers appropriate, agrees to a request under Article 8 in relation to the adult.

9.

(1) This paragraph applies where jurisdiction is exercisable under this Schedule in connection with a matter which involves a Convention country other than England and Wales.

(2) Any Article on which the jurisdiction is based applies in relation to the matter in so far as it involves the other country (and the court must, accordingly, comply with any duty conferred on it as a result).

(3) Article 12 also applies, so far as its provisions allow, in relation to the matter in so far as it involves the other country.

10. A reference in this Schedule to the exercise of jurisdiction under this Schedule is to the exercise of functions under this Act as a result of this Part of this Schedule.

PART 3

APPLICABLE LAW

11. In exercising jurisdiction under this Schedule, the court may, if it thinks that the matter has a substantial connection with a country other than England and Wales, apply the law of that other country.

12. Where a protective measure is taken in one country but implemented in another, the conditions of implementation are governed by the law of the other country.

13.

(1) If the donor of a lasting power is habitually resident in England and Wales at the time of granting the power, the law applicable to the existence, extent, modification or extinction of the power is—

(a) the law of England and Wales, or

(b) if he specifies in writing the law of a connected country for the purpose, that law.

(2) If he is habitually resident in another country at that time, but England and Wales is a connected country, the law applicable in that respect is—

(a) the law of the other country, or

(b) if he specifies in writing the law of England and Wales for the purpose, that law.

(3) A country is connected, in relation to the donor, if it is a country—

(a) of which he is a national,

(b) in which he was habitually resident, or

(c) in which he has property.

(4) Where this paragraph applies as a result of sub-paragraph (3)(c), it applies only in relation to the property which the donor has in the connected country.

(5) The law applicable to the manner of the exercise of a lasting power is the law of the country where it is exercised.

(6) In this Part of this Schedule, "lasting power" means—

(a) a lasting power of attorney (see section 9),

(b) an enduring power of attorney within the meaning of Schedule 4, or

(c) any other power of like effect.

14.

(1) Where a lasting power is not exercised in a manner sufficient to guarantee the protection of the person or property of the donor, the court, in exercising jurisdiction under this Schedule, may disapply or modify the power.

(2) Where, in accordance with this Part of this Schedule, the law applicable to the power is, in one or more respects, that of a country other than England and Wales, the court must, so far as possible, have regard to the law of the other country in that respect (or those respects).

15. Regulations may provide for Schedule 1 (lasting powers of attorney: formalities) to apply with modifications in relation to a lasting power which comes within paragraph 13(6)(c) above.

16.

(1) This paragraph applies where a person (a representative) in purported exercise of an authority to act on behalf of an adult enters into a transaction with a third party.

(2) The validity of the transaction may not be questioned in proceedings, nor may the third party be held liable, merely because—

(a) where the representative and third party are in England and Wales when entering into the transaction, sub-paragraph (3) applies;

(b) where they are in another country at that time, sub-paragraph (4) applies.

(3) This sub-paragraph applies if—

(a) the law applicable to the authority in one or more respects is, as a result of this Schedule, the law of a country other than England and Wales, and

(b) the representative is not entitled to exercise the authority in that respect (or those respects) under the law of that other country.

(4) This sub-paragraph applies if—

(a) the law applicable to the authority in one or more respects is, as a result of this Part of this Schedule, the law of England and Wales, and

(b) the representative is not entitled to exercise the authority in that respect (or those respects) under that law.

(5) This paragraph does not apply if the third party knew or ought to have known that the applicable law was—

(a) in a case within sub-paragraph (3), the law of the other country;

(b) in a case within sub-paragraph (4), the law of England and Wales.

17. Where the court is entitled to exercise jurisdiction under this Schedule, the mandatory provisions of the law of England and Wales apply, regardless of any system of law which would otherwise apply in relation to the matter.

18. Nothing in this Part of this Schedule requires or enables the application in England and Wales of a provision of the law of another country if its application would be manifestly contrary to public policy.

PART 4

RECOGNITION AND ENFORCEMENT

19.

(1) A protective measure taken in relation to an adult under the law of a country other than England and Wales is to be recognised in England and Wales if it was taken on the ground that the adult is habitually resident in the other country.

(2) A protective measure taken in relation to an adult under the law of a Convention country other than England and Wales is to be recognised in England and Wales if it was taken on a ground mentioned in Chapter 2 (jurisdiction).

(3) But the court may disapply this paragraph in relation to a measure if it thinks that—

(a) the case in which the measure was taken was not urgent,

(b) the adult was not given an opportunity to be heard, and

(c) that omission amounted to a breach of natural justice.

(4) It may also disapply this paragraph in relation to a measure if it thinks that—

(a) recognition of the measure would be manifestly contrary to public policy,

(b) the measure would be inconsistent with a mandatory provision of the law of England and Wales, or

(c) the measure is inconsistent with one subsequently taken, or recognised, in England and Wales in relation to the adult.

(5) And the court may disapply this paragraph in relation to a measure taken under the law of a Convention country in a matter to which Article 33 applies, if the court thinks that that Article has not been complied with in connection with that matter.

20.

(1) An interested person may apply to the court for a declaration as to whether a protective measure taken under the law of a country other than England and Wales is to be recognised in England and Wales.

(2) No permission is required for an application to the court under this paragraph.

21. For the purposes of paragraphs 19 and 20, any finding of fact relied on when the measure was taken is conclusive.

22.

(1) An interested person may apply to the court for a declaration as to whether a protective measure taken under the law of, and enforceable in, a country other than England and Wales is enforceable, or to be registered, in England and Wales in accordance with Court of Protection Rules.

(2) The court must make the declaration if—

(a) the measure comes within sub-paragraph (1) or (2) of paragraph 19, and

(b) the paragraph is not disapplied in relation to it as a result of sub-paragraph (3), (4) or (5).

(3) A measure to which a declaration under this paragraph relates is enforceable in England and Wales as if it were a measure of like effect taken by the court.

23.

(1) This paragraph applies where—

    (a) provision giving effect to, or otherwise deriving from, the Convention in a country other than England and Wales applies in relation to a person who has not reached 16, and

    (b) a measure is taken in relation to that person in reliance on that provision.

(2) This Part of this Schedule applies in relation to that measure as it applies in relation to a protective measure taken in relation to an adult under the law of a Convention country other than England and Wales.

24. The court may not review the merits of a measure taken outside England and Wales except to establish whether the measure complies with this Schedule in so far as it is, as a result of this Schedule, required to do so.

25. Court of Protection Rules may make provision about an application under paragraph 20 or 22.

PART 5

CO-OPERATION

26.

(1) This paragraph applies where a public authority proposes to place an adult in an establishment in a Convention country other than England and Wales.

(2) The public authority must consult an appropriate authority in that other country about the proposed placement and, for that purpose, must send it—

    (a) a report on the adult, and

    (b) a statement of its reasons for the proposed placement.

(3) If the appropriate authority in the other country opposes the proposed placement within a reasonable time, the public authority may not proceed with it.

27. A proposal received by a public authority under Article 33 in relation to an adult is to proceed unless the authority opposes it within a reasonable time.

28.

(1) This paragraph applies if a public authority is told that an adult—

    (a) who is in serious danger, and

    (b) in relation to whom the public authority has taken, or is considering taking, protective measures,

is, or has become resident, in a Convention country other than England and Wales.

(2) The public authority must tell an appropriate authority in that other country about—

    (a) the danger, and

    (b) the measures taken or under consideration.

29. A public authority may not request from, or send to, an appropriate authority in a Convention country information in accordance with Chapter 5 (co-operation) in relation to an adult if it thinks that doing so—

    (a) would be likely to endanger the adult or his property, or

    (b) would amount to a serious threat to the liberty or life of a member of the adult's family.

PART 6

GENERAL

30. A certificate given under Article 38 by an authority in a Convention country other than England and Wales is, unless the contrary is shown, proof of the matters contained in it.

31. Her Majesty may by Order in Council confer on the Lord Chancellor, the court or another public authority functions for enabling the Convention to be given effect in England and Wales.

32.

(1) Regulations may make provision—

    (a) giving further effect to the Convention, or

    (b) otherwise about the private international law of England and Wales in relation to the protection of adults.

(2) The regulations may—

    (a) confer functions on the court or another public authority;

    (b) amend this Schedule;

    (c) provide for this Schedule to apply with specified modifications;

    (d) make provision about countries other than Convention countries.

33. Nothing in this Schedule applies, and no provision made under paragraph 32 is to apply, to any matter to which the Convention, as a result of Article 4, does not apply.

34. A reference in this Schedule to regulations or an order (other than an Order in Council) is to regulations or an order made for the purposes of this Schedule by the Lord Chancellor.

35. The following provisions of this Schedule have effect only if the Convention is in force in accordance with Article 57—

    (a) paragraph 8,

    (b) paragraph 9,

    (c) paragraph 19(2) and (5),

    (d) Part 5,

    (e) paragraph 30.

DEFINITIONS

"property": s.64(1)

"the court": s.64(1)

"Court of Protection Rules": s.64(1)

GENERAL NOTE

See the notes to s.63. This Schedule is divided into six parts. Part 1 contains definitions and introductory provisions. Part 2 provides the grounds, based on Arts 5-11 of the Hague Convention on the International Protection of Adults, on which the Court of Protection will exercise its jurisdiction under this Act when dealing with cases with an international element. Part 3 makes provision as to the law of which country is to apply in various situations. It also provides protection for a third party who enters into a transaction with a representative on behalf of a person, where that representative was actually not entitled so to act under the law of a country other than England and Wales applicable by virtue of Pt 3. Part 4 provides for the recognition and enforcement of protective measures taken in other countries. Part 5 provides for co-operation between authorities in England and Wales and authorities in other Convention countries. Part 6 includes powers to make further provision as to private international by Order in Council and regulations and provisions on commencement.

SCHEDULE 4 - Section 66(3)

PROVISIONS APPLYING TO EXISTING ENDURING POWERS OF ATTORNEY

PART I

ENDURING POWERS OF ATTORNEY

1. Enduring power of attorney to survive mental incapacity of donor

(1) Where an individual has created a power of attorney which is an enduring power within the meaning of this Schedule—

    (a) the power is not revoked by any subsequent mental incapacity of his,

(b) upon such incapacity supervening, the donee of the power may not do anything under the authority of the power except as provided by sub-paragraph (2) unless or until the instrument creating the power is registered under paragraph 13, and

(c) if and so long as paragraph (b) operates to suspend the donee's authority to act under the power, section 5 of the Powers of Attorney Act 1971 (c. 27) (protection of donee and third persons), so far as applicable, applies as if the power had been revoked by the donor's mental incapacity,

and, accordingly, section 1 of this Act does not apply.

(2) Despite sub-paragraph (1)(b), where the attorney has made an application for registration of the instrument then, until it is registered, the attorney may take action under the power—

(a) to maintain the donor or prevent loss to his estate, or

(b) to maintain himself or other persons in so far as paragraph 3(2) permits him to do so.

(3) Where the attorney purports to act as provided by sub-paragraph (2) then, in favour of a person who deals with him without knowledge that the attorney is acting otherwise than in accordance with sub-paragraph (2)(a) or (b), the transaction between them is as valid as if the attorney were acting in accordance with sub-paragraph (2)(a) or (b).

2. Characteristics of an enduring power of attorney

(1) Subject to sub-paragraphs (5) and (6) and paragraph 20, a power of attorney is an enduring power within the meaning of this Schedule if the instrument which creates the power—

(a) is in the prescribed form,

(b) was executed in the prescribed manner by the donor and the attorney, and

(c) incorporated at the time of execution by the donor the prescribed explanatory information.

(2) In this paragraph, "prescribed" means prescribed by such of the following regulations as applied when the instrument was executed—

(a) the Enduring Powers of Attorney (Prescribed Form) Regulations 1986 (S.I. 1986/126),

(b) the Enduring Powers of Attorney (Prescribed Form) Regulations 1987 (S.I. 1987/1612),

(c) the Enduring Powers of Attorney (Prescribed Form) Regulations 1990 (S.I. 1990/1376),

(d) the Enduring Powers of Attorney (Welsh Language Prescribed Form) Regulations 2000 (S.I. 2000/289).

(3) An instrument in the prescribed form purporting to have been executed in the prescribed manner is to be taken, in the absence of evidence to the contrary, to be a document which incorporated at the time of execution by the donor the prescribed explanatory information.

(4) If an instrument differs in an immaterial respect in form or mode of expression from the prescribed form it is to be treated as sufficient in point of form and expression.

(5) A power of attorney cannot be an enduring power unless, when he executes the instrument creating it, the attorney is—

(a) an individual who has reached 18 and is not bankrupt, or

(b) a trust corporation.

(6) A power of attorney which gives the attorney a right to appoint a substitute or successor cannot be an enduring power.

(7) An enduring power is revoked by the bankruptcy of the donor or attorney.

(8) But where the donor or attorney is bankrupt merely because an interim bankruptcy restrictions order has effect in respect of him, the power is suspended for so long as the order has effect.

(9) An enduring power is revoked if the court—

(a) exercises a power under sections 16 to 20 in relation to the donor, and

(b) directs that the enduring power is to be revoked.

(10) No disclaimer of an enduring power, whether by deed or otherwise, is valid unless and until the attorney gives notice of it to the donor or, where paragraph 4(6) or 15(1) applies, to the Public Guardian.

3. Scope of authority etc. of attorney under enduring power

(1) If the instrument which creates an enduring power of attorney is expressed to confer general authority on the attorney, the instrument operates to confer, subject to—

(a) the restriction imposed by sub-paragraph (3), and

(b) any conditions or restrictions contained in the instrument,

authority to do on behalf of the donor anything which the donor could lawfully do by an attorney at the time when the donor executed the instrument.

(2) Subject to any conditions or restrictions contained in the instrument, an attorney under an enduring power, whether general or limited, may (without obtaining any consent) act under the power so as to benefit himself or other persons than the donor to the following extent but no further—

(a) he may so act in relation to himself or in relation to any other person if the donor might be expected to provide for his or that person's needs respectively, and

(b) he may do whatever the donor might be expected to do to meet those needs.

(3) Without prejudice to sub-paragraph (2) but subject to any conditions or restrictions contained in the instrument, an attorney under an enduring power, whether general or limited, may (without obtaining any consent) dispose of the property of the donor by way of gift to the following extent but no further—

(a) he may make gifts of a seasonal nature or at a time, or on an anniversary, of a birth, a marriage or the formation of a civil partnership, to persons (including himself) who are related to or connected with the donor, and

(b) he may make gifts to any charity to whom the donor made or might be expected to make gifts,

provided that the value of each such gift is not unreasonable having regard to all the circumstances and in particular the size of the donor's estate.

PART 2

ACTION ON ACTUAL OR IMPENDING INCAPACITY OF DONOR

4. Duties of attorney in event of actual or impending incapacity of donor

(1) Sub-paragraphs (2) to (6) apply if the attorney under an enduring power has reason to believe that the donor is or is becoming mentally incapable.

(2) The attorney must, as soon as practicable, make an application to the Public Guardian for the registration of the instrument creating the power.

(3) Before making an application for registration the attorney must comply with the provisions as to notice set out in Part 3 of this Schedule.

(4) An application for registration—

(a) must be made in the prescribed form, and

(b) must contain such statements as may be prescribed.

(5) The attorney—

(a) may, before making an application for the registration of the instrument, refer to the court for its determination any question as to the validity of the power, and

(b) must comply with any direction given to him by the court on that determination.

(6) No disclaimer of the power is valid unless and until the attorney gives notice of it to the Public Guardian; and the Public Guardian must notify the donor if he receives a notice under this sub-paragraph.

(7) A person who, in an application for registration, makes a statement which he knows to be false in a material particular is guilty of an offence and is liable—

(a) on summary conviction, to imprisonment for a term not exceeding 12 months or a fine not exceeding the statutory maximum or both;

(b) on conviction on indictment, to imprisonment for a term not exceeding 2 years or a fine or both.

(8) In this paragraph, "prescribed" means prescribed by regulations made for the purposes of this Schedule by the Lord Chancellor.

PART 3

NOTIFICATION PRIOR TO REGISTRATION

5. Subject to paragraph 7, before making an application for registration the attorney must give notice of his intention to do so to all those persons (if any) who are entitled to receive notice by virtue of paragraph 6.

6.

(1) Subject to sub-paragraphs (2) to (4), persons of the following classes (relatives) are entitled to receive notice under paragraph 5—

(a) the donor's spouse or civil partner,

(b) the donor's children,

(c) the donor's parents,

(d) the donor's brothers and sisters, whether of the whole or half blood,

(e) the widow, widower or surviving civil partner of a child of the donor,

(f) the donor's grandchildren,

(g) the children of the donor's brothers and sisters of the whole blood,

(h) the children of the donor's brothers and sisters of the half blood,

(i) the donor's uncles and aunts of the whole blood,

(j) the children of the donor's uncles and aunts of the whole blood.

(2) A person is not entitled to receive notice under paragraph 5 if—

(a) his name or address is not known to the attorney and cannot be reasonably ascertained by him, or

(b) the attorney has reason to believe that he has not reached 18 or is mentally incapable.

(3) Except where sub-paragraph (4) applies—

(a) no more than 3 persons are entitled to receive notice under paragraph 5, and

(b) in determining the persons who are so entitled, persons falling within the class in sub-paragraph (1)(a) are to be preferred to persons falling within the class in sub-paragraph (1)(b), those falling within the class in sub-paragraph (1)(b) are to be preferred to those falling within the class in sub-paragraph (1)(c), and so on.

(4) Despite the limit of 3 specified in sub-paragraph (3), where—

(a) there is more than one person falling within any of classes (a) to (j) of sub-paragraph (1), and

(b) at least one of those persons would be entitled to receive notice under paragraph 5,

then, subject to sub-paragraph (2), all the persons falling within that class are entitled to receive notice under paragraph 5.

7.

(1) An attorney is not required to give notice under paragraph 5—

(a) to himself, or

(b) to any other attorney under the power who is joining in making the application,

even though he or, as the case may be, the other attorney is entitled to receive notice by virtue of paragraph 6.

(2) In the case of any person who is entitled to receive notice by virtue of paragraph 6, the attorney, before applying for registration, may make an application to the court to be dispensed from the requirement to give him notice; and the court must grant the application if it is satisfied—

(a) that it would be undesirable or impracticable for the attorney to give him notice, or

(b) that no useful purpose is likely to be served by giving him notice.

8.

(1) Subject to sub-paragraph (2), before making an application for registration the attorney must give notice of his intention to do so to the donor.

(2) Paragraph 7(2) applies in relation to the donor as it applies in relation to a person who is entitled to receive notice under paragraph 5.

9. A notice to relatives under this Part of this Schedule must—

(a) be in the prescribed form,

(b) state that the attorney proposes to make an application to the Public Guardian for the registration of the instrument creating the enduring power in question,

(c) inform the person to whom it is given of his right to object to the registration under paragraph 13(4), and

(d) specify, as the grounds on which an objection to registration may be made, the grounds set out in paragraph 13(9).

10. A notice to the donor under this Part of this Schedule—

(a) must be in the prescribed form,

(b) must contain the statement mentioned in paragraph 9(b), and

(c) must inform the donor that, while the instrument remains registered, any revocation of the power by him will be ineffective unless and until the revocation is confirmed by the court.

11.

(1) Subject to sub-paragraph (2), before making an application for registration an attorney under a joint and several power must give notice of his intention to do so to any other attorney under the power who is not joining in making the application; and paragraphs 7(2) and 9 apply in relation to attorneys entitled to receive notice by virtue of this paragraph as they apply in relation to persons entitled to receive notice by virtue of paragraph 6.

(2) An attorney is not entitled to receive notice by virtue of this paragraph if—

(a) his address is not known to the applying attorney and cannot reasonably be ascertained by him, or

(b) the applying attorney has reason to believe that he has not reached 18 or is mentally incapable.

12. Despite section 7 of the Interpretation Act 1978 (c. 30) (construction of references to service by post), for the purposes of this Part of this Schedule a notice given by post is to be regarded as given on the date on which it was posted.

PART 4

REGISTRATION

13. Registration of instrument creating power

(1) If an application is made in accordance with paragraph 4(3) and (4) the Public Guardian must, subject to the provisions of this paragraph, register the instrument to which the application relates.

(2) If it appears to the Public Guardian that—
   (a) there is a deputy appointed for the donor of the power created by the instrument, and
   (b) the powers conferred on the deputy would, if the instrument were registered, to any extent conflict with the powers conferred on the attorney,
the Public Guardian must not register the instrument except in accordance with the court's directions.

(3) The court may, on the application of the attorney, direct the Public Guardian to register an instrument even though notice has not been given as required by paragraph 4(3) and Part 3 of this Schedule to a person entitled to receive it, if the court is satisfied—
   (a) that it was undesirable or impracticable for the attorney to give notice to that person, or
   (b) that no useful purpose is likely to be served by giving him notice.

(4) Sub-paragraph (5) applies if, before the end of the period of 5 weeks beginning with the date (or the latest date) on which the attorney gave notice under paragraph 5 of an application for registration, the Public Guardian receives a valid notice of objection to the registration from a person entitled to notice of the application.

(5) The Public Guardian must not register the instrument except in accordance with the court's directions.

(6) Sub-paragraph (7) applies if, in the case of an application for registration—
   (a) it appears from the application that there is no one to whom notice has been given under paragraph 5, or
   (b) the Public Guardian has reason to believe that appropriate inquiries might bring to light evidence on which he could be satisfied that one of the grounds of objection set out in sub-paragraph (9) was established.

(7) The Public Guardian—
   (a) must not register the instrument, and
   (b) must undertake such inquiries as he thinks appropriate in all the circumstances.

(8) If, having complied with sub-paragraph (7)(b), the Public Guardian is satisfied that one of the grounds of objection set out in sub-paragraph (9) is established—
   (a) the attorney may apply to the court for directions, and
   (b) the Public Guardian must not register the instrument except in accordance with the court's directions.

(9) A notice of objection under this paragraph is valid if made on one or more of the following grounds—
   (a) that the power purported to have been created by the instrument was not valid as an enduring power of attorney,
   (b) that the power created by the instrument no longer subsists,
   (c) that the application is premature because the donor is not yet becoming mentally incapable,
   (d) that fraud or undue pressure was used to induce the donor to create the power,
   (e) that, having regard to all the circumstances and in particular the attorney's relationship to or connection with the donor, the attorney is unsuitable to be the donor's attorney.

(10) If any of those grounds is established to the satisfaction of the court it must direct the Public Guardian not to register the instrument, but if not so satisfied it must direct its registration.

(11) If the court directs the Public Guardian not to register an instrument because it is satisfied that the ground in sub-paragraph (9)(d) or (e) is established, it must by order revoke the power created by the instrument.

(12) If the court directs the Public Guardian not to register an instrument because it is satisfied that any ground in sub-paragraph (9) except that in paragraph (c) is established, the instrument must be delivered up to be cancelled unless the court otherwise directs.

14. Register of enduring powers

The Public Guardian has the function of establishing and maintaining a register of enduring powers for the purposes of this Schedule.

PART 5

LEGAL POSITION AFTER REGISTRATION

15. Effect and proof of registration

(1) The effect of the registration of an instrument under paragraph 13 is that—
   (a) no revocation of the power by the donor is valid unless and until the court confirms the revocation under paragraph 16(3);
   (b) no disclaimer of the power is valid unless and until the attorney gives notice of it to the Public Guardian;
   (c) the donor may not extend or restrict the scope of the authority conferred by the instrument and no instruction or consent given by him after registration, in the case of a consent, confers any right and, in the case of an instruction, imposes or confers any obligation or right on or creates any liability of the attorney or other persons having notice of the instruction or consent.

(2) Sub-paragraph (1) applies for so long as the instrument is registered under paragraph 13 whether or not the donor is for the time being mentally incapable.

(3) A document purporting to be an office copy of an instrument registered under this Schedule is, in any part of the United Kingdom, evidence of—
   (a) the contents of the instrument, and
   (b) the fact that it has been so registered.

(4) Sub-paragraph (3) is without prejudice to section 3 of the Powers of Attorney Act 1971 (c. 27) (proof by certified copies) and to any other method of proof authorised by law.

16. Functions of court with regard to registered power

(1) Where an instrument has been registered under paragraph 13, the court has the following functions with respect to the power and the donor of and the attorney appointed to act under the power.

(2) The court may—
   (a) determine any question as to the meaning or effect of the instrument;
   (b) give directions with respect to—
      (i) the management or disposal by the attorney of the property and affairs of the donor;
      (ii) the rendering of accounts by the attorney and the production of the records kept by him for the purpose;
      (iii) the remuneration or expenses of the attorney whether or not in default of or in accordance with any provision made by the instrument, including directions for the repayment of excessive or the payment of additional remuneration;
   (c) require the attorney to supply information or produce documents or things in his possession as attorney;
   (d) give any consent or authorisation to act which the attorney would have to obtain from a mentally capable donor;
   (e) authorise the attorney to act so as to benefit himself or other persons than the donor otherwise than in accordance with paragraph 3(2) and (3) (but subject to any conditions or restrictions contained in the instrument);
   (f) relieve the attorney wholly or partly from any liability which he has or may have incurred on account of a breach of his duties as attorney.

(3) On application made for the purpose by or on behalf of the donor, the court must confirm the revocation of the power if satisfied that the donor—
   (a) has done whatever is necessary in law to effect an express revocation of the power, and
   (b) was mentally capable of revoking a power of attorney when he did so (whether or not he is so when the court considers the application).

(4) The court must direct the Public Guardian to cancel the registration of an instrument registered under paragraph 13 in any of the following circumstances—
   (a) on confirming the revocation of the power under sub-paragraph (3),
   (b) on directing under paragraph 2(9)(b) that the power is to be revoked,
   (c) on being satisfied that the donor is and is likely to remain mentally capable,

(d) on being satisfied that the power has expired or has been revoked by the mental incapacity of the attorney,

(e) on being satisfied that the power was not a valid and subsisting enduring power when registration was effected,

(f) on being satisfied that fraud or undue pressure was used to induce the donor to create the power,

(g) on being satisfied that, having regard to all the circumstances and in particular the attorney's relationship to or connection with the donor, the attorney is unsuitable to be the donor's attorney.

(5) If the court directs the Public Guardian to cancel the registration of an instrument on being satisfied of the matters specified in sub-paragraph (4)(f) or (g) it must by order revoke the power created by the instrument.

(6) If the court directs the cancellation of the registration of an instrument under sub-paragraph (4) except paragraph (c) the instrument must be delivered up to the Public Guardian to be cancelled, unless the court otherwise directs.

17. Cancellation of registration by Public Guardian

The Public Guardian must cancel the registration of an instrument creating an enduring power of attorney—

(a) on receipt of a disclaimer signed by the attorney;

(b) if satisfied that the power has been revoked by the death or bankruptcy of the donor or attorney or, if the attorney is a body corporate, by its winding up or dissolution;

(c) on receipt of notification from the court that the court has revoked the power;

(d) on confirmation from the court that the donor has revoked the power.

PART 6

PROTECTION OF ATTORNEY AND THIRD PARTIES

18. Protection of attorney and third persons where power is invalid or revoked

(1) Sub-paragraphs (2) and (3) apply where an instrument which did not create a valid power of attorney has been registered under paragraph 13 (whether or not the registration has been cancelled at the time of the act or transaction in question).

(2) An attorney who acts in pursuance of the power does not incur any liability (either to the donor or to any other person) because of the non-existence of the power unless at the time of acting he knows—

(a) that the instrument did not create a valid enduring power,

(b) that an event has occurred which, if the instrument had created a valid enduring power, would have had the effect of revoking the power, or

(c) that, if the instrument had created a valid enduring power, the power would have expired before that time.

(3) Any transaction between the attorney and another person is, in favour of that person, as valid as if the power had then been in existence, unless at the time of the transaction that person has knowledge of any of the matters mentioned in sub-paragraph (2).

(4) If the interest of a purchaser depends on whether a transaction between the attorney and another person was valid by virtue of sub-paragraph (3), it is conclusively presumed in favour of the purchaser that the transaction was valid if—

(a) the transaction between that person and the attorney was completed within 12 months of the date on which the instrument was registered, or

(b) that person makes a statutory declaration, before or within 3 months after the completion of the purchase, that he had no reason at the time of the transaction to doubt that the attorney had authority to dispose of the property which was the subject of the transaction.

(5) For the purposes of section 5 of the Powers of Attorney Act 1971 (c. 27) (protection where power is revoked) in its application to an enduring power the revocation of which by the donor is by virtue of paragraph 15 invalid unless and until confirmed by the court under paragraph 16—

(a) knowledge of the confirmation of the revocation is knowledge of the revocation of the power, but

(b) knowledge of the unconfirmed revocation is not.

19. Further protection of attorney and third persons

(1) If—

(a) an instrument framed in a form prescribed as mentioned in paragraph 2(2) creates a power which is not a valid enduring power, and

(b) the power is revoked by the mental incapacity of the donor,

sub-paragraphs (2) and (3) apply, whether or not the instrument has been registered.

(2) An attorney who acts in pursuance of the power does not, by reason of the revocation, incur any liability (either to the donor or to any other person) unless at the time of acting he knows—

(a) that the instrument did not create a valid enduring power, and

(b) that the donor has become mentally incapable.

(3) Any transaction between the attorney and another person is, in favour of that person, as valid as if the power had then been in existence, unless at the time of the transaction that person knows—

(a) that the instrument did not create a valid enduring power, and

(b) that the donor has become mentally incapable.

(4) Paragraph 18(4) applies for the purpose of determining whether a transaction was valid by virtue of sub-paragraph (3) as it applies for the purpose or determining whether a transaction was valid by virtue of paragraph 18(3).

PART 7

JOINT AND JOINT AND SEVERAL ATTORNEYS

20. Application to joint and joint and several attorneys

(1) An instrument which appoints more than one person to be an attorney cannot create an enduring power unless the attorneys are appointed to act—

(a) jointly, or

(b) jointly and severally.

(2) This Schedule, in its application to joint attorneys, applies to them collectively as it applies to a single attorney but subject to the modifications specified in paragraph 21.

(3) This Schedule, in its application to joint and several attorneys, applies with the modifications specified in sub-paragraphs (4) to (7) and in paragraph 22.

(4) A failure, as respects any one attorney, to comply with the requirements for the creation of enduring powers—

(a) prevents the instrument from creating such a power in his case, but

(b) does not affect its efficacy for that purpose as respects the other or others or its efficacy in his case for the purpose of creating a power of attorney which is not an enduring power.

(5) If one or more but not both or all the attorneys makes or joins in making an application for registration of the instrument—

(a) an attorney who is not an applicant as well as one who is may act pending the registration of the instrument as provided in paragraph 1(2),

(b) notice of the application must also be given under Part 3 of this Schedule to the other attorney or attorneys, and

(c) objection may validly be taken to the registration on a ground relating to an attorney or to the power of an attorney who is not an applicant as well as to one or the power of one who is an applicant.

(6) The Public Guardian is not precluded by paragraph 13(5) or (8) from registering an instrument and the court must not direct him not to do so under paragraph 13(10) if an enduring power subsists as respects some attorney who is not affected by the ground or grounds of the objection in question; and where the Public Guardian registers an instrument in that case, he must make against the registration an entry in the prescribed form.

(7) Sub-paragraph (6) does not preclude the court from revoking a power in so far as it confers a power on any other attorney in respect of whom the ground in paragraph 13(9)(d) or (e) is established; and where any ground in paragraph 13(9) affecting any other attorney is established the court must direct the Public Guardian to make against the registration an entry in the prescribed form.

(8) In sub-paragraph (4), "the requirements for the creation of enduring powers" means the provisions of—

(a) paragraph 2 other than sub-paragraphs (8) and (9), and

(b) the regulations mentioned in paragraph 2.

21. Joint attorneys

(1) In paragraph 2(5), the reference to the time when the attorney executes the instrument is to be read as a reference to the time when the second or last attorney executes the instrument.

(2) In paragraph 2(6) to (8), the reference to the attorney is to be read as a reference to any attorney under the power.

(3) Paragraph 13 has effect as if the ground of objection to the registration of the instrument specified in sub-paragraph (9)(e) applied to any attorney under the power.

(4) In paragraph 16(2), references to the attorney are to be read as including references to any attorney under the power.

(5) In paragraph 16(4), references to the attorney are to be read as including references to any attorney under the power.

(6) In paragraph 17, references to the attorney are to be read as including references to any attorney under the power.

22. Joint and several attorneys

(1) In paragraph 2(7), the reference to the bankruptcy of the attorney is to be read as a reference to the bankruptcy of the last remaining attorney under the power; and the bankruptcy of any other attorney under the power causes that person to cease to be an attorney under the power.

(2) In paragraph 2(8), the reference to the suspension of the power is to be read as a reference to its suspension in so far as it relates to the attorney in respect of whom the interim bankruptcy restrictions order has effect.

(3) The restriction upon disclaimer imposed by paragraph 4(6) applies only to those attorneys who have reason to believe that the donor is or is becoming mentally incapable.

PART 8

INTERPRETATION

23.

(1) In this Schedule—

"enduring power" is to be construed in accordance with paragraph 2,

"mentally incapable" or "mental incapacity", except where it refers to revocation at common law, means in relation to any person, that he is incapable by reason of mental disorder (within the meaning of the Mental Health Act) of managing and administering his property and affairs and "mentally capable" and "mental capacity" are to be construed accordingly,

"notice" means notice in writing, and

"prescribed", except for the purposes of paragraph 2, means prescribed by regulations made for the purposes of this Schedule by the Lord Chancellor.

(2) Any question arising under or for the purposes of this Schedule as to what the donor of the power might at any time be expected to do is to be determined by assuming that he had full mental capacity at the time but otherwise by reference to the circumstances existing at that time.

DEFINITIONS

"bankrupt": s.64(3)

"trust corporation": s.64(1)

"Public Guardian": s.64(1)

"the court": s.64(1)

"deputy": s.64(1)

"property": s.64(1)

"purchaser": s.64(1)

"Mental Health Act": s.64(1)

GENERAL NOTE

This Schedule has effect in relation to enduring powers of attorney (EPAs) created before the implementation of this Act. It ensures that such instruments will continue to have the same legal effect as they had at the time they were made. They will also continue to be governed by the same legal rules and procedures which were in place at the time they were made. The Schedule therefore reproduces, with amendments, the relevant provisions of the Enduring Powers of Attorney Act 1985, which is repealed by Sch.7, and provides that the principles set out in s.1 shall not retrospectively apply to EPAs. The amendments are directed to the way in which tasks performed by the replaced Court of Protection will, on implementation of this Act, be divided between the new Court of Protection and the office of Public Guardian. The 1985 Act is considered by S.M.Cretney and D.Lush in *Enduring Powers of Attorney*, Jordans, 2001.

SCHEDULE 5 - **Section 66(4)**

TRANSITIONAL PROVISIONS AND SAVINGS

PART I

REPEAL OF PART 7 OF THE MENTAL HEALTH ACT 1983

1. **Existing receivers**

   (1) This paragraph applies where, immediately before the commencement day, there is a receiver (R) for a person (P) appointed under section 99 of the Mental Health Act.

   (2) On and after that day—

      (a) this Act applies as if R were a deputy appointed for P by the court, but with the functions that R had as receiver immediately before that day, and

      (b) a reference in any other enactment to a deputy appointed by the court includes a person appointed as a deputy as a result of paragraph (a).

   (3) On any application to it by R, the court may end R's appointment as P's deputy.

   (4) Where, as a result of section 20(1), R may not make a decision on behalf of P in relation to a relevant matter, R must apply to the court.

   (5) If, on the application, the court is satisfied that P is capable of managing his property and affairs in relation to the relevant matter—

      (a) it must make an order ending R's appointment as P's deputy in relation to that matter, but

      (b) it may, in relation to any other matter, exercise in relation to P any of the powers which it has under sections 15 to 19.

   (6) If it is not satisfied, the court may exercise in relation to P any of the powers which it has under sections 15 to 19.

   (7) R's appointment as P's deputy ceases to have effect if P dies.

   (8) "Relevant matter" means a matter in relation to which, immediately before the commencement day, R was authorised to act as P's receiver.

   (9) In sub-paragraph (1), the reference to a receiver appointed under section 99 of the Mental Health Act includes a reference to a person who by virtue of Schedule 5 to that Act was deemed to be a receiver appointed under that section.

2. **Orders, appointments etc**

   (1) Any order or appointment made, direction or authority given or other thing done which has, or by virtue of Schedule 5 to the Mental Health Act was deemed to have, effect under Part 7 of the Act immediately before the commencement day is to continue to have effect despite the repeal of Part 7.

   (2) In so far as any such order, appointment, direction, authority or thing could have been made, given or done under sections 15 to 20 if those sections had then been in force—

      (a) it is to be treated as made, given or done under those sections, and

      (b) the powers of variation and discharge conferred by section 16(7) apply accordingly.

   (3) Sub-paragraph (1)—

      (a) does not apply to nominations under section 93(1) or (4) of the Mental Health Act, and

      (b) as respects receivers, has effect subject to paragraph 1.

   (4) This Act does not affect the operation of section 109 of the Mental Health Act (effect and proof of orders etc.) in relation to orders made and directions given under Part 7 of that Act.

   (5) This paragraph is without prejudice to section 16 of the Interpretation Act 1978 (c. 30) (general savings on repeal).

3. Pending proceedings

(1) Any application for the exercise of a power under Part 7 of the Mental Health Act which is pending immediately before the commencement day is to be treated, in so far as a corresponding power is exercisable under sections 16 to 20, as an application for the exercise of that power.

(2) For the purposes of sub-paragraph (1) an application for the appointment of a receiver is to be treated as an application for the appointment of a deputy.

4. Appeals

(1) Part 7 of the Mental Health Act and the rules made under it are to continue to apply to any appeal brought by virtue of section 105 of that Act which has not been determined before the commencement day.

(2) If in the case of an appeal brought by virtue of section 105(1) (appeal to nominated judge) the judge nominated under section 93 of the Mental Health Act has begun to hear the appeal, he is to continue to do so but otherwise it is to be heard by a puisne judge of the High Court nominated under section 46.

5. Fees

All fees and other payments which, having become due, have not been paid to the former Court of Protection before the commencement day, are to be paid to the new Court of Protection.

6. Court records

(1) The records of the former Court of Protection are to be treated, on and after the commencement day, as records of the new Court of Protection and are to be dealt with accordingly under the Public Records Act 1958 (c. 51).

(2) On and after the commencement day, the Public Guardian is, for the purpose of exercising any of his functions, to be given such access as he may require to such of the records mentioned in sub-paragraph (1) as relate to the appointment of receivers under section 99 of the Mental Health Act.

7. Existing charges

This Act does not affect the operation in relation to a charge created before the commencement day of—

    (a) so much of section 101(6) of the Mental Health Act as precludes a charge created under section 101(5) from conferring a right of sale or foreclosure during the lifetime of the patient, or

    (b) section 106(6) of the Mental Health Act (charge created by virtue of section 106(5) not to cause interest to fail etc.).

8. Preservation of interests on disposal of property

Paragraph 8(1) of Schedule 2 applies in relation to any disposal of property (within the meaning of that provision) by a person living on 1st November 1960, being a disposal effected under the Lunacy Act 1890 (c. 5) as it applies in relation to the disposal of property effected under sections 16 to 20.

9. Accounts

Court of Protection Rules may provide that, in a case where paragraph 1 applies, R is to have a duty to render accounts—

    (a) while he is receiver;

    (b) after he is discharged.

10. Interpretation

In this Part of this Schedule—

    (a) "the commencement day" means the day on which section 66(1)(a) (repeal of Part 7 of the Mental Health Act) comes into force,

    (b) "the former Court of Protection" means the office abolished by section 45, and

    (c) "the new Court of Protection" means the court established by that section.

PART 2

REPEAL OF THE ENDURING POWERS OF ATTORNEY ACT 1985

11. Orders, determinations, etc

(1) Any order or determination made, or other thing done, under the 1985 Act which has effect immediately before the commencement day continues to have effect despite the repeal of that Act.

(2) In so far as any such order, determination or thing could have been made or done under
Schedule 4 if it had then been in force—

(a) it is to be treated as made or done under that Schedule, and

(b) the powers of variation and discharge exercisable by the court apply accordingly.

(3) Any instrument registered under the 1985 Act is to be treated as having been registered by the
Public Guardian under Schedule 4.

(4) This paragraph is without prejudice to section 16 of the Interpretation Act 1978 (c. 30) (general
savings on repeal).

12. Pending proceedings

(1) An application for the exercise of a power under the 1985 Act which is pending immediately
before the commencement day is to be treated, in so far as a corresponding power is exercisable
under Schedule 4, as an application for the exercise of that power.

(2) For the purposes of sub-paragraph (1)—

(a) a pending application under section 4(2) of the 1985 Act for the registration of an instrument
is to be treated as an application to the Public Guardian under paragraph 4 of Schedule 4 and
any notice given in connection with that application under Schedule 1 to the 1985 Act is to
be treated as given under Part 3 of Schedule 4,

(b) a notice of objection to the registration of an instrument is to be treated as a notice of
objection under paragraph 13 of Schedule 4, and

(c) pending proceedings under section 5 of the 1985 Act are to be treated as proceedings on an
application for the exercise by the court of a power which would become exercisable in
relation to an instrument under paragraph 16(2) of Schedule 4 on its registration.

13. Appeals

(1) The 1985 Act and, so far as relevant, the provisions of Part 7 of the Mental Health Act and the
rules made under it as applied by section 10 of the 1985 Act are to continue to have effect in
relation to any appeal brought by virtue of section 10(1)(c) of the 1985 Act which has not been
determined before the commencement day.

(2) If, in the case of an appeal brought by virtue of section 105(1) of the Mental Health Act as
applied by section 10(1)(c) of the 1985 Act (appeal to nominated judge), the judge nominated under
section 93 of the Mental Health Act has begun to hear the appeal, he is to continue to do so but
otherwise the appeal is to be heard by a puisne judge of the High Court nominated under section
46.

14. Exercise of powers of donor as trustee

(1) Section 2(8) of the 1985 Act (which prevents a power of attorney under section 25 of the Trustee
Act 1925 (c. 19) as enacted from being an enduring power) is to continue to apply to any enduring
power—

(a) created before 1st March 2000, and

(b) having effect immediately before the commencement day.

(2) Section 3(3) of the 1985 Act (which entitles the donee of an enduring power to exercise the
donor's powers as trustee) is to continue to apply to any enduring power to which, as a result of
the provision mentioned in sub-paragraph (3), it applies immediately before the commencement
day.

(3) The provision is section 4(3)(a) of the Trustee Delegation Act 1999 (c. 15) (which provides for
section 3(3) of the 1985 Act to cease to apply to an enduring power when its registration is
cancelled, if it was registered in response to an application made before 1st March 2001).

(4) Even though section 4 of the 1999 Act is repealed by this Act, that section is to continue to
apply in relation to an enduring power—

(a) to which section 3(3) of the 1985 Act applies as a result of sub-paragraph (2), or

(b) to which, immediately before the repeal of section 4 of the 1999 Act, section 1 of that Act
applies as a result of section 4 of it.

(5) The reference in section 1(9) of the 1999 Act to section 4(6) of that Act is to be read with sub-paragraphs (2) to (4).

15. Interpretation

In this Part of this Schedule, "the commencement day" means the day on which section 66(1)(b) (repeal of the 1985 Act) comes into force.

DEFINITIONS
"Mental Health Act": s.64(1)
"deputy": s.64(1)
"the court": s.64(1)
"enactment": s.64(1)
"property": s.64(1)
"Public Guardian": s.64(1)
"Court of Protection Rules": s.64(1)
"the 1985 Act": s.64(1)

SCHEDULE 6 - **Section 67(1)**

MINOR AND CONSEQUENTIAL AMENDMENTS

1. **Fines and Recoveries Act 1833 (c. 74)**

(1) The Fines and Recoveries Act 1833 (c. 74) is amended as follows.

(2) In section 33 (case where protector of settlement lacks capacity to act), for the words from "shall be incapable" to "is incapable as aforesaid" substitute "lacks capacity (within the meaning of the Mental Capacity Act 2005) to manage his property and affairs, the Court of Protection is to take his place as protector of the settlement while he lacks capacity".

(3) In sections 48 and 49 (mental health jurisdiction), for each reference to the judge having jurisdiction under Part 7 of the Mental Health Act substitute a reference to the Court of Protection.

2. **Improvement of Land Act 1864 (c. 114)**

In section 68 of the Improvement of Land Act 1864 (c. 114) (apportionment of rentcharges)—

    (a) for ", curator, or receiver of" substitute "or curator of, or a deputy with powers in relation to property and affairs appointed by the Court of Protection for,", and

    (b) for "or patient within the meaning of Part VII of the Mental Health Act 1983" substitute "person who lacks capacity (within the meaning of the Mental Capacity Act 2005) to receive the notice".

3. **Trustee Act 1925 (c. 19)**

(1) The Trustee Act 1925 (c. 19) is amended as follows.

(2) In section 36 (appointment of new trustee)—

    (a) in subsection (6C), for the words from "a power of attorney" to the end, substitute "an enduring power of attorney or lasting power of attorney registered under the Mental Capacity Act 2005", and

    (b) in subsection (9)—

        (i) for the words from "is incapable" to "exercising" substitute "lacks capacity to exercise", and

        (ii) for the words from "the authority" to the end substitute "the Court of Protection".

(3) In section 41(1) (power of court to appoint new trustee) for the words from "is incapable" to "exercising" substitute "lacks capacity to exercise".

(4) In section 54 (mental health jurisdiction)—

    (a) for subsection (1) substitute—

        "(1) Subject to subsection (2), the Court of Protection may not make an order, or give a direction or authority, in relation to a person who lacks capacity to exercise his functions as trustee, if the High Court may make an order to that effect under this Act.",

    (b) in subsection (2)—

(i) for the words from the beginning to "of a receiver" substitute "Where a person lacks capacity to exercise his functions as a trustee and a deputy is appointed for him by the Court of Protection or an application for the appointment of a deputy",

(ii) for "the said authority", in each place, substitute "the Court of Protection", and

(iii) for "the patient", in each place, substitute "the person concerned", and

(c) omit subsection (3).

(5) In section 55 (order made on particular allegation to be conclusive evidence of it)—

(a) for the words from "Part VII" to "Northern Ireland" substitute "sections 15 to 20 of the Mental Capacity Act 2005 or any corresponding provisions having effect in Northern Ireland", and

(b) for paragraph (a) substitute—

"(a) that a trustee or mortgagee lacks capacity in relation to the matter in question;".

(6) In section 68 (definitions), at the end add—

"(3) Any reference in this Act to a person who lacks capacity in relation to a matter is to a person—

(a) who lacks capacity within the meaning of the Mental Capacity Act 2005 in relation to that matter, or

(b) in respect of whom the powers conferred by section 48 of that Act are exercisable and have been exercised in relation to that matter.".

4. Law of Property Act 1925 (c. 20)

(1) The Law of Property Act 1925 (c. 20) is amended as follows.

(2) In section 22 (conveyances on behalf of persons who lack capacity)—

(a) in subsection (1)—

(i) for the words from "in a person suffering" to "is acting" substitute ", either solely or jointly with any other person or persons, in a person lacking capacity (within the meaning of the Mental Capacity Act 2005) to convey or create a legal estate, a deputy appointed for him by the Court of Protection or (if no deputy is appointed)", and

(ii) for "the authority having jurisdiction under Part VII of the Mental Health Act 1983" substitute "the Court of Protection",

(b) in subsection (2), for "is incapable, by reason of mental disorder, of exercising" substitute "lacks capacity (within the meaning of that Act) to exercise", and

(c) in subsection (3), for the words from "an enduring power" to the end substitute "an enduring power of attorney or lasting power of attorney (within the meaning of the 2005 Act) is entitled to act for the trustee who lacks capacity in relation to the dealing.".

(3) In section 205(1) (interpretation), omit paragraph (xiii).

5. Administration of Estates Act 1925 (c. 23)

(1) The Administration of Estates Act 1925 (c. 23) is amended as follows.

(2) In section 41(1) (powers of personal representatives to appropriate), in the proviso—

(a) in paragraph (ii)—

(i) for the words from "is incapable" to "the consent" substitute "lacks capacity (within the meaning of the Mental Capacity Act 2005) to give the consent, it", and

(ii) for "or receiver" substitute "or a person appointed as deputy for him by the Court of Protection", and

(b) in paragraph (iv), for "no receiver is acting for a person suffering from mental disorder" substitute "no deputy is appointed for a person who lacks capacity to consent".

(3) Omit section 55(1)(viii) (definitions of person of unsound mind and defective).

6. National Assistance Act 1948 (c. 29)

In section 49 of the National Assistance Act 1948 (c. 29) (expenses of council officers acting for persons who lack capacity)—

(a) for the words from "applies" to "affairs of a patient" substitute "applies for appointment by the Court of Protection as a deputy", and

(b) for "such functions" substitute "his functions as deputy".

7. U.S.A. Veterans' Pensions (Administration) Act 1949 (c. 45)

In section 1 of the U.S.A. Veterans' Pensions (Administration) Act 1949 (c. 45) (administration of pensions)—

(a) in subsection (4), omit the words from "or for whom" to "1983", and

(b) after subsection (4), insert—

"(4A) An agreement under subsection (1) is not to be made in relation to a person who lacks capacity (within the meaning of the Mental Capacity Act 2005) for the purposes of this Act if—

(a) there is a donee of an enduring power of attorney or lasting power of attorney (within the meaning of the 2005 Act), or a deputy appointed for the person by the Court of Protection, and

(b) the donee or deputy has power in relation to the person for the purposes of this Act.

(4B) The proviso at the end of subsection (4) also applies in relation to subsection (4A).".

8. Intestates' Estates Act 1952 (c. 64)

In Schedule 2 to the Intestates' Estates Act 1952 (c. 64) (rights of surviving spouse or civil partner in relation to home), for paragraph 6(1) substitute—

"(1) Where the surviving spouse or civil partner lacks capacity (within the meaning of the Mental Capacity Act 2005) to make a requirement or give a consent under this Schedule, the requirement or consent may be made or given by a deputy appointed by the Court of Protection with power in that respect or, if no deputy has that power, by that court.".

9. Variation of Trusts Act 1958 (c. 53)

In section 1 of the Variation of Trusts Act 1958 (c. 53) (jurisdiction of courts to vary trusts)—

(a) in subsection (3), for the words from "shall be determined" to the end substitute "who lacks capacity (within the meaning of the Mental Capacity Act 2005) to give his assent is to be determined by the Court of Protection", and

(b) in subsection (6), for the words from "the powers" to the end substitute "the powers of the Court of Protection".

10. Administration of Justice Act 1960 (c. 65)

In section 12(1)(b) of the Administration of Justice Act 1960 (c. 65) (contempt of court to publish information about proceedings in private relating to persons with incapacity) for the words from "under Part VIII" to "that Act" substitute "under the Mental Capacity Act 2005, or under any provision of the Mental Health Act 1983".

11. Industrial and Provident Societies Act 1965 (c. 12)

In section 26 of the Industrial and Provident Societies Act 1965 (c. 12) (payments for mentally incapable people), for subsection (2) substitute—

"(2) Subsection (1) does not apply where the member or person concerned lacks capacity (within the meaning of the Mental Capacity Act 2005) for the purposes of this Act and—

(a) there is a donee of an enduring power of attorney or lasting power of attorney (within the meaning of the 2005 Act), or a deputy appointed for the member or person by the Court of Protection, and

(b) the donee or deputy has power in relation to the member or person for the purposes of this Act.".

12. Compulsory Purchase Act 1965 (c. 56)

In Schedule 1 to the Compulsory Purchase Act 1965 (c. 56) (persons without power to sell their interests), for paragraph 1(2)(b) substitute—

"(b) do not have effect in relation to a person who lacks capacity (within the meaning of the Mental Capacity Act 2005) for the purposes of this Act if—

(i) there is a donee of an enduring power of attorney or lasting power of attorney (within the meaning of the 2005 Act), or a deputy appointed for the person by the Court of Protection, and

(ii) the donee or deputy has power in relation to the person for the purposes of this Act.".

13. Leasehold Reform Act 1967 (c. 88)

(1) For section 26(2) of the Leasehold Reform Act 1967 (c. 88) (landlord lacking capacity) substitute—

"(2) Where a landlord lacks capacity (within the meaning of the Mental Capacity Act 2005) to exercise his functions as a landlord, those functions are to be exercised—

(a) by a donee of an enduring power of attorney or lasting power of attorney (within the meaning of the 2005 Act), or a deputy appointed for him by the Court of Protection, with power to exercise those functions, or

(b) if no donee or deputy has that power, by a person authorised in that respect by that court.".

(2) That amendment does not affect any proceedings pending at the commencement of this paragraph in which a receiver or a person authorised under Part 7 of the Mental Health Act is acting on behalf of the landlord.

14. Medicines Act 1968 (c. 67)

In section 72 of the Medicines Act 1968 (c. 67) (pharmacist lacking capacity)—

(a) in subsection (1)(c), for the words from "a receiver" to "1959" substitute "he becomes a person who lacks capacity (within the meaning of the Mental Capacity Act 2005) to carry on the business",

(b) after subsection (1) insert—

"(1A) In subsection (1)(c), the reference to a person who lacks capacity to carry on the business is to a person—

(a) in respect of whom there is a donee of an enduring power of attorney or lasting power of attorney (within the meaning of the Mental Capacity Act 2005), or

(b) for whom a deputy is appointed by the Court of Protection,

and in relation to whom the donee or deputy has power for the purposes of this Act.",

(c) in subsection (3)(d)—

(i) for "receiver" substitute "deputy", and

(ii) after "guardian" insert "or from the date of registration of the instrument appointing the donee", and

(d) in subsection (4)(c), for "receiver" substitute "donee, deputy".

15. Family Law Reform Act 1969 (c. 46)

For section 21(4) of the Family Law Reform Act 1969 (c. 46) (consent required for taking of bodily sample from person lacking capacity), substitute—

"(4) A bodily sample may be taken from a person who lacks capacity (within the meaning of the Mental Capacity Act 2005) to give his consent, if consent is given by the court giving the direction under section 20 or by—

(a) a donee of an enduring power of attorney or lasting power of attorney (within the meaning of that Act), or

(b) a deputy appointed, or any other person authorised, by the Court of Protection,

with power in that respect.".

16. Local Authority Social Services Act 1970 (c. 42)

(1) Schedule 1 to the Local Authority Social Services Act 1970 (c. 42) (enactments conferring functions assigned to social services committee) is amended as follows.

(2) In the entry for section 49 of the National Assistance Act 1948 (expenses of local authority officer appointed for person who lacks capacity) for "receiver" substitute "deputy".

(3) At the end, insert—

"Mental Capacity Act 2005	
Section 39	Instructing independent mental capacity advocate before providing accommodation for person lacking capacity.
Section 49	Reports in proceedings."

17. Courts Act 1971 (c. 23)

In Part 1A of Schedule 2 to the Courts Act 1971 (c. 23) (office-holders eligible for appointment as circuit judges), omit the reference to a Master of the Court of Protection.

18. Local Government Act 1972 (c. 70)

(1) Omit section 118 of the Local Government Act 1972 (c. 70) (payment of pension etc. where recipient lacks capacity).

(2) Sub-paragraph (3) applies where, before the commencement of this paragraph, a local authority has, in respect of a person referred to in that section as "the patient", made payments under that section—

(a) to an institution or person having the care of the patient, or

(b) in accordance with subsection (1)(a) or (b) of that section.

(3) The local authority may, in respect of the patient, continue to make payments under that section to that institution or person, or in accordance with subsection (1)(a) or (b) of that section, despite the repeal made by sub-paragraph (1).

19. Matrimonial Causes Act 1973 (c. 18)

In section 40 of the Matrimonial Causes Act 1973 (c. 18) (payments to person who lacks capacity) (which becomes subsection (1))—

(a) for the words from "is incapable" to "affairs" substitute "("P") lacks capacity (within the meaning of the Mental Capacity Act 2005) in relation to the provisions of the order",

(b) for "that person under Part VIII of that Act" substitute "P under that Act",

(c) for the words from "such persons" to the end substitute "such person ("D") as it may direct", and

(d) at the end insert—

"(2) In carrying out any functions of his in relation to an order made under subsection (1), D must act in P's best interests (within the meaning of that Act).".

20. Juries Act 1974 (c. 23)

In Schedule 1 to the Juries Act 1974 (c. 23) (disqualification for jury service), for paragraph 3 substitute—

"**3.** A person who lacks capacity, within the meaning of the Mental Capacity Act 2005, to serve as a juror.".

21. Consumer Credit Act 1974 (c. 39)

For section 37(1)(c) of the Consumer Credit Act 1974 (c. 39) (termination of consumer credit licence if holder lacks capacity) substitute—

"(c) becomes a person who lacks capacity (within the meaning of the Mental Capacity Act 2005) to carry on the activities covered by the licence.".

22. Solicitors Act 1974 (c. 47)

(1) The Solicitors Act 1974 (c. 47) is amended as follows.

(2) For section 12(1)(j) (application for practising certificate by solicitor lacking capacity) substitute—

"(j) while he lacks capacity (within the meaning of the Mental Capacity Act 2005) to act as a solicitor and powers under sections 15 to 20 or section 48 of that Act are exercisable in relation to him;".

(3) In section 62(4) (contentious business agreements made by clients) for paragraphs (c) and (d) substitute—

"(c) as a deputy for him appointed by the Court of Protection with powers in relation to his property and affairs, or

(d) as another person authorised under that Act to act on his behalf.".

(4) In paragraph 1(1) of Schedule 1 (circumstances in which Law Society may intervene in solicitor's practice), for paragraph (f) substitute—

"(f) a solicitor lacks capacity (within the meaning of the Mental Capacity Act 2005) to act as a solicitor and powers under sections 15 to 20 or section 48 of that Act are exercisable in relation to him;".

23. Local Government (Miscellaneous Provisions) Act 1976 (c. 57)

In section 31 of the Local Government (Miscellaneous Provisions) Act 1976 (c. 57) (the title to which becomes Indemnities for local authority officers appointed as deputies or administrators), for the words from "as a receiver" to "1959" substitute "as a deputy for a person by the Court of Protection".

24. Sale of Goods Act 1979 (c. 54)

In section 3(2) of the Sale of Goods Act 1979 (c. 54) (capacity to buy and sell) the words "mental incapacity or" cease to have effect in England and Wales.

25.   Limitation Act 1980 (c. 58)

In section 38 of the Limitation Act 1980 (c. 58) (interpretation) substitute—
   (a) in subsection (2) for "of unsound mind" substitute "lacks capacity (within the meaning of the Mental Capacity Act 2005) to conduct legal proceedings", and
   (b) omit subsections (3) and (4).

26.   Public Passenger Vehicles Act 1981 (c. 14)

In section 57(2)(c) of the Public Passenger Vehicles Act 1981 (c. 14) (termination of public service vehicle licence if holder lacks capacity) for the words from "becomes a patient" to "or" substitute "becomes a person who lacks capacity (within the meaning of the Mental Capacity Act 2005) to use a vehicle under the licence, or".

27.   Judicial Pensions Act 1981 (c. 20)

In Schedule 1 to the Judicial Pensions Act 1981 (c. 20) (pensions of Supreme Court officers, etc.), in paragraph 1, omit the reference to a Master of the Court of Protection except in the case of a person holding that office immediately before the commencement of this paragraph or who had previously retired from that office or died.

28.   Supreme Court Act 1981 (c. 54)

In Schedule 2 to the Supreme Court Act 1981 (c. 54) (qualifications for appointment to office in Supreme Court), omit paragraph 11 (Master of the Court of Protection).

29.   Mental Health Act 1983 (c. 20)

   (1) The Mental Health Act is amended as follows.
   (2) In section 134(3) (cases where correspondence of detained patients may not be withheld) for paragraph (b) substitute—
           "(b) any judge or officer of the Court of Protection, any of the Court of Protection Visitors or any person asked by that Court for a report under section 49 of the Mental Capacity Act 2005 concerning the patient;".
   (3) In section 139 (protection for acts done in pursuance of 1983 Act), in subsection (1), omit from "or in, or in pursuance" to "Part VII of this Act,".
   (4) Section 142 (payment of pension etc. where recipient lacks capacity) ceases to have effect in England and Wales.
   (5) Sub-paragraph (6) applies where, before the commencement of sub-paragraph (4), an authority has, in respect of a person referred to in that section as "the patient", made payments under that section—
           (a) to an institution or person having the care of the patient, or
           (b) in accordance with subsection (2)(a) or (b) of that section.
   (6) The authority may, in respect of the patient, continue to make payments under that section to that institution or person, or in accordance with subsection (2)(a) or (b) of that section, despite the amendment made by sub-paragraph (4).
   (7) In section 145(1) (interpretation), in the definition of patient, omit "(except in Part VII of this Act)".
   (8) In section 146 (provisions having effect in Scotland), omit from "104(4)" to "section),".
   (9) In section 147 (provisions having effect in Northern Ireland), omit from "104(4)" to "section),".

30.   Administration of Justice Act 1985 (c. 61)

In section 18(3) of the Administration of Justice Act 1985 (c. 61) (licensed conveyancer who lacks capacity), for the words from "that person" to the end substitute "he becomes a person who lacks capacity (within the meaning of the Mental Capacity Act 2005) to practise as a licensed conveyancer.".

31.   Insolvency Act 1986 (c. 45)

   (1) The Insolvency Act 1986 (c. 45) is amended as follows.
   (2) In section 389A (people not authorised to act as nominee or supervisor in voluntary arrangement), in subsection (3)—
           (a) omit the "or" immediately after paragraph (b),
           (b) in paragraph (c), omit "Part VII of the Mental Health Act 1983 or", and
           (c) after that paragraph, insert
                  ", or
                  (d) he lacks capacity (within the meaning of the Mental Capacity Act 2005) to act as nominee or supervisor".

(3) In section 390 (people not qualified to be insolvency practitioners), in subsection (4)—
   (a) omit the "or" immediately after paragraph (b),
   (b) in paragraph (c), omit "Part VII of the Mental Health Act 1983 or", and
   (c) after that paragraph, insert
      ", or
            (d) he lacks capacity (within the meaning of the Mental Capacity Act 2005) to act as an insolvency practitioner.".

32. Building Societies Act 1986 (c. 53)

In section 102D(9) of the Building Societies Act 1986 (c. 53) (references to a person holding an account on trust for another)—
   (a) in paragraph (a), for "Part VII of the Mental Health Act 1983" substitute "the Mental Capacity Act 2005", and
   (b) for paragraph (b) substitute—
            "(b) to an attorney holding an account for another person under—
                  (i) an enduring power of attorney or lasting power of attorney registered under the Mental Capacity Act 2005, or
                  (ii) an enduring power registered under the Enduring Powers of Attorney (Northern Ireland) Order 1987;".

33. Public Trustee and Administration of Funds Act 1986 (c. 57)

In section 3 of the Public Trustee and Administration of Funds Act 1986 (c. 57) (functions of the Public Trustee)—
   (a) for subsections (1) to (5) substitute—
            "(1) The Public Trustee may exercise the functions of a deputy appointed by the Court of Protection.",
   (b) in subsection (6), for "the 1906 Act" substitute "the Public Trustee Act 1906", and
   (c) omit subsection (7).

34. Patronage (Benefices) Measure 1986 (No.3)

(1) The Patronage (Benefices) Measure 1986 (No. 3) is amended as follows.
(2) In section 5 (rights of patronage exercisable otherwise than by registered patron), after subsection (3) insert—
      "(3A) The reference in subsection (3) to a power of attorney does not include an enduring power of attorney or lasting power of attorney (within the meaning of the Mental Capacity Act 2005)."
(3) In section 9 (information to be sent to designated officer when benefice becomes vacant), after subsection (5) insert—
      "(5A) Subsections (5B) and (5C) apply where the functions of a registered patron are, as a result of paragraph 10 of Schedule 2 to the Mental Capacity Act 2005 (patron's loss of capacity to discharge functions), to be discharged by an individual appointed by the Court of Protection.
      (5B) If the individual is a clerk in Holy Orders, subsection (5) applies to him as it applies to the registered patron.
      (5C) If the individual is not a clerk in Holy Orders, subsection (1) (other than paragraph (b)) applies to him as it applies to the registered patron."

35. Courts and Legal Services Act 1990 (c. 41)

(1) The Courts and Legal Services Act 1990 (c. 41) is amended as follows.
(2) In Schedule 11 (judges etc. barred from legal practice), for the reference to a Master of the Court of Protection substitute a reference to each of the following—
   (a) Senior Judge of the Court of Protection,
   (b) President of the Court of Protection,
   (c) Vice-President of the Court of Protection.
(3) In paragraph 5(3) of Schedule 14 (exercise of powers of intervention in registered foreign lawyer's practice), for paragraph (f) substitute—
            "(f) he lacks capacity (within the meaning of the Mental Capacity Act 2005) to act as a registered foreign lawyer and powers under sections 15 to 20 or section 48 are exercisable in relation to him;".

36. Child Support Act 1991 (c. 48)

In section 50 of the Child Support Act 1991 (c. 48) (unauthorised disclosure of information)—

(a) in subsection (8)—

    (i) immediately after paragraph (a), insert "or",

    (ii) omit paragraphs (b) and (d) and the "or" immediately after paragraph (c), and

    (iii) for ", receiver, custodian or appointee" substitute "or custodian", and

(b) after that subsection, insert—

    "(9) Where the person to whom the information relates lacks capacity (within the meaning of the Mental Capacity Act 2005) to consent to its disclosure, the appropriate person is—

        (a) a donee of an enduring power of attorney or lasting power of attorney (within the meaning of that Act), or

        (b) a deputy appointed for him, or any other person authorised, by the Court of Protection,

    with power in that respect.".

37. Social Security Administration Act 1992 (c. 5)

In section 123 of the Social Security Administration Act 1992 (c. 5) (unauthorised disclosure of information)—

(a) in subsection (10), omit—

    (i) in paragraph (b), "a receiver appointed under section 99 of the Mental Health Act 1983 or",

    (ii) in paragraph (d)(i), "sub-paragraph (a) of rule 41(1) of the Court of Protection Rules 1984 or",

    (iii) in paragraph (d)(ii), "a receiver ad interim appointed under sub-paragraph (b) of the said rule 41(1) or", and

    (iv) "receiver,", and

(b) after that subsection, insert—

    "(11) Where the person to whom the information relates lacks capacity (within the meaning of the Mental Capacity Act 2005) to consent to its disclosure, the appropriate person is—

        (a) a donee of an enduring power of attorney or lasting power of attorney (within the meaning of that Act), or

        (b) a deputy appointed for him, or any other person authorised, by the Court of Protection,

    with power in that respect.".

38. Judicial Pensions and Retirement Act 1993 (c. 8)

(1) The Judicial Pensions and Retirement Act 1993 (c. 8) is amended as follows.

(2) In Schedule 1 (qualifying judicial offices), in Part 2, under the cross-heading Court officers, omit the reference to a Master of the Court of Protection except in the case of a person holding that office immediately before the commencement of this sub-paragraph or who had previously retired from that office or died.

(3) In Schedule 5 (retirement: the relevant offices), omit the entries relating to the Master and Deputy or temporary Master of the Court of Protection, except in the case of a person holding any of those offices immediately before the commencement of this sub-paragraph.

(4) In Schedule 7 (retirement: transitional provisions), omit paragraph 5(5)(i)(g) except in the case of a person holding office as a deputy or temporary Master of the Court of Protection immediately before the commencement of this sub-paragraph.

39. Leasehold Reform, Housing and Urban Development Act 1993 (c. 28)

(1) For paragraph 4 of Schedule 2 to the Leasehold Reform, Housing and Urban Development Act 1993 (c. 28) (landlord under a disability), substitute—

    "**4.**

    (1) This paragraph applies where a Chapter I or Chapter II landlord lacks capacity (within the meaning of the Mental Capacity Act 2005) to exercise his functions as a landlord.

    (2) For the purposes of the Chapter concerned, the landlord's place is to be taken—

        (a) by a donee of an enduring power of attorney or lasting power of attorney (within the meaning of the 2005 Act), or a deputy appointed for him by the Court of Protection, with power to exercise those functions, or

        (b) if no deputy or donee has that power, by a person authorised in that respect by that court.".

(2) That amendment does not affect any proceedings pending at the commencement of this paragraph in which a receiver or a person authorised under Part 7 of the Mental Health Act 1983 (c. 20) is acting on behalf of the landlord.

40. Goods Vehicles (Licensing of Operators) Act 1995 (c. 23)

(1) The Goods Vehicles (Licensing of Operators) Act 1995 (c. 23) is amended as follows.

(2) In section 16(5) (termination of licence), for "he becomes a patient within the meaning of Part VII of the Mental Health Act 1983" substitute "he becomes a person who lacks capacity (within the meaning of the Mental Capacity Act 2005) to use a vehicle under the licence".

(3) In section 48 (licence not to be transferable, etc.)—

    (a) in subsection (2)—

        (i) for "or become a patient within the meaning of Part VII of the Mental Health Act 1983" substitute ", or become a person who lacks capacity (within the meaning of the Mental Capacity Act 2005) to use a vehicle under the licence,", and

        (ii) in paragraph (a), for "became a patient" substitute "became a person who lacked capacity in that respect", and

    (b) in subsection (5), for "a patient within the meaning of Part VII of the Mental Health Act 1983" substitute "a person lacking capacity".

41. Disability Discrimination Act 1995 (c. 50)

In section 20(7) of the Disability Discrimination Act 1995 (c. 50) (regulations to disapply provisions about incapacity), in paragraph (b), for "Part VII of the Mental Health Act 1983" substitute "the Mental Capacity Act 2005".

42. Trusts of Land and Appointment of Trustees Act 1996 (c. 47)

(1) The Trusts of Land and Appointment of Trustees Act 1996 (c. 47) is amended as follows.

(2) In section 9 (delegation by trustees), in subsection (6), for the words from "an enduring power" to the end substitute "an enduring power of attorney or lasting power of attorney within the meaning of the Mental Capacity Act 2005".

(3) In section 20 (the title to which becomes Appointment of substitute for trustee who lacks capacity)—

    (a) in subsection (1)(a), for "is incapable by reason of mental disorder of exercising" substitute "lacks capacity (within the meaning of the Mental Capacity Act 2005) to exercise", and

    (b) in subsection (2)—

        (i) for paragraph (a) substitute—

            "(a) a deputy appointed for the trustee by the Court of Protection,",

        (ii) in paragraph (b), for the words from "a power of attorney" to the end substitute "an enduring power of attorney or lasting power of attorney registered under the Mental Capacity Act 2005", and

        (iii) in paragraph (c), for the words from "the authority" to the end substitute "the Court of Protection".

43. Human Rights Act 1998 (c. 42)

In section 4(5) of the Human Rights Act 1998 (c. 42) (courts which may make declarations of incompatibility), after paragraph (e) insert—

        "(f) the Court of Protection, in any matter being dealt with by the President of the Family Division, the Vice-Chancellor or a puisne judge of the High Court."

44. Access to Justice Act 1999 (c. 22)

In paragraph 1 of Schedule 2 to the Access to Justice Act 1999 (c. 22) (services excluded from the Community Legal Service), after paragraph (e) insert—

        "(ea) the creation of lasting powers of attorney under the Mental Capacity Act 2005,

        (eb) the making of advance decisions under that Act,".

45. Adoption and Children Act 2002 (c. 38)

In section 52(1)(a) of the Adoption and Children Act 2002 (c. 38) (parental consent to adoption), for "is incapable of giving consent" substitute "lacks capacity (within the meaning of the Mental Capacity Act 2005) to give consent".

46. Licensing Act 2003 (c. 17)

(1) The Licensing Act 2003 (c.17) is amended as follows.

(2) In section 27(1) (lapse of premises licence), for paragraph (b) substitute—

> "(b) becomes a person who lacks capacity (within the meaning of the Mental Capacity Act 2005) to hold the licence,".

(3) In section 47 (interim authority notice in relation to premises licence)—

(a) in subsection (5), for paragraph (b) substitute—

> "(b) the former holder lacks capacity (within the meaning of the Mental Capacity Act 2005) to hold the licence and that person acts for him under an enduring power of attorney or lasting power of attorney registered under that Act,"

, and

(b) in subsection (10), omit the definition of "mentally incapable".

47. Courts Act 2003 (c. 39)

(1) The Courts Act 2003 (c. 39) is amended as follows.

(2) In section 1(1) (the courts in relation to which the Lord Chancellor must discharge his general duty), after paragraph (a) insert—

> "(aa) the Court of Protection,".

(3) In section 64(2) (judicial titles which the Lord Chancellor may by order alter)—

(a) omit the reference to a Master of the Court of Protection, and

(b) at the appropriate place insert a reference to each of the following—

> (i) Senior Judge of the Court of Protection,
> (ii) President of the Court of Protection,
> (iii) Vice-president of the Court of Protection.

SCHEDULE 7 - **Section 67(2)**

REPEALS

Short title and chapter	Extent of repeal
Trustee Act 1925 (c. 19)	Section 54(3).
Law of Property Act 1925 (c. 20)	Section 205(1)(xiii).
Administration of Estates Act 1925 (c. 23)	Section 55(1)(viii)
U.S.A. Veterans' Pensions (Administration) Act 1949 (c. 45)	In section 1(4), the words from "or for whom" to "1983".
Mental Health Act 1959 (c. 72)	In Schedule 7, in Part 1, the entries relating to— section 33 of the Fines and Recoveries Act 1833, section 68 of the Improvement of Land Act 1864, section 55 of the Trustee Act 1925, section 205(1) of the Law of Property Act 1925, section 49 of the National Assistance Act 1948, and section 1 of the Variation of Trusts Act 1958.
Courts Act 1971 (c. 23)	In Schedule 2, in Part 1A, the words "Master of the Court of Protection".
Local Government Act 1972 (c. 70)	Section 118.
Limitation Act 1980 (c. 58)	Section 38(3) and (4).
Supreme Court Act 1981 (c. 54)	In Schedule 2, in Part 2, paragraph 11.
Mental Health Act 1983 (c. 20)	Part 7. In section 139(1) the words from "or in, or in pursuance" to "Part VII of this Act,". In section 145(1), in the definition of patient the words "(except in Part VII of this Act)". In sections 146 and 147 the words from "104(4)" to "section),". Schedule 3.

Short title and chapter	Extent of repeal
	In Schedule 4, paragraph 1, 2, 4, 5, 7, 9, 14, 20, 22, 25, 32, 38, 55 and 56. In Schedule 5, paragraphs 26, 43, 44 and 45.
Enduring Powers of Attorney Act 1985 (c. 29)	The whole Act.
Insolvency Act 1986 (c. 45)	In section 389A(3)— the "or" immediately after paragraph (b), and in paragraph (c), the words "Part VII of the Mental Health Act 1983 or". In section 390(4)— the "or" immediately after paragraph (b), and in paragraph (c), the words "Part VII of the Mental Health Act 1983 or".
Public Trustee and Administration of Funds Act 1986 (c. 57)	Section 2. Section 3(7).
Child Support Act 1991 (c. 48)	In section 50(8)— paragraphs (b) and (d), and the "or" immediately after paragraph (c).
Social Security Administration Act 1992 (c. 5)	In section 123(10)— in paragraph (b), "a receiver appointed under section 99 of the Mental Health Act 1983 or", in paragraph (d)(i), "sub-paragraph (a) of rule 41(1) of the Court of Protection Rules Act 1984 or", in paragraph (d)(ii), "a receiver and interim appointed under sub-paragraph (b) of the said rule 41(1) or", and "receiver,".
Trustee Delegation Act 1999 (c. 15)	Section 4. Section 6. In section 7(3), the words "in accordance with section 4 above".
Care Standards Act 2000 (c. 14)	In Schedule 4, paragraph 8.
Licensing Act 2003 (c. 17)	In section 47(10), the definition of "mentally incapable".
Courts Act 2003 (c. 64)	In section 64(2), the words "Master of the Court of Protection".

ANNEX A

COUNCIL OF EUROPE

COMMITTEE OF MINISTERS

RECOMMENDATION NO. R (99) 4

OF THE COMMITTEE OF MINISTERS TO MEMBER STATES ON PRINCIPLES CONCERNING THE LEGAL PROTECTION OF INCAPABLE ADULTS

(Adopted by the Committee of Ministers on 23 February 1999, at the 660th meeting of the Ministers' Deputies)

The Committee of Ministers, under the terms of Article 15.*b* of the Statute of the Council of Europe,

Bearing in mind the Universal Declaration of Human Rights proclaimed by the General Assembly of the United Nations on 10 December 1948;

Bearing in mind the International Covenant on Civil and Political Rights and the International Covenant on Economic, Social and Cultural Rights of 16 December 1966;

Bearing in mind the Convention for the Protection of Human Rights and Fundamental Freedoms of 4 November 1950;

Bearing in mind the Convention for the Protection of Human Rights and Dignity of the Human Being with regard to the Application of Biology and Medicine: Convention on Human Rights and Biomedicine of 4 April 1997;

Considering that the aim of the Council of Europe is to achieve a greater unity between its members, in particular by promoting the adoption of common rules in legal matters;

Noting that demographic and medical changes have resulted in an increased number of people who, although of full age, are incapable of protecting their interests by reason of an impairment or insufficiency of their personal faculties;

Noting also that social changes have resulted in an increased need for adequate legislation to ensure the protection of such people;

Noting that legislative reforms on the protection, by representation or assistance, of incapable adults have been introduced or are under consideration in a number of member states and that these reforms have common features;

Recognising, however, that wide disparities in the legislation of member states in this area still exist;

Convinced of the importance in this context of respect for human rights and for the dignity of each person as a human being,

Recommends the governments of member states to take or reinforce, in their legislation and practice, all measures they consider necessary with a view to the implementation of the following principles:

PRINCIPLES

PART I

SCOPE OF APPLICATION

1. The following principles apply to the protection of adults who, by reason of an impairment or insufficiency of their personal faculties, are incapable of making, in an autonomous way, decisions concerning any or all of their personal or economic affairs, or understanding, expressing or acting upon such decisions, and who consequently cannot protect their interests.

2. The incapacity may be due to a mental disability, a disease or a similar reason.

3. The principles apply to measures of protection or other legal arrangements enabling such adults to benefit from representation or assistance in relation to those affairs.

4. In these principles "adult" means a person who is treated as being of full age under the applicable law on capacity in civil matters.

5. In these principles "intervention in the health field" means any act performed professionally on a person for reasons of health. It includes, in particular, interventions for the purposes of preventive care, diagnosis, treatment, rehabilitation or research.

PART II

GOVERNING PRINCIPLES

PRINCIPLE 1
RESPECT FOR HUMAN RIGHTS

In relation to the protection of incapable adults the fundamental principle, underlying all the other principles, is respect for the dignity of each person as a human being. The laws, procedures and practices relating to the protection of incapable adults shall be based on respect for their human rights and fundamental freedoms, taking into account any qualifications on those rights contained in the relevant international legal instruments.

PRINCIPLE 2
FLEXIBILITY IN LEGAL RESPONSE

1. The measures of protection and other legal arrangements available for the protection of the personal and economic interests of incapable adults should be sufficient, in scope or flexibility, to enable a suitable legal response to be made to different degrees of incapacity and various situations.

2. Appropriate measures of protection or other legal arrangements should be available in cases of emergency.

3. The law should provide for simple and inexpensive measures of protection or other legal arrangements.

4. The range of measures of protection should include, in appropriate cases, those which do not restrict the legal capacity of the person concerned.

5. The range of measures of protection should include those which are limited to one specific act without requiring the appointment of a representative or a representative with continuing powers.

6. Consideration should be given to the inclusion of measures under which the appointed person acts jointly with the adult concerned, and of measures involving the appointment of more than one representative.

7. Consideration should be given to the need to provide for, and regulate, legal arrangements which a person who is still capable can take to provide for any subsequent incapacity.

8. Consideration should be given to the need to provide expressly that certain decisions, particularly those of a minor or routine nature relating to health or personal welfare, may be taken for an incapable adult by those deriving their powers from the law rather than from a judicial or administrative measure.

PRINCIPLE 3

MAXIMUM PRESERVATION OF CAPACITY

1. The legislative framework should, so far as possible, recognise that different degrees of incapacity may exist and that incapacity may vary from time to time. Accordingly, a measure of protection should not result automatically in a complete removal of legal capacity. However, a restriction of legal capacity should be possible where it is shown to be necessary for the protection of the person concerned.

2. In particular, a measure of protection should not automatically deprive the person concerned of the right to vote, or to make a will, or to consent or refuse consent to any intervention in the health field, or to make other decisions of a personal character at any time when his or her capacity permits him or her to do so.

3. Consideration should be given to legal arrangements whereby, even when representation in a particular area is necessary, the adult may be permitted, with the representative's consent, to undertake specific acts or acts in a specific area.

4. Whenever possible the adult should be enabled to enter into legally effective transactions of an everyday nature.

PRINCIPLE 4

PUBLICITY

The disadvantage of automatically giving publicity to measures of protection or similar legal arrangements should be weighed in the balance against any protection which might be afforded to the adult concerned or to third parties.

PRINCIPLE 5

NECESSITY AND SUBSIDIARITY

1. No measure of protection should be established for an incapable adult unless the measure is necessary, taking into account the individual circumstances and the needs of the person concerned. A measure of protection may be established, however, with the full and free consent of the person concerned.

2. In deciding whether a measure of protection is necessary, account should be taken of any less formal arrangements which might be made, and of any assistance which might be provided by family members or by others.

PRINCIPLE 6

PROPORTIONALITY

1. Where a measure of protection is necessary it should be proportional to the degree of capacity of the person concerned and tailored to the individual circumstances and needs of the person concerned.

2. The measure of protection should interfere with the legal capacity, rights and freedoms of the person concerned to the minimum extent which is consistent with achieving the purpose of the intervention.

PRINCIPLE 7

PROCEDURAL FAIRNESS AND EFFICIENCY

1. There should be fair and efficient procedures for the taking of measures for the protection of incapable adults.

2. There should be adequate procedural safeguards to protect the human rights of the persons concerned and to prevent possible abuses.

PRINCIPLE 8

PARAMOUNTCY OF INTERESTS AND WELFARE OF THE PERSON CONCERNED

1. In establishing or implementing a measure of protection for an incapable adult the interests and welfare of that person should be the paramount consideration.

2. This principle implies, in particular, that the choice of any person to represent or assist an incapable adult should be governed primarily by the suitability of that person to safeguard and promote the adult's interests and welfare.

3. This principle also implies that the property of the incapable adult should be managed and used for the benefit of the person concerned and to secure his or her welfare.

PRINCIPLE 9

RESPECT FOR WISHES AND FEELINGS OF THE PERSON CONCERNED

1. In establishing or implementing a measure of protection for an incapable adult the past and present wishes and feelings of the adult should be ascertained so far as possible, and should be taken into account and given due respect.

2. This principle implies, in particular, that the wishes of the adult as to the choice of any person to represent or assist him or her should be taken into account and, as far as possible, given due respect.

3. It also implies that a person representing or assisting an incapable adult should give him or her adequate information, whenever this is possible and appropriate, in particular concerning any major decision affecting him or her, so that he or she may express a view.

PRINCIPLE 10

CONSULTATION

In the establishment and implementation of a measure of protection there should be consultation, so far as reasonable and practicable, with those having a close interest in the welfare of the adult concerned, whether as representative, close family member or otherwise. It is for national law to determine which persons should be consulted and the effects of consultation or its absence.

PART III

PROCEDURAL PRINCIPLES

PRINCIPLE 11

INSTITUTION OF PROCEEDINGS

1. The list of those entitled to institute proceedings for the taking of measures for the protection of incapable adults should be sufficiently wide to ensure that measures of protection can be considered in all cases where they are necessary. It may, in particular, be necessary to provide for proceedings to be initiated by a

public official or body, or by the court or other competent authority on its own motion.

2. The person concerned should be informed promptly in a language, or by other means, which he or she understands of the institution of proceedings which could affect his or her legal capacity, the exercise of his or her rights or his or her interests unless such information would be manifestly without meaning to the person concerned or would present a severe danger to the health of the person concerned.

PRINCIPLE 12

INVESTIGATION AND ASSESSMENT

1. There should be adequate procedures for the investigation and assessment of the adult's personal faculties.

2. No measure of protection which restricts the legal capacity of an incapable adult should be taken unless the person taking the measure has seen the adult or is personally satisfied as to the adult's condition and an up-to-date report from at least one suitably qualified expert has been submitted. The report should be in writing or recorded in writing.

PRINCIPLE 13

RIGHT TO BE HEARD IN PERSON

The person concerned should have the right to be heard in person in any proceedings which could affect his or her legal capacity.

PRINCIPLE 14

DURATION, REVIEW AND APPEAL

1. Measures of protection should, whenever possible and appropriate, be of limited duration. Consideration should be given to the institution of periodical reviews.

2. Measures of protection should be reviewed on a change of circumstances and, in particular, on a change in the adult's condition. They should be terminated if the conditions for them are no longer fulfilled.

3. There should be adequate rights of appeal.

PRINCIPLE 15

PROVISIONAL MEASURES IN CASE OF EMERGENCY

If a provisional measure is needed in a case of emergency, principles 11 to 14 should be applicable as far as possible according to the circumstances.

PRINCIPLE 16

ADEQUATE CONTROL

There should be adequate control of the operation of measures of protection and of the acts and decisions of representatives.

PRINCIPLE 17

QUALIFIED PERSONS

1. Steps should be taken with a view to providing an adequate number of suitably qualified persons for the representation and assistance of incapable adults.

2. Consideration should be given, in particular, to the establishment or support of associations or other bodies with the function of providing and training such people.

PART IV

THE ROLE OF REPRESENTATIVES

PRINCIPLE 18

CONTROL OF POWERS ARISING BY OPERATION OF LAW

1. Consideration should be given to the need to ensure that any powers conferred on any person by operation of law, without the intervention of a judicial or administrative authority, to act or take decisions on behalf of an incapable adult are limited and their exercise controlled.

2. The conferment of any such powers should not deprive the adult of legal capacity.

3. Any such powers should be capable of being modified or terminated at any time by a measure of protection taken by a judicial or administrative authority.

4. Principles 8 to 10 apply to the exercise of such powers as they apply to the implementation of measures of protection.

PRINCIPLE 19

LIMITATION OF POWERS OF REPRESENTATIVES

1. It is for national law to determine which juridical acts are of such a highly personal nature that they can not be done by a representative.

2. It is also for national law to determine whether decisions by a representative on certain serious matters should require the specific approval of a court or other body.

PRINCIPLE 20

LIABILITY

1. Representatives should be liable, in accordance with national law, for any loss or damage caused by them to incapable adults while exercising their functions.

2. In particular, the laws on liability for wrongful acts, negligence or maltreatment should apply to representatives and others involved in the affairs of incapable adults.

PRINCIPLE 21

REMUNERATION AND EXPENSES

1. National law should address the questions of the remuneration and the reimbursement of expenses of those appointed to represent or assist incapable adults.

2. Distinctions may be made between those acting in a professional capacity and those acting in other capacities, and between the management of personal matters of the incapable adult and the management of his or her economic matters.

PART V

INTERVENTIONS IN THE HEALTH FIELD

PRINCIPLE 22

CONSENT

1. Where an adult, even if subject to a measure of protection, is in fact capable of giving free and informed consent to a given intervention in the health field, the

intervention may only be carried out with his or her consent. The consent should be solicited by the person empowered to intervene.

2. Where an adult is not in fact capable of giving free and informed consent to a given intervention, the intervention may, nonetheless, be carried out provided that:

— it is for his or her direct benefit, and

— authorisation has been given by his or her representative or by an authority or a person or body provided for by law.

3. Consideration should be given to the designation by the law of appropriate authorities, persons or bodies for the purpose of authorising interventions of different types, when adults who are incapable of giving free and informed consent do not have a representative with appropriate powers. Consideration should also be given to the need to provide for the authorisation of a court or other competent body in the case of certain serious types of intervention.

4. Consideration should be given to the establishment of mechanisms for the resolution of any conflicts between persons or bodies authorised to consent or refuse consent to interventions in the health field in relation to adults who are incapable of giving consent.

PRINCIPLE 23

CONSENT (ALTERNATIVE RULES)

If the government of a member state does not apply the rules contained in paragraphs 1 and 2 of Principle 22, the following rules should be applicable:

Where an adult is subject to a measure of protection under which a given intervention in the health field can be carried out only with the authorisation of a body or a person provided for by law, the consent of the adult should nonetheless be sought if he or she has the capacity to give it.

2. Where, according to the law, an adult is not in a position to give free and informed consent to an intervention in the health field, the intervention may nonetheless be carried out if:

— it is for his or her direct benefit, and

— authorisation has been given by his or her representative or by an authority or a person or body provided for by law.

3. The law should provide for remedies allowing the person concerned to be heard by an independent official body before any important medical intervention is carried out.

PRINCIPLE 24

EXCEPTIONAL CASES

1. Special rules may be provided by national law, in accordance with relevant international instruments, in relation to interventions which, because of their special nature, require the provision of additional protection for the person concerned.

2. Such rules may involve a limited derogation from the criterion of direct benefit provided that the additional protection is such as to minimise the possibility of any abuse or irregularity.

PRINCIPLE 25

PROTECTION OF ADULTS WITH A MENTAL DISORDER

Subject to protective conditions prescribed by law, including supervisory, control and appeal procedures, an adult who has a mental disorder of a serious nature may be subjected, without his or her consent, to an intervention aimed at treating his or her mental disorder only where, without such treatment, serious harm is likely to result to his or her health.

PRINCIPLE 26

PERMISSIBILITY OF INTERVENTION IN EMERGENCY SITUATION

When, because of an emergency situation, the appropriate consent or authorisation cannot be obtained, any medically necessary intervention may be carried out immediately for the benefit of the health of the person concerned.

PRINCIPLE 27

APPLICABILITY OF CERTAIN PRINCIPLES APPLYING TO MEASURES OF PROTECTION

1. Principles 8 to 10 apply to any intervention in the health field concerning an incapable adult as they apply to measures of protection.

2. In particular, and in accordance with principle 9, the previously expressed wishes relating to a medical intervention by a patient who is not, at the time of the intervention, in a state to express his or her wishes should be taken into account.

PRINCIPLE 28

PERMISSIBILITY OF SPECIAL RULES ON CERTAIN MATTERS

Special rules may be provided by national law, in accordance with relevant international instruments, in relation to interventions which are necessary in a democratic society in the interest of public safety, for the prevention of crime, for the protection of public health or for the protection of the rights and freedom of others.

GENERAL NOTE

Each Member State of the Council of Europe has one representative on the Committee of Ministers which is "the organ which acts on behalf of the Council" (Statute of the Council of Europe, Art.13). The United Kingdom is a member of the Council of Europe and is therefore represented on the Committee of Ministers. The function of the Committee is to consider the action required to further the aims of the Council. In "appropriate cases, the conclusions of the Committee may take the form of recommendations to the Governments of Members and the Committee may request the Governments of Members to inform it of the action taken by them with regard to such recommendations" (Art.15(b)). Recommendations of the Committee of Ministers are not legally binding on Member States.

The Draft Mental Incapacity Bill, which formed Appendix A to the Law Commission's Report on Mental Incapacity (Law Comm. No.231), fed into the United Kingdom's negotiations on Recommendation (99)4. The Recommendation was subsequently taken into account during the development of policy that cumulated in the publication of the Draft Mental Incapacity Bill in June 2003. It is reproduced here as it might on occasion assist with the interpretation of the Act. The Recommendation is accompanied by an "Explanatory Memorandum" which can be accessed at the Council's website (*www.coe.int*).

ANNEX B

CONVENTION FOR THE PROTECTION OF HUMAN RIGHTS AND DIGNITY OF THE HUMAN BEING WITH REGARD TO THE APPLICATION OF BIOLOGY AND MEDICINE:

CONVENTION ON HUMAN RIGHTS AND BIOMEDICINE

European Treaty Series – No. 164

OVIEDO, 4.IV.1997

Preamble

The member States of the Council of Europe, the other States and the European Community, signatories hereto,

Bearing in mind the Universal Declaration of Human Rights proclaimed by the General Assembly of the United Nations on 10 December 1948;

Bearing in mind the Convention for the Protection of Human Rights and Fundamental Freedoms of 4 November 1950;

Bearing in mind the European Social Charter of 18 October 1961;

Bearing in mind the International Covenant on Civil and Political Rights and the International Covenant on Economic, Social and Cultural Rights of 16 December 1966;

Bearing in mind the Convention for the Protection of Individuals with regard to Automatic Processing of Personal Data of 28 January 1981;

Bearing also in mind the Convention on the Rights of the Child of 20 November 1989;

Considering that the aim of the Council of Europe is the achievement of a greater unity between its members and that one of the methods by which that aim is to be pursued is the maintenance and further realisation of human rights and fundamental freedoms;

Conscious of the accelerating developments in biology and medicine;

Convinced of the need to respect the human being both as an individual and as a member of the human species and recognising the importance of ensuring the dignity of the human being;

Conscious that the misuse of biology and medicine may lead to acts endangering human dignity;

Affirming that progress in biology and medicine should be used for the benefit of present and future generations;

Stressing the need for international co-operation so that all humanity may enjoy the benefits of biology and medicine;

Recognising the importance of promoting a public debate on the questions posed by the application of biology and medicine and the responses to be given thereto;

Wishing to remind all members of society of their rights and responsibilities;

Taking account of the work of the Parliamentary Assembly in this field, including Recommendation 1160 (1991) on the preparation of a convention on bioethics;

Resolving to take such measures as are necessary to safeguard human dignity and the fundamental rights and freedoms of the individual with regard to the application of biology and medicine,

Have agreed as follows:

CHAPTER I

GENERAL PROVISIONS

ARTICLE 1

PURPOSE AND OBJECT

Parties to this Convention shall protect the dignity and identity of all human beings and guarantee everyone, without discrimination, respect for their integrity and other rights and fundamental freedoms with regard to the application of biology and medicine.

Each Party shall take in its internal law the necessary measures to give effect to the provisions of this Convention.

ARTICLE 2

PRIMACY OF THE HUMAN BEING

The interests and welfare of the human being shall prevail over the sole interest of society or science.

ARTICLE 3

EQUITABLE ACCESS TO HEALTH CARE

Parties, taking into account health needs and available resources, shall take appropriate measures with a view to providing, within their jurisdiction, equitable access to health care of appropriate quality.

ARTICLE 4

PROFESSIONAL STANDARDS

Any intervention in the health field, including research, must be carried out in accordance with relevant professional obligations and standards.

CHAPTER II

CONSENT

ARTICLE 5

GENERAL RULE

An intervention in the health field may only be carried out after the person concerned has given free and informed consent to it.

This person shall beforehand be given appropriate information as to the purpose and nature of the intervention as well as on its consequences and risks.

The person concerned may freely withdraw consent at any time.

ARTICLE 6

PROTECTION OF PERSONS NOT ABLE TO CONSENT

1. Subject to Articles 17 and 20 below, an intervention may only be carried out on a person who does not have the capacity to consent, for his or her direct benefit.

2. Where, according to law, a minor does not have the capacity to consent to an intervention, the intervention may only be carried out with the authorisation of his or her representative or an authority or a person or body provided for by law.

The opinion of the minor shall be taken into consideration as an increasingly determining factor in proportion to his or her age and degree of maturity.

3. Where, according to law, an adult does not have the capacity to consent to an intervention because of a mental disability, a disease or for similar reasons, the intervention may only be carried out with the authorisation of his or her representative or an authority or a person or body provided for by law.

The individual concerned shall as far as possible take part in the authorisation procedure.

4. The representative, the authority, the person or the body mentioned in paragraphs 2 and 3 above shall be given, under the same conditions, the information referred to in Article 5.

5. The authorisation referred to in paragraphs 2 and 3 above may be withdrawn at any time in the best interests of the person concerned.

ARTICLE 7

PROTECTION OF PERSONS WHO HAVE A MENTAL DISORDER

Subject to protective conditions prescribed by law, including supervisory, control and appeal procedures, a person who has a mental disorder of a serious nature may be subjected, without his or her consent, to an intervention aimed at treating his or her mental disorder only where, without such treatment, serious harm is likely to result to his or her health.

ARTICLE 8

EMERGENCY SITUATION

When because of an emergency situation the appropriate consent cannot be obtained, any medically necessary intervention may be carried out immediately for the benefit of the health of the individual concerned.

ARTICLE 9

PREVIOUSLY EXPRESSED WISHES

The previously expressed wishes relating to a medical intervention by a patient who is not, at the time of the intervention, in a state to express his or her wishes shall be taken into account.

CHAPTER III

PRIVATE LIFE AND RIGHT TO INFORMATION

ARTICLE 10

PRIVATE LIFE AND RIGHT TO INFORMATION

1. Everyone has the right to respect for private life in relation to information about his or her health.

2. Everyone is entitled to know any information collected about his or her health. However, the wishes of individuals not to be so informed shall be observed.

3. In exceptional cases, restrictions may be placed by law on the exercise of the rights contained in paragraph 2 in the interests of the patient.

CHAPTER IV

HUMAN GENOME

ARTICLE 11

NON-DISCRIMINATION

Any form of discrimination against a person on grounds of his or her genetic heritage is prohibited.

ARTICLE 12

PREDICTIVE GENETIC TESTS

Tests which are predictive of genetic diseases or which serve either to identify the subject as a carrier of a gene responsible for a disease or to detect a genetic predisposition or susceptibility to a disease may be performed only for health purposes or for scientific research linked to health purposes, and subject to appropriate genetic counselling.

ARTICLE 13

INTERVENTIONS ON THE HUMAN GENOME

An intervention seeking to modify the human genome may only be undertaken for preventive, diagnostic or therapeutic purposes and only if its aim is not to introduce any modification in the genome of any descendants.

ARTICLE 14

NON-SELECTION OF SEX

The use of techniques of medically assisted procreation shall not be allowed for the purpose of choosing a future child's sex, except where serious hereditary sex-related disease is to be avoided.

CHAPTER V

SCIENTIFIC RESEARCH

ARTICLE 15

GENERAL RULE

Scientific research in the field of biology and medicine shall be carried out freely, subject to the provisions of this Convention and the other legal provisions ensuring the protection of the human being.

ARTICLE 16

PROTECTION OF PERSONS UNDERGOING RESEARCH

Research on a person may only be undertaken if all the following conditions are met:

i   there is no alternative of comparable effectiveness to research on humans;

ii   the risks which may be incurred by that person are not disproportionate to the potential benefits of the research;

iii   the research project has been approved by the competent body after independent examination of its scientific merit, including assessment of the importance of the aim of the research, and multidisciplinary review of its ethical acceptability,

iv   the persons undergoing research have been informed of their rights and the safeguards prescribed by law for their protection;

v   the necessary consent as provided for under Article 5 has been given expressly, specifically and is documented. Such consent may be freely withdrawn at any time.

ARTICLE 17

PROTECTION OF PERSONS NOT ABLE TO CONSENT TO RESEARCH

1. Research on a person without the capacity to consent as stipulated in Article 5 may be undertaken only if all the following conditions are met:

i   the conditions laid down in Article 16, sub-paragraphs i to iv, are fulfilled;

ii   the results of the research have the potential to produce real and direct benefit to his or her health;

iii   research of comparable effectiveness cannot be carried out on individuals capable of giving consent;

iv   the necessary authorisation provided for under Article 6 has been given specifically and in writing; and

v   the person concerned does not object.

2. Exceptionally and under the protective conditions prescribed by law, where the research has not the potential to produce results of direct benefit to the health of the person concerned, such research may be authorised subject to the conditions laid down in paragraph 1, sub-paragraphs i, iii, iv and v above, and to the following additional conditions:

i   the research has the aim of contributing, through significant improvement in the scientific understanding of the individual's condition, disease or disorder, to the ultimate attainment of results capable of conferring benefit to the person concerned or to other persons in the same age category or afflicted with the same disease or disorder or having the same condition;

ii   the research entails only minimal risk and minimal burden for the individual concerned.

ARTICLE 18

RESEARCH ON EMBRYOS *IN VITRO*

1. Where the law allows research on embryos *in vitro*, it shall ensure adequate protection of the embryo.
2. The creation of human embryos for research purposes is prohibited.

CHAPTER VI

ORGAN AND TISSUE REMOVAL FROM LIVING DONORS FOR TRANSPLANTATION PURPOSES

ARTICLE 19

GENERAL RULE

1. Removal of organs or tissue from a living person for transplantation purposes may be carried out solely for the therapeutic benefit of the recipient and where there is no suitable organ or tissue available from a deceased person and no other alternative therapeutic method of comparable effectiveness.

2. The necessary consent as provided for under Article 5 must have been given expressly and specifically either in written form or before an official body.

ARTICLE 20

PROTECTION OF PERSONS NOT ABLE TO CONSENT TO ORGAN REMOVAL

1. No organ or tissue removal may be carried out on a person who does not have the capacity to consent under Article 5.

2. Exceptionally and under the protective conditions prescribed by law, the removal of regenerative tissue from a person who does not have the capacity to consent may be authorised provided the following conditions are met:

i   there is no compatible donor available who has the capacity to consent;

ii   the recipient is a brother or sister of the donor;

iii   the donation must have the potential to be life-saving for the recipient;

iv   the authorisation provided for under paragraphs 2 and 3 of Article 6 has been given specifically and in writing, in accordance with the law and with the approval of the competent body;

v   the potential donor concerned does not object.

CHAPTER VII

PROHIBITION OF FINANCIAL GAIN AND DISPOSAL OF A PART OF THE HUMAN BODY

ARTICLE 21

PROHIBITION OF FINANCIAL GAIN

The human body and its parts shall not, as such, give rise to financial gain.

ARTICLE 22

DISPOSAL OF A REMOVED PART OF THE HUMAN BODY

When in the course of an intervention any part of a human body is removed, it may be stored and used for a purpose other than that for which it was removed, only if this is done in conformity with appropriate information and consent procedures.

CHAPTER VIII

INFRINGEMENTS OF THE PROVISIONS OF THE CONVENTION

ARTICLE 23

INFRINGEMENT OF THE RIGHTS OR PRINCIPLES

The Parties shall provide appropriate judicial protection to prevent or to put a stop to an unlawful infringement of the rights and principles set forth in this Convention at short notice.

ARTICLE 24

COMPENSATION FOR UNDUE DAMAGE

The person who has suffered undue damage resulting from an intervention is entitled to fair compensation according to the conditions and procedures prescribed by law.

ARTICLE 25

SANCTIONS

Parties shall provide for appropriate sanctions to be applied in the event of infringement of the provisions contained in this Convention.

CHAPTER IX

RELATION BETWEEN THIS CONVENTION AND OTHER PROVISIONS

ARTICLE 26

RESTRICTIONS ON THE EXERCISE OF THE RIGHTS

1. No restrictions shall be placed on the exercise of the rights and protective provisions contained in this Convention other than such as are prescribed by law and are necessary in a democratic society in the interest of public safety, for the prevention of crime, for the protection of public health or for the protection of the rights and freedoms of others.
    2. The restrictions contemplated in the preceding paragraph may not be placed on Articles 11, 13, 14, 16, 17, 19, 20 and 21.

ARTICLE 27

WIDER PROTECTION

None of the provisions of this Convention shall be interpreted as limiting or otherwise affecting the possibility for a Party to grant a wider measure of protection with regard to the application of biology and medicine than is stipulated in this Convention.

CHAPTER X

PUBLIC DEBATE

ARTICLE 28
PUBLIC DEBATE

Parties to this Convention shall see to it that the fundamental questions raised by the developments of biology and medicine are the subject of appropriate public discussion in the light, in particular, of relevant medical, social, economic, ethical and legal implications, and that their possible application is made the subject of appropriate consultation.

CHAPTER XI

INTERPRETATION AND FOLLOW-UP OF THE CONVENTION

ARTICLE 29
INTERPRETATION OF THE CONVENTION

The European Court of Human Rights may give, without direct reference to any specific proceedings pending in a court, advisory opinions on legal questions concerning the interpretation of the present Convention at the request of:

— the Government of a Party, after having informed the other Parties;

— the Committee set up by Article 32, with membership restricted to the Representatives of the Parties to this Convention, by a decision adopted by a two-thirds majority of votes cast.

ARTICLE 30
REPORTS ON THE APPLICATION OF THE CONVENTION

On receipt of a request from the Secretary General of the Council of Europe any Party shall furnish an explanation of the manner in which its internal law ensures the effective implementation of any of the provisions of the Convention.

CHAPTER XII

PROTOCOLS

ARTICLE 31
PROTOCOLS

Protocols may be concluded in pursuance of Article 32, with a view to developing, in specific fields, the principles contained in this Convention.

The Protocols shall be open for signature by Signatories of the Convention. They shall be subject to ratification, acceptance or approval. A Signatory may not ratify, accept or approve Protocols without previously or simultaneously ratifying accepting or approving the Convention.

CHAPTERS XII TO XIV

[*Not reproduced.*]

GENERAL NOTE

This Council of Europe Convention (the "Oviedo Convention") was drafted with the intention of defining and safeguarding fundamental rights in biomedical research, in particular of those participating in research. Although the United Kingdom is not a signatory to the Convention, "the Government has been supportive of it and recognises its importance in setting out a common approach toward bioethical issues" (Joint Committee on Human Rights 4th Report, Appendix 4, letter of Baroness Ashton of Upholland to the Chair, para.56). Frequent references were made to the terms of the Convention during the Parliamentary debates on the research clauses of the Bill. The Convention is accompanied by an "Explanatory Report" which can be accessed at the Council's website (*www.coe.int*).

Paragraph 7 of the Explanatory Report states:

"The Convention sets out only the most important principles. Additional standards and more detailed questions should be dealt with in additional protocols. The Convention as a whole will thus provide a common framework for the protection of human rights and human dignity in both longstanding and developing areas concerning the application of biology and medicine."

The first Additional Protocol to the Convention, which was opened for signature by the signatories to the Convention on January 25, 2005, expands on, and in some cases qualifies, the provisions of the Convention. It is reproduced as Annex C.

When considering whether a national authority's regulatory framework relating to consent to treatment meets the requirements of Art.8(2) of the European Convention on Human Rights, the European Court of Human Rights will judge the framework against the standards laid down in the Convention (*Glass v United Kingdom,* App. No.61827/00, March 9, 2004, para.75).

Recognition of the tension that exists between the potential benefits of research and the potential for abuse led to the "Helsinki Declaration" on the ethical principles for medical research involving human subjects by the World Medical Association in 1964. The Declaration has been regularly amended, most recently in Edinburgh in 2000. The Declaration states that it "is the duty of the physician in medical research to protect the life, health, privacy, and dignity of the human subject" (para.B.10). Paragraphs B.24 to 26 are concerned with research involving the mentally incapacitated:

"24. For a research subject who is legally incompetent, physically or mentally incapable of giving consent or is a legally incompetent minor, the investigator must obtain informed consent from the legally authorised representative in accordance with applicable law. These groups should not be included in research unless the research is necessary to promote the health of the population represented and this research cannot instead be performed on legally competent persons.

25. When a subject deemed legally incompetent, such as a minor child, is able to give assent to decisions about participation in research, the investigator must obtain that assent in addition to the consent of the legally authorised representative.

26. Research on individuals from whom it is not possible to obtain consent, including proxy or advance consent, should be done only if the physical/mental condition that prevents obtaining informed consent is a necessary characteristic of the research population. The specific reasons for involving research subjects with a condition that renders them unable to give informed consent should be stated in the experimental protocol for consideration and approval of the review committee. The protocol should state that consent to remain in the research should be obtained as soon as possible from the individual or a legally authorised surrogate."

ANNEX C

ADDITIONAL PROTOCOL TO THE CONVENTION ON HUMAN RIGHTS AND BIOMEDICINE, CONCERNING BIOMEDICAL RESEARCH

Council of Europe Treaty Series – No. 195

STRASBOURG, 25.I.2005

Preamble

The member States of the Council of Europe, the other States and the European Community signatories to this Additional Protocol to the Convention for the Protection of Human Rights and Dignity of the Human Being with regard to the Application of Biology and Medicine (hereinafter referred to as "the Convention"),

Considering that the aim of the Council of Europe is the achievement of greater unity between its members and that one of the methods by which this aim is pursued is the maintenance and further realisation of human rights and fundamental freedoms;

Considering that the aim of the Convention, as defined in Article 1, is to protect the dignity and identity of all human beings and guarantee everyone, without discrimination, respect for their integrity and other rights and fundamental freedoms with regard to the application of biology and medicine;

Considering that progress in medical and biological sciences, in particular advances obtained through biomedical research, contributes to saving lives and improving quality of life;

Conscious of the fact that the advancement of biomedical science and practice is dependent on knowledge and discovery which necessitates research on human beings;

Stressing that such research is often transdisciplinary and international;

Taking into account national and international professional standards in the field of biomedical research and the previous work of the Committee of Ministers and the Parliamentary Assembly of the Council of Europe in this field;

Convinced that biomedical research that is contrary to human dignity and human rights should never be carried out;

Stressing the paramount concern to be the protection of the human being participating in research;

Affirming that particular protection shall be given to human beings who may be vulnerable in the context of research;

Recognising that every person has a right to accept or refuse to undergo biomedical research and that no one should be forced to undergo such research;

Resolving to take such measures as are necessary to safeguard human dignity and the fundamental rights and freedoms of the individual with regard to biomedical research,

Have agreed as follows:

CHAPTER I

OBJECT AND SCOPE

ARTICLE 1

OBJECT AND PURPOSE

Parties to this Protocol shall protect the dignity and identity of all human beings and guarantee everyone, without discrimination, respect for their integrity and other rights and fundamental freedoms with regard to any research involving interventions on human beings in the field of biomedicine.

ARTICLE 2

SCOPE

1. This Protocol covers the full range of research activities in the health field involving interventions on human beings.

2. This Protocol does not apply to research on embryos *in vitro*. It does apply to research on foetuses and embryos *in vivo*.

3. For the purposes of this Protocol, the term "intervention" includes:

i   a physical intervention, and

ii   any other intervention in so far as it involves a risk to the psychological health of the person concerned.

CHAPTER II

GENERAL PROVISIONS

ARTICLE 3

PRIMACY OF THE HUMAN BEING

The interests and welfare of the human being participating in research shall prevail over the sole interest of society or science.

ARTICLE 4

GENERAL RULE

Research shall be carried out freely, subject to the provisions of this Protocol and the other legal provisions ensuring the protection of the human being.

ARTICLE 5

ABSENCE OF ALTERNATIVES

Research on human beings may only be undertaken if there is no alternative of comparable effectiveness.

ARTICLE 6

RISKS AND BENEFITS

1. Research shall not involve risks and burdens to the human being disproportionate to its potential benefits.

2. In addition, where the research does not have the potential to produce results of direct benefit to the health of the research participant, such research may only be undertaken if the research entails no more than acceptable risk and acceptable

burden for the research participant. This shall be without prejudice to the provision contained in Article 15 paragraph 2, sub-paragraph ii for the protection of persons not able to consent to research.

ARTICLE 7

APPROVAL

Research may only be undertaken if the research project has been approved by the competent body after independent examination of its scientific merit, including assessment of the importance of the aim of research, and multidisciplinary review of its ethical acceptability.

ARTICLE 8

SCIENTIFIC QUALITY

Any research must be scientifically justified, meet generally accepted criteria of scientific quality and be carried out in accordance with relevant professional obligations and standards under the supervision of an appropriately qualified researcher.

CHAPTER III

ETHICS COMMITTEE

ARTICLE 9

INDEPENDENT EXAMINATION BY AN ETHICS COMMITTEE

1. Every research project shall be submitted for independent examination of its ethical acceptability to an ethics committee. Such projects shall be submitted to independent examination in each State in which any research activity is to take place.

2. The purpose of the multidisciplinary examination of the ethical acceptability of the research project shall be to protect the dignity, rights, safety and well-being of research participants. The assessment of the ethical acceptability shall draw on an appropriate range of expertise and experience adequately reflecting professional and lay views.

3. The ethics committee shall produce an opinion containing reasons for its conclusion.

ARTICLE 10

INDEPENDENCE OF THE ETHICS COMMITTEE

1. Parties to this Protocol shall take measures to assure the independence of the ethics committee. That body shall not be subject to undue external influences.

2. Members of the ethics committee shall declare all circumstances that might lead to a conflict of interest. Should such conflicts arise, those involved shall not participate in that review.

ARTICLE 11

INFORMATION FOR THE ETHICS COMMITTEE

1. All information which is necessary for the ethical assessment of the research project shall be given in written form to the ethics committee.

2. In particular, information on items contained in the appendix to this Protocol shall be provided, in so far as it is relevant for the research project. The appendix

may be amended by the Committee set up by Article 32 of the Convention by a two-thirds majority of the votes cast.

ARTICLE 12

UNDUE INFLUENCE

The ethics committee must be satisfied that no undue influence, including that of a financial nature, will be exerted on persons to participate in research. In this respect, particular attention must be given to vulnerable or dependent persons.

CHAPTER IV

INFORMATION AND CONSENT

ARTICLE 13

INFORMATION FOR RESEARCH PARTICIPANTS

1. The persons being asked to participate in a research project shall be given adequate information in a comprehensible form. This information shall be documented.

2. The information shall cover the purpose, the overall plan and the possible risks and benefits of the research project, and include the opinion of the ethics committee. Before being asked to consent to participate in a research project, the persons concerned shall be specifically informed, according to the nature and purpose of the research:

i of the nature, extent and duration of the procedures involved, in particular, details of any burden imposed by the research project;

ii of available preventive, diagnostic and therapeutic procedures;

iii of the arrangements for responding to adverse events or the concerns of research participants;

iv of arrangements to ensure respect for private life and ensure the confidentiality of personal data;

v of arrangements for access to information relevant to the participant arising from the research and to its overall results;

vi of the arrangements for fair compensation in the case of damage;

vii of any foreseen potential further uses, including commercial uses, of the research results, data or biological materials;

viii of the source of funding of the research project.

3. In addition, the persons being asked to participate in a research project shall be informed of the rights and safeguards prescribed by law for their protection, and specifically of their right to refuse consent or to withdraw consent at any time without being subject to any form of discrimination, in particular regarding the right to medical care.

ARTICLE 14

CONSENT

1. No research on a person may be carried out, subject to the provisions of both Chapter V and Article 19, without the informed, free, express, specific and

documented consent of the person. Such consent may be freely withdrawn by the person at any phase of the research.

2. Refusal to give consent or the withdrawal of consent to participation in research shall not lead to any form of discrimination against the person concerned, in particular regarding the right to medical care.

3. Where the capacity of the person to give informed consent is in doubt, arrangements shall be in place to verify whether or not the person has such capacity.

CHAPTER V

PROTECTION OF PERSONS NOT ABLE TO CONSENT TO RESEARCH

ARTICLE 15

PROTECTION OF PERSONS NOT ABLE TO CONSENT TO RESEARCH

1. Research on a person without the capacity to consent to research may be undertaken only if all the following specific conditions are met:

i   the results of the research have the potential to produce real and direct benefit to his or her health;

ii   research of comparable effectiveness cannot be carried out on individuals capable of giving consent;

iii   the person undergoing research has been informed of his or her rights and the safeguards prescribed by law for his or her protection, unless this person is not in a state to receive the information;

iv   the necessary authorisation has been given specifically and in writing by the legal representative or an authority, person or body provided for by law, and after having received the information required by Article 16, taking into account the person's previously expressed wishes or objections. An adult not able to consent shall as far as possible take part in the authorisation procedure. The opinion of a minor shall be taken into consideration as an increasingly determining factor in proportion to age and degree of maturity;

v   the person concerned does not object.

2. Exceptionally and under the protective conditions prescribed by law, where the research has not the potential to produce results of direct benefit to the health of the person concerned, such research may be authorised subject to the conditions laid down in paragraph 1, sub-paragraphs ii, iii, iv, and v above, and to the following additional conditions:

i   the research has the aim of contributing, through significant improvement in the scientific understanding of the individual's condition, disease or disorder, to the ultimate attainment of results capable of conferring benefit to the person concerned or to other persons in the same age category or afflicted with the same disease or disorder or having the same condition;

ii   the research entails only minimal risk and minimal burden for the individual concerned; and any consideration of additional potential benefits of the research shall not be used to justify an increased level of risk or burden.

3. Objection to participation, refusal to give authorisation or the withdrawal of authorisation to participate in research shall not lead to any form of discrimination against the person concerned, in particular regarding the right to medical care.

Article 16

Information prior to authorisation

1. Those being asked to authorise participation of a person in a research project shall be given adequate information in a comprehensible form. This information shall be documented.

2. The information shall cover the purpose, the overall plan and the possible risks and benefits of the research project, and include the opinion of the ethics committee. They shall further be informed of the rights and safeguards prescribed by law for the protection of those not able to consent to research and specifically of the right to refuse or to withdraw authorisation at any time, without the person concerned being subject to any form of discrimination, in particular regarding the right to medical care. They shall be specifically informed according to the nature and purpose of the research of the items of information listed in Article 13.

3. The information shall also be provided to the individual concerned, unless this person is not in a state to receive the information.

Article 17

Research with minimal risk and minimal burden

1. For the purposes of this Protocol it is deemed that the research bears a minimal risk if, having regard to the nature and scale of the intervention, it is to be expected that it will result, at the most, in a very slight and temporary negative impact on the health of the person concerned.

2. It is deemed that it bears a minimal burden if it is to be expected that the discomfort will be, at the most, temporary and very slight for the person concerned. In assessing the burden for an individual, a person enjoying the special confidence of the person concerned shall assess the burden where appropriate.

CHAPTER VI

SPECIFIC SITUATIONS

Article 18

Research during pregnancy or breastfeeding

1. Research on a pregnant woman which does not have the potential to produce results of direct benefit to her health, or to that of her embryo, foetus or child after birth, may only be undertaken if the following additional conditions are met:

i   the research has the aim of contributing to the ultimate attainment of results capable of conferring benefit to other women in relation to reproduction or to other embryos, foetuses or children;

ii   research of comparable effectiveness cannot be carried out on women who are not pregnant;

iii   the research entails only minimal risk and minimal burden.

2. Where research is undertaken on a breastfeeding woman, particular care shall be taken to avoid any adverse impact on the health of the child.

ARTICLE 19

RESEARCH ON PERSONS IN EMERGENCY CLINICAL SITUATIONS

1. The law shall determine whether, and under which protective additional conditions, research in emergency situations may take place when:

i   a person is not in a state to give consent, and

ii   because of the urgency of the situation, it is impossible to obtain in a sufficiently timely manner, authorisation from his or her representative or an authority or a person or body which would in the absence of an emergency situation be called upon to give authorisation.

2. The law shall include the following specific conditions:

i   research of comparable effectiveness cannot be carried out on persons in non-emergency situations;

ii   the research project may only be undertaken if it has been approved specifically for emergency situations by the competent body;

iii any relevant previously expressed objections of the person known to the researcher shall be respected;

iv   where the research has not the potential to produce results of direct benefit to the health of the person concerned, it has the aim of contributing, through significant improvement in the scientific understanding of the individual's condition, disease or disorder, to the ultimate attainment of results capable of conferring benefit to the person concerned or to other persons in the same category or afflicted with the same disease or disorder or having the same condition, and entails only minimal risk and minimal burden.

3. Persons participating in the emergency research project or, if applicable, their representatives shall be provided with all the relevant information concerning their participation in the research project as soon as possible. Consent or authorisation for continued participation shall be requested as soon as reasonably possible.

ARTICLE 20

RESEARCH ON PERSONS DEPRIVED OF LIBERTY

Where the law allows research on persons deprived of liberty, such persons may participate in a research project in which the results do not have the potential to produce direct benefit to their health only if the following additional conditions are met:

i   research of comparable effectiveness cannot be carried out without the participation of persons deprived of liberty;

ii   the research has the aim of contributing to the ultimate attainment of results capable of conferring benefit to persons deprived of liberty;

iii the research entails only minimal risk and minimal burden.

CHAPTER VII

SAFETY AND SUPERVISION

ARTICLE 21

MINIMISATION OF RISK AND BURDEN

1. All reasonable measures shall be taken to ensure safety and to minimise risk and burden for the research participants.

2. Research may only be carried out under the supervision of a clinical professional who possesses the necessary qualifications and experience.

ARTICLE 22

ASSESSMENT OF HEALTH STATUS

1. The researcher shall take all necessary steps to assess the state of health of human beings prior to their inclusion in research, to ensure that those at increased risk in relation to participation in a specific project be excluded.

2. Where research is undertaken on persons in the reproductive stage of their lives, particular consideration shall be given to the possible adverse impact on a current or future pregnancy and the health of an embryo, foetus or child.

ARTICLE 23

NON-INTERFERENCE WITH NECESSARY CLINICAL INTERVENTIONS

1. Research shall not delay nor deprive participants of medically necessary preventive, diagnostic or therapeutic procedures.

2. In research associated with prevention, diagnosis or treatment, participants assigned to control groups shall be assured of proven methods of prevention, diagnosis or treatment.

3. The use of placebo is permissible where there are no methods of proven effectiveness, or where withdrawal or withholding of such methods does not present an unacceptable risk or burden.

ARTICLE 24

NEW DEVELOPMENTS

1. Parties to this Protocol shall take measures to ensure that the research project is re-examined if this is justified in the light of scientific developments or events arising in the course of the research.

2. The purpose of the re-examination is to establish whether:

i   the research needs to be discontinued or if changes to the research project are necessary for the research to continue;

ii   research participants, or if applicable their representatives, need to be informed of the developments or events;

iii   additional consent or authorisation for participation is required.

3. Any new information relevant to their participation shall be conveyed to the research participants, or, if applicable, to their representatives, in a timely manner.

4. The competent body shall be informed of the reasons for any premature termination of a research project.

CHAPTER VIII

CONFIDENTIALITY AND RIGHT TO INFORMATION

ARTICLE 25

CONFIDENTIALITY

1. Any information of a personal nature collected during biomedical research shall be considered as confidential and treated according to the rules relating to the protection of private life.

2. The law shall protect against inappropriate disclosure of any other information related to a research project that has been submitted to an ethics committee in compliance with this Protocol.

ARTICLE 26

RIGHT TO INFORMATION

1. Research participants shall be entitled to know any information collected on their health in conformity with the provisions of Article 10 of the Convention.

2. Other personal information collected for a research project will be accessible to them in conformity with the law on the protection of individuals with regard to processing of personal data.

ARTICLE 27

DUTY OF CARE

If research gives rise to information of relevance to the current or future health or quality of life of research participants, this information must be offered to them. That shall be done within a framework of health care or counselling. In communication of such information, due care must be taken in order to protect confidentiality and to respect any wish of a participant not to receive such information.

ARTICLE 28

AVAILABILITY OF RESULTS

1. On completion of the research, a report or summary shall be submitted to the ethics committee or the competent body.

2. The conclusions of the research shall be made available to participants in reasonable time, on request.

3. The researcher shall take appropriate measures to make public the results of research in reasonable time.

CHAPTER IX

RESEARCH IN STATES NOT PARTIES TO THIS PROTOCOL

ARTICLE 29

RESEARCH IN STATES NOT PARTIES TO THIS PROTOCOL

Sponsors or researchers within the jurisdiction of a Party to this Protocol that plan to undertake or direct a research project in a State not party to this Protocol shall ensure that, without prejudice to the provisions applicable in that State, the research project complies with the principles on which the provisions of this

Protocol are based. Where necessary, the Party shall take appropriate measures to that end.

CHAPTER X

INFRINGEMENT OF THE PROVISIONS OF THE PROTOCOL

ARTICLE 30

INFRINGEMENT OF THE RIGHTS OR PRINCIPLES

The Parties shall provide appropriate judicial protection to prevent or to put a stop to an unlawful infringement of the rights or principles set forth in this Protocol at short notice.

ARTICLE 31

COMPENSATION FOR DAMAGE

The person who has suffered damage as a result of participation in research shall be entitled to fair compensation according to the conditions and procedures pre-scribed by law.

ARTICLE 32

SANCTIONS

Parties shall provide for appropriate sanctions to be applied in the event of infringe-ment of the provisions contained in this Protocol.

CHAPTER XI

RELATION BETWEEN THIS PROTOCOL AND OTHER PROVISIONS AND RE-EXAMINATION OF THE PROTOCOL

ARTICLE 33

RELATION BETWEEN THIS PROTOCOL AND THE CONVENTION

As between the Parties, the provisions of Articles 1 to 32 of this Protocol shall be regarded as additional articles to the Convention, and all the provisions of the Convention shall apply accordingly.

ARTICLE 34

WIDER PROTECTION

None of the provisions of this Protocol shall be interpreted as limiting or otherwise affecting the possibility for a Party to grant research participants a wider measure of protection than is stipulated in this Protocol.

ARTICLE 35

RE-EXAMINATION OF THE PROTOCOL

In order to monitor scientific developments, the present Protocol shall be examined within the Committee referred to in Article 32 of the Convention no later than five years from the entry into force of this Protocol and thereafter at such intervals as the Committee may determine.

CHAPTER XII

[Not reproduced.]

APPENDIX TO THE ADDITIONAL PROTOCOL ON BIOMEDICAL RESEARCH

Information to be given to the ethics committee

Information on the following items shall be provided to the ethics committee, in so far as it is relevant for the research project:

Description of the project

i   the name of the principal researcher, qualifications and experience of researchers and, where appropriate, the clinically responsible person, and funding arrangements;

ii   the aim and justification for the research based on the latest state of scientific knowledge;

iii   methods and procedures envisaged, including statistical and other analytical techniques;

iv   a comprehensive summary of the research project in lay language;

v   a statement of previous and concurrent submissions of the research project for assessment or approval and the outcome of those submissions;

Participants, consent and information

vi   justification for involving human beings in the research project;

vii   the criteria for inclusion or exclusion of the categories of persons for participation in the research project and how those persons are to be selected and recruited;

viii   reasons for the use or the absence of control groups;

ix   a description of the nature and degree of foreseeable risks that may be incurred through participating in research;

x   the nature, extent and duration of the interventions to be carried out on the research participants, and details of any burden imposed by the research project;

xi   arrangements to monitor, evaluate and react to contingencies that may have consequences for the present or future health of research participants;

xii   the timing and details of information for those persons who would participate in the research project and the means proposed for provision of this information;

xiii   documentation intended to be used to seek consent or, in the case of persons not able to consent, authorisation for participation in the research project;

xiv   arrangements to ensure respect for the private life of those persons who would participate in research and ensure the confidentiality of personal data;

xv arrangements foreseen for information which may be generated and be relevant to the present or future health of those persons who would participate in research and their family members;

Other information

xvi details of all payments and rewards to be made in the context of the research project;

xvii details of all circumstances that might lead to conflicts of interest that may affect the independent judgement of the researchers;

xviii details of any foreseen potential further uses, including commercial uses, of the research results, data or biological materials;

xix details of all other ethical issues, as perceived by the researcher;

xx details of any insurance or indemnity to cover damage arising in the context of the research project.

The ethics committee may request additional information necessary for evaluation of the research project.

GENERAL NOTE
See the General Note to Annex B.

INDEX

References are to sections and Schedules